101
BUSINESSES
YOU CAN
START ON THE
INTERNET

Other VNR Business Technology/Communications Books. . . .

- **Designing TCP/IP Internetworks**
  by Geoff Bennett

- **Cases in Network Implementation: Enterprise Networking**
  by William E. Bracker, Jr. and Ray Sarch

- **Information Proficiency: The Key To The Information Age**
  by Thomas J. Buckholtz

- **Doing More Business on the Internet**
  by Mary J. Cronin

- **Currid's Guide to Business Technology**
  by Cheryl C. Currid

- **Networking Device Drivers**
  by Sanjay Dhawan

- **Routing in Today's Internetworks**
  by Mark Dickie

- **Spinning the Web: How To Provide Information On The Internet**
  by Andrew Ford

- **Digital Signal Processing in Communications**
  by Marvin E. Frerking

- **The Complete Cyberspace Reference and Directory**
  by Gilbert Held

- **Working With NetWare: For Network Supervisors and Users**
  by Gilbert Held

- **Global Expansion In The Information Age: Big Planet, Small World**
  by Thomas J. Howard

- **Online Marketing Handbook: How To Sell, Advertise, Publicize, and Promote Your Products and Services On the Internet and Commercial Online Systems**
  by Daniel S. Janal

- **Digital Telephony and Network Integration, 2nd Edition**
  by Bernhard E. Keiser and Eugene Strange

- **Internet Trainer's Guide**
  by Diane K. Kovacs

- **Low-Cost E-Mail With UUCP: Integrating UNIX, DOS, Windows and MAC**
  by Thomas Wm. Madron

- **The Illustrated Network Book: A Graphic Guide to Understanding Computer Networks**
  by Matthew G. Naugle

- **Making Telecommuting Happen: A Guide for Telemanagers and Telecommuters**
  by Jack M. Nilles

- **JPEG Still Image Data Compression Standard**
  by William B. Pennebaker and Joan L. Mitchell

- **Successful Reengineering: An Implementation Guide To Using Information Technology**
  by Daniel Petrozzo and John C. Stepper

- **Reducing the Cost of LAN Ownership: The Business of Running a Network**
  by Salvatore L. Salamone and Greg Gianforte

- **Using Wireless Communications in Business**
  by Andrew M. Seybold

- **Fax Power: High Leverage Business Communications**
  by Philip C. W. Sih

- **Applications for Distributed Systems and Network Management**
  by Kornel Terplan and Jill Huntington-Lee

- **SNMP Application Developer's Manual**
  by Robert L. Townsend

- **A Network of Objects: How To Lower Your Computing Cost and Improve Your Applications Delivery**
  by Thomas C. Tsai

- **Communications Standard Dictionary, 2nd Edition**
  by Martin H. Weik, DSc.

- **Enterprise Networking for Information Systems Professionals**
  by Norman Witkin

101 BUSINESSES YOU CAN START ON THE INTERNET

Daniel S. Janal

VAN NOSTRAND REINHOLD
I(T)P™ A Division of International Thomson Publishing Inc.

New York • Albany • Bonn • Boston • Detroit • London • Madrid • Melbourne
Mexico City • Paris • San Francisco • Singapore • Tokyo • Toronto

Copyright © 1996 by Daniel S. Janal

I⊤P™   Van Nostrand Reinhold is a division of International Thomson Publishing,Inc.
The ITP logo is a trademark under license

Printed in the United States of America

ISBN: 0442–02202–6

For more information, contact:

Van Nostrand Reinhold
115 Fifth Avenue
New York, N.Y. 10003

International Thomson Publishing
GmbH
Königswinterer Strasse 418
353227 Bonn
Germany

International Thomson Publishing Europe
Berkshire House 168-173
High Holborn
London WCIV 7AA
England

International Thomson Publishing Asia
221 Henderson Road #05-10
Henderson Building
Singapore 0315

Thomas Nelson Australia
102 Dodds Street
South Melbourne, 3205
Victoria, Australia

International Thomson Publishing Japan
Hirakawacho Kyowa Building, 3F
2-2-1 Hirakawacho
Chiyoda-ku, 102 Tokyo
Japan

Nelson Canada
1120 Birchmount Road
Scarborough, Ontario
Canada M1K 5G4

International Thomson Editores
Campos Eliseos 385, Piso 7
Col. Polanco
11560 Mexico D.F. Mexico

1 2 3 4 5 6 7 8 9 10 QEBFF 01 00 99 98 97 96 95

Library of Congress Cataloging-in-Publication Data
Available upon request.

Dedicated to my wife, Susan.

TABLE OF CONTENTS

FOREWORD

by Paul & Sarah Edwards

Every so often there is a window in time that opens onto wide vistas of never–before–possible opportunities. This century has been rich with such moments. We have seen the mass production of automobiles, air travel, and the advent of radio, television, and the personal computer. Each of these technological breakthroughs has ushered in a brief period of time of unlimited possibilities for those with the imagination, courage, and spunk to seize them. And so it is with today's information highway.

Over the months to come, the online world will host whole new industries, spawn many new kinds of businesses, and provide new venues to pursue dreams otherwise waylaid along more crowded and conventional roadways. As you will see in this book, it's already happening. Already there is a flurry of people doing business on the Internet. And it's fertile and ripe for more.

The best thing about these special moments in time is that often anyone who wants to pioneer their possibilities can do so. There are no college degrees required, no formal training needed, no dues to be paid, and no mentors to be courted. So times like these empower individuals, and as such are the perfect occasion for aspiring and existing small and home businesses to leap into action. Often, as one and two-person businesses, our imagination, agility, and flexibility enable us to leap ahead of other larger, slower moving groups on these new frontiers.

This book shows you that, indeed, the Internet is one of these new frontiers, and making money there, while still being tested and explored, is already a reality. The new pioneers featured in this book are people like yourself. You will find out how they came up with their ideas and what specific steps they took to turn those ideas into reality. Some are well underway. Others are just beginning. But at whatever stage they are in, you will sense their excitement and enthusiasm for the new world that's opening up for them.

You will find many ideas for starting such activities yourself. You'll learn about the characteristics of the unique new terrain called the Internet and the practical realities of how to traverse its unfamiliar geography. Dan makes you feel comfortable with the Internet's otherwise "techie" elements. You will quickly become familiar with its language and the rules of its road. You'll learn many tips for marketing and selling your products and services in accord with these new rules.

We've known Dan since the early days of our operating the Working from Home Forum on CompuServe, which we started in 1983. We know him as a skilled practitioner in marketing on the information highway. Over these years, he has recognized opportunity, seized it and, as a public relations professional, helped others to do so too. So he's earned his spurs to be your guide to this newest of electronic frontiers.

Paul & Sarah Edwards
Santa Monica, Calif.

August 1995

PREFACE

OVERVIEW—WHY YOU SHOULD READ THIS BOOK

The Internet will dramatically change the way people do business—from prospecting to building image to making the all-important sale. We are at the dawn of this era. Like the pioneers of the Wild West, these early settlers will bear the greatest rewards simply by being there first. You could be among the first.

The purpose of this book is to give you the ideas and inspiration to start your own new business on the Internet, or expand your current business onto the Internet and reach new audiences around the country and around the world.

This book provides you with an overview of the benefits you could attain by putting your store onto the Internet and adopting an online marketing program. It then shows you how 101 businesses and products are being sold on the Internet today. You will get an insider's look and learn from more than fourty in-depth case studies and dozens of other insightful interviews. By learning from others, you'll see exactly what it is like to run a business on the Internet—everything from the financial costs to the personal costs. You will also get a good feel for the daily routine and the ins and outs of starting a business on the Internet.

Unlike other books that promise the sky and are filled with the hype that accompanies any new medium or technology, this book tries to separate fact from fiction. It shows you what works and what doesn't work. We want to help you, not hype you.

This book is an idea generator. In that spirit, this book gives you the business overview so you can get your business up and running on the Internet quickly and inexpensively. After reading and browsing this book, you should be able to say, "Gee, I can do that!"

You'll also get a primer on marketing and advertising in this new media and several publicity and marketing strategies you can perform yourself. You'll also be exposed to inside information on how Internet advertising agencies price their services. In fact, those firms will probably hate the fact that this book is being written! You'll learn a lot of their secrets!

This book is decidedly not technical. You don't have to be a programming geek to get your store online. We are not going to give you a step-by-step description of how to configure a server to communicate directly with the Internet. You can hire experts to do that.

You might think of this book as a tour book. Imagine you want to go on a cross-country driving vacation and you have to get ideas on where to visit. The main point of the book is to introduce you to places that people have enjoyed visiting. The book also would be wise to tell you to have your oil changed, carburetor cleaned, and engine tuned before you hit the road. However, the book wouldn't tell you how to do each of those steps and which torque wrench setting to use! You would take your car to a garage and have the mechanics do it for you.

The same is true with this book. You are looking to see what works and doesn't work from companies that have begun to travel this path. This book is for you if you want ideas, inspiration, vision, and tips on sales and marketing. You want an overview of the technology of the Internet in order to understand the terms and its structure, but you don't want to tinker with everything under the hood. You want to be able to understand their words so you can communicate with the technicians. After all, you want to do what you do best and enjoy most—sell your products or professional services.

After all, if you opened a store on Main Street, would you get on your knees to install the carpeting, climb the rafters to hook up the electricity and lights, or go under the building to run the plumbing lines? No way! You would hire people who do this for you—experienced craftsmen who do these tasks hundreds of times a year—so you can concentrate on running your business.

If you are the kind of person who likes to tinker under the hood, we'll point you to other technical books and online resources that will show you how to build your online store step-by-step. You can have the choice of being your own handyman contractor, or hiring others so you can do what you like to do best.

In any case, you will get a lot of practical information that you can use and save a ton of money by not hiring professionals, so you can allocate your resources where it will help you the most.

How to Use This Book

Remember your boring sixth grade history book? You had to read it from cover to cover, with each chapter in order to follow the timeline of history? You couldn't jump around and read about the stuff that interested you. Instead you had to follow the strict order of events. That ordeal won't be repeated in this book.

You can have a rich experience reading this book even if you don't read it chapter by chapter or from cover to cover. In fact, smart readers will skim through the book first and find the material that interests them. You will probably want to skip entire chapters because they don't contain information that is essential to running your business. That advice makes this large book easy to get through!

This book is divided into two sections. The first section contains three chapters explaining why you should consider starting a business on the Internet, what the Internet is all about and the marketing tools you can use, and how to understand the new marketing paradigms involved in this new media. You will want to read these chapters to get a good understanding of the nuts and bolts of marketing on the Internet. You can read it first, or skip directly to the second section.

This second section contains examples of 101 businesses you can start and products you can sell on the Internet. It is chock full of practical advice, case studies of online entrepreneurs, and interviews with people who are in the trenches of online marketing. You'll find a lot of inspirational stories, as well as useful tips on how to run the business and pitfalls to watch out for.

The businesses are arranged in chapters that contain information about related businesses, such as products, professional services, artists, real estate, and food. One chapter even contains information on how to pursue a career in the Internet industries. You might want to read the chapter that relates to your particular interest first and then skim the rest of the chapters for words of wisdom and practical advice. Then read the first section to find out how to minimize your downside risks and increase your chances for succeeding as an online marketer. Whichever approach you choose, you have control over the material.

By the way, we have taken a new approach to give you access to information at your fingertips. Instead of lumping all sources for additional information at the end the book in an appendix, you'll find all the sources for information listed near the first reference. We've also listed e–mail addresses of interview subjects and many of their phone numbers if they've said they would happy to correspond via e–mailwith readers of this book, in the spirit of entrepreneuriship. We didn't print the numbers of the handful of people who asked for privacy.

Interactive Books

Online marketers learn to inject interactivity into their material so that each reader can have a rewarding experience. We've tried to do that here so you'll have an engaging experience as well, given the limitations of paper.

This book is a living product. It grows each day on the Internet. If you would like to visit the online stores, businesses and products mentioned in this book, you can either type in their address (which is called a URL, Uniform Resource Locator), or go to my Home Page and click on the addresses there. My Home Page URL is:

```
http://www.janal-communications.com
```

If you should happen to notice that a company has changed its address or gone out of business, please send me a note at update@janalpr.com or 76004.1046@compuserve.com and I'll update the listing.

Also, if you operate a successful business on the Internet, please let me know and I'll be happy to add you to my listings for free. Who knows, your company might be included in the next edition!

Happy browsing!

Conventions Used in This Book

If you want to see the Web Sites and Home Pages listed in the book, you can type in the URL or address listed. Please note that you must type the information exactly as it appears. The Internet is a finicky taskmaster and won't do what you want it to do if you leave out a forward slash or a comma. However, be careful NOT to include commas or periods at the end of the address that would normally appear in proper grammar. For example, don't type the final period in this demonstration because it is the period that belongs at the end of the sentence.

To find out if your competitors are on the Internet, check to see if they are listed with a directory, like `Yahoo`, `http://www.yahoo.com`.

At the risk of being redundant, you would type:

```
http://www.yahoo.com
```

not

```
http://www.yahoo.com.
```

Got it?

About the Author

Daniel S. Janal is one of the most popular speakers and consultants on the topic of marketing on the Internet. He teaches Internet marketing classes at the University of California at Berkeley and the University of California at Santa Cruz, in addition to consulting with large and small companies on how to create their Home Pages and virtual storefronts on the World Wide Web.

He is one of the pioneers of personal computer public relations in the United States. He has consulted with more than 100 companies over twelve years, including launching Grolier's Multimedia Encyclopedia, the first piece of consumer software available on CD-ROM. He also helped launch America Online. Other clients include AT&T Multimedia Software Solutions, Bell Atlantic Creative Services, Prentice-Hall Home Software, The Learning Company and Equis International. His company, Janal Communications, is located in Danville, CA (510-831-0900). He is considered an expert in providing online marketing solutions for companies.

He is the author of the best-selling Online Marketing Handbook: How to Sell, Advertise, Publicize and Promote Your Products on the Internet and Commercial Online Services; (Van Nostrand Reinhold, 1995) and How to Publicize High Tech Products and Services (10K Press/Janal

Communications, 1991), considered the definitive training manual of public relations novices in the computer industry. He is the codeveloper of Publicity Builder Software (JIAN, 1993). He has contributed articles to numerous trade magazines, including InfoWorld, Computer Dealer, MicroAge Journal, and Compute. He also writes and publishes a newsletter, Online Marketing Update, available online and in print.

One of the most sought-after speakers on the topic of Internet marketing, Mr. Janal conducts lively, interactive sessions that offer tools that participants can use immediately. His enthusiastic, energetic style has entertained and informed audiences at the national meeting of the Public Relations Society of America, Software Publishers Association, Home Office Computing, Softex 2000 in Rio de Janeiro, Soft-letter Marketing Summit, and many others. He is available for speaking engagements and private consultations.

Before starting a career in public relations, Mr. Janal was an award-winning newspaper reporter and business news editor for Gannett Newspapers in Florida and New York. He has won writing awards from the National Education Association and the Hearst Foundation.

He holds bachelor's and master's degrees from Northwestern University's Medill School of Journalism.

For more information about Janal Communications, visit our Home Page http://www.janal-communications.com. To contact Daniel Janal: email to :

update@janalpr.com
76004.1046@compuserve.com
510-831-0900
or snail mail (U.S. Post Office) to:

Janal Communications
P.O. Box 2642
Danville, CA 94526.

ACKNOWLEDGEMENTS

This book is a collaboration of great minds who consented to share their wisdom and experience. In addition to the people interviewed for the book, I'd like to thank these people who have helped me over the years. We learn from our experiences and chance encounters. Sometimes it amazes me how much we really do learn from each other and how the most trivial of information gained one day can play an important role in our lives years later.

Leslie Laredo, Michael Kolowich, Jennifer Christensen, David DeJean at AT&T Interchange Online Network; Steve Case, Pam McCraw, and Doug Rekenthaler at America Online; Regina Brady, Keith Arnold, Michele Moran, and Kathy Gerber at CompuServe; Carol Wallace at Prodigy.

Pam Alexander, Christina Tavella, and Brian Johnson at Alexander Communications; Connie Connors and Lydia Trettis at Connnors Communications; Barbara Thomas, Ed Niehaus, Bill Ryan, Marcos Sanchez, and Skye Ketonen at Niehaus Ryan Haller; Kim Bayne of wolfeBayne Communications. Marty Winston of Winston & Winston; Ron Solberg and Bill Lutholtz of PRSIG.

Greg Jarboe, Charlie Cooper, Ryck Lent, Chris Shipley, Robin Raskin, and Bill Machrone. Tanya Mazarowski of Mecklermedia; Lorraine Sileo and Chris Elwell of Simba Information; Jeff Silverstein and Maureen Flemming of Digital Information Group; Kristin Zhivago at Zhivago Marketing Partners.

Launch Point Associates—Alan Crofut, Cliff Bernstein and Rory McDonough; The Internet Roundtable Society—Bob Lash, Wendi Bernstein Lash, Michael Fremont and Scott Shanks; Ameet Zaveri, Terri Lonier, and James McHugh for reviewing the manuscript.

Michael Krieger, Ken Skier, Maurice Hamoy, Brad Peppard, Tom Stitt, Gary Jose, Keith Hendrick, Jim Nichols, Jackie Clark, Eric Robichaud, Lynne Marcus, Mark Bruce, Bruce Freeman, Mark O'Deady, Peggy Watt, Sharyn Fitzpatrick, Pat Meier, Charlie Valeston, Frank Tzeng, Steve Hersee, Leigh Mariner, Ivan Levison, Larry Parks, Jonathan Parks, Howard Zack, Dave Arganbright, Joe Szczepaniak, Maryanne Piazza, Alan Penchansky, Tim Bajarin, T Steve Hersee, Richard Goswick, David Toner, Irv Brechner, Marty Shenman, Jeff Tarter, Jane Farber, Allison Shapiro, Bob Kersey, Colleen Coletta, Jerry Duro, John Cole, Ken Wasch, Dave McClure, Greg Doench, John Kilcullen, Carol Rizzardi, Babbette Griffis, Mary Stanley. Thanks to Joel Strasser and Tom Richmond who gave me my start in PR.

Thanks to reporters who like a good story: Lance Elko, Selby Bateman, Pete Scicso, David English, Mike Hudnall, Bob Schwabach, Larry Shannon, Pete Lewis, Steve Manes, Keith Ferrell, Kathy Yakal, Ted Needleman, Bob Scott, Kerri Karvetski, Heather Clancy, Alan Bechtold, Dave Haskin, Jerry Olsen, Barry Brenesal, Gayle Ehrenmann, Ephraim Schwartz, John Blackford, Arlan Levitan, Matt Lake, Yael Li Ron, Jon Zilber, Scott Finnie, Adam Meyerson, Donna Meyerson, Michael Penwarden, Gina Smith, Leo Laporte, John Dvorak, Fred Fishkin, Mike Langberg, Michael Antonoff, Fred Abatemarco, Nancy Trespasz, Fred Langa, Jim Forbes, Paul Schindler, Phil Albinus, Donna Tapellini, Rich

Malloy, Dan Rosenbaum, Dennis Allen, Rick Manning, Rich Santalesa, David Coursey, Tim Bajarin, and Scott Mace.

My trusted associates, Susan Morrow, Mark Bruce, and Bruce Freeman.

My mentor, Sandy Hartman. Great friends like Gordy Allen, Wally Bock, Roberta Morgan, and Dave Arnold.

Friends for life, Steven Kessler, Stuart Gruber, Barry Block, Alan Schindler, Phil Albinus, Donna Tapellini, Rich Malloy, Dan Rosenbaum, Dennis Allen, Rick Manning, Rich Santalesa, David Coursey, Tim Bajarin, and Scott Mace.

My trusted associates, Susan Morrow, Mark Bruce, and Bruce Freeman.

Dauber, Alan Penchansky, and Len Zandrow.

The excellent staff at Van Nostrand Reinhold: Neil Levine, Mike Sherry, Lesley Rock, Judith Steinbaum, John Boyd, and Marianne Russell; Matt Wagner at Waterside Productions. Thanks to Paul and Sarah Edwards for their excellent foreword.

Thanks for feedback and encouragement from George Thibault and Steve Leon.

Special thanks to Susan Tracy. May all your fortune cookies come true.

SECTION 1

This section will explain the benefits and risks of starting a business on the Internet. You will also learn how marketing, sales, and advertising are different in the interative, mulitmedia environment of the Internet. Finally, you will gain valuable step—by—step instructions for attracting people to your cyberstore.

1 WHY YOU SHOULD OPEN A BUSINESS ON THE INTERNET

OVERVIEW-OPENING YOUR INTERNET STORE

Who is making money on the Internet?

Lots of people. People like you.

They operate businesses from their spare bedroom at home, professional suites in office parks, and retail storefronts on Main Street. They sell products ranging from flowers and condoms, to boats and travel services, to research reports and matchmaking services, to lobsters and hand-made jewelry. They are professionals like lawyers and accountants. They are artists like musicians, writers, and actors. They are merchants and entrepreneurs.

They represent virtually every age from a sixteen-year-old cartoonist to a senior citizen selling a book about grandparenting. There is a father and son team that sells baseball cards on the Internet and others who work together and feel like family. They are all over the world, from a Canadian speakers bureau to an Australian software publisher.

Some people started businesses on the Internet because they are opportunity-driven entrepreneurs, while others were desperate victims of corporate downsizing. Some hold college degrees and others are still in high school. Two things are for sure: the ones who majored in marketing do not make fun of computer geeks anymore; the computer majors wish they had minored in business administration. They are a diverse lot that has many different reasons for being online.

Dennis DeAndre gave up a six-figure income selling commercial real estate like shopping centers and apartment complexes in San Francisco to create a real estate listing service on the Internet. "I am leaving because of the opportunities on the Internet to transform my field. I think the Internet will downsize a number of industries that offer personal services, including real estate, travel agents, stock brokers, and banks. Instead of being on the side that is being downsized, I plan to take full advantage and capitalize on the new technology. That is where the growth and opportunities are," he says, e-mail: dennis@wco.com. He is just beginning to work on creating his store on the Internet and does not expect to make money for a year.

Some are making a ton of money, like CyberSource's software.net, which grosses $60,000 a month selling computer software—after starting the business only a few months earlier. Company president and CEO Bill McKiernan expects the company to gross $2 million in its first year.

Other companies are trying to break even or are waiting for their first sale. Some companies have invested tens of thousands of dollars, others have invested their beer money.

They are working hard. They are having a lot of fun. They want to be the first ones on the Internet's business areas to stake out their claims so even if the majority of Americans do not have Internet accounts yet.

These entrepreneurs expect a tidal wave of buyers and they want to be prepared for when these consumers do come. These entrepreneurs do not want to be left behind.

Some general interest stores are swamped with 10,000 to 100,000 people visiting each day. Other sites are waiting for more people in their target audience to discover the benefits of online commerce.

"A lot of us are setting up Web sites in anticipation of the rush to online commerce. However, it is like we have set up for the party but it is still very early and most of the guests still have not arrived," says Cliff Bernstein, who runs Internet Health Resources, a successful company that creates Web sites for companies in the health care industry in the San Francisco Bay Area, cliffb@hooked.net, http://www.ihr.com.

Like an early attendee at a party, these pioneers are thinking they will have a great time, but feel a little uncomfortable until more people show up. Of course, they also get the first shot at the best food!

While most people hope to make money, Giselle Aguiar, who runs the Christian Singles Dating Service, looks for an even greater reward. "The first wedding will be the greatest," she says, http://www.christsin-gles.com/Two4Christ/.

There is reason to believe this is the best of times to open a business on the Internet and the worst of times. It is the best of times because there is little competition in major product and service categories, so you can stake your claim to be the first and because prices for services to get online are much lower than opening a storefront on Main Street. It is the worst of times because there are not any established rules to follow or guidelines for success in this new wilderness. No one knows what to charge for providing technical or creative consulting to get online. No one knows how many people are online or who they are, or whether enough of those people need your products to make the venture financially rewarding.

Yet, research firms say there were $25 million to $250 million of goods and services sold on the Internet in 1994. A reporter for Fortune magazine said this figure was inconsequential, as the traditional mail-order business is ninety-nine times larger than the best estimate of Internet sales figures. But I ask you, how much of that $250 billion do not you want?

The figure is expected to reach the billions by the turn of the century, according to virtually every analyst covering the online market. That is an important reason for your store to be on the Internet.

ARE YOU THE RIGHT PERSON TO OPEN A STORE?

Let's take a quick quiz to measure your sales ability:

- Do you hate to sell?
- Would you rather not have to deal with the public face-to-face?
- Does the thought of making cold calls make you break out into a sweat?
- Do you have good ideas?
- Are you capable of completing tasks?
- Can you write a decent letter, or adapt one from a book of sample letters?
- Can you learn from your mistakes?
- Are you stuck in a dead-end job, or about to become a victim of corporate downsizing?
- Do you have a good understanding of how to run a business, including marketing and financial operations?

If you answered "yes" to most of these questions, you have the makings of becoming a great success as an online entrepreneur by opening a storefront on the Internet.

That is because the key skills in sales and marketing in the off-line world aggressiveness, persistence, and false-friendliness do not really matter in the online world of the Internet where faceless transactions are the rule, not the exception, where consumers want information instead of persuasion, and where numerous customers hate to deal with salespeople.

The Internet is a world in which the cream rises to the top and merit counts more than flash. If you are the type of person who always says, "I have a great idea, but I need someone to sell it," then this book-and the Internet are for you.

The way to sell on the Internet is through the soft sell, not the hard sell you see in consumer electronic stores and at car dealerships. On the Internet you merely tell your story, present your information, show pictures of the product, and provide an order form or telephone numbers so the person can call when he is ready to buy. You might never see the person face-to-face or have any dialogue whatsoever with your prospects. In this way, you will not have to deal with the fear of rejection that is the number one fear of would-be salespeople (myself included)!

By the way, if you answered "no" to these questions, do not worry, you too can be a success on the Internet! Having good skills in sales, marketing, and social graces can only help you succeed as an online marketer. As long as you are committed to helping your customers be happy and successful, then you have a good chance of being successful as well.

So, whether you are you a natural-born salesperson or tongue-tied; whether you know the five essential closes preached by every sales guru on the seminar circuit or think that people will buy when they are good and ready, the Internet has a place for you!

This book is designed to help these kinds of people:

- *Wannabees*—You are stuck in a boring, mindless job, or one that has limited opportunities for advancement, earnings, and creativity; or you have been a victim of downsizing and corporate engineering and want to learn how to make money on the Internet. You might be a household professional taking care of the kids on a full-time basis and make jewelry and crafts that you sell at flea markets on the weekends. Welcome to the Internet, the ultimate flea market.

- *Current Business Owners*—You already run a business on Main Street or a professional service in the Office Park and want to reach new markets of people around the world who are on the Internet.

- *Entrepreneurs*—You have read all the hype about the Information Superhighway and want the straight truth about what works and does not work in online marketing. You want good ideas on businesses to start, products to sell, and industry groups to invest in.

- *College Students*—You have surfed the Internet for eight hours every day for the past year and want to see how you can make a career of it.

Basic Questions

Let us cut to the chase. If you are flipping through this book, there are four questions you want answered before reading anything else:

How much time will this take?

Running a business takes time. The people interviewed for this book spend between twenty to sixty hours a week running their Internet store.

Do I have to quit my day job?

Entrepreneuring provides you with many opportunities to conduct a moonlight business while you continue your present employment, or take care of the kids during the day. You can start a business on the Internet and handle the operations at night and on weekends. You might decide never to leave your day job and just operate the Internet business as a sideline, or you might find that business online is so good that you can devote your career to it.

How much money do I need to get started?

You will see by the case studies that some people started with just a few hundred dollars, while others spent considerable sums. To take a ballpark average, it takes about $2,500 in computer equipment to get started, as well as another $2,500 for someone to create your online store. Then there is inventory, which varies store by store. An information business might not have any inventory costs at all, while a mail-order gardening tools catalog might have to invest tens of thousands of dollars. You also need to consider the costs of doing business, such as marketing, legal and accounting service, business permits, and taxes. The bottom line, then, is a minimum average of $5,000 to start a minimal operation, with no upward limit. If you have a computer, your additional investment is limited to business permits, professional legal and accounting advice, and online startup fees.

If you really want to test the waters, you could open a store on the Internet via Prodigy or America Online for $9.95 a month. You will learn about those options in Chapter 2.

How much money can I make?

That question really cannot be answered with a specific number, but you knew that anyway! The answer depends partially on how many people want your product or service, how many of those people are on the Internet, whether they can find you, and can you offer them an attractive price. Fortunately, the indicators are very positive.

There are approximately 30 million people on the Internet, that is, they can access e-mail accounts at the very least. Of those people about, 7-10 million have access to the World Wide Web (also called WWW or the Web), which houses all the storefronts and commercial spaces. Many millions more will jump online in the short term, as the commercial online services (CompuServe, America Online, Prodigy, Microsoft Network, AT&T Interchange, Delphi, and others) offer their 10 million-plus members access to the commercial activities on the Web. These people are affluent (with average income about $60,000), college graduates, overwhelmingly married, and male (by a 2-to-1 ratio). They collectively bought between $50-$200 million of products in 1994, a figure that is expected to increase to $2.5 billion by 1998, according to Simba Research of Wilton, Connecticut.

A survey by MasterCard International `http://www.mastercard.com` in June 1995 showed:

- 66 percent of respondents use the Internet to shop.
- 59 percent rate the Internet as an important outlet when looking for merchandise.
- 28 percent bought products or services on the Internet.
- 17 percent spend an average of one to two hours looking at merchandise each time they shop on the Internet.

According to these numbers, people want to shop on the Internet. If your customers are there, should not you be there as well?

Summary

You can start a business on the Internet either full time or part time. You can also place your existing business on the Internet to open a new sales channel. Start-up costs can range from pocket change to tens of thousands of dollars, depending on your needs. Your earning potential is limited to your ideas, your market, and your ability to convince them to invest in your product or service.

With those preliminaries out of the way, let us look at why you should sell your products or services on the Internet, whether you are an established business, a start up, or have a great idea.

19 REASONS TO START A BUSINESS ON THE INTERNET

If you are thinking about making a commitment to running an online store, you should be aware of the advantages and disadvantages. Let us look first at the reasons to open your storefront on the Internet.

The Internet offers many advantages for companies that want to sell products, whether they are expanding an existing storefront on Main Street, or creating a company that exists only in cyberspace. Here are several reasons for a company to have an online store:

- Reach a worldwide audience
- Do business with an affluent market
- No barrier of time zones, you are open twenty-four hours a day
- Reach consumers when they are ready to buy
- Open a new channel of distribution for your company
- ... Or sell products only on the Internet
- Offer lower costs to consumers and beat competition
- Beat competition to new markets because they aren't online

- Make additional sales more easily
- Create cost-effective catalogs that are long on details
- Low cost of doing business
- Low cost of entry
- No or low rent.
- Interact with customers
- Engage the senses by using audio, video, and multimedia to create relationships and sell products

Let us look at each of these factors.

Reach a worldwide audience

More than 30 million people from around the world are on the Internet. I have received orders for my books from such far flung and exotic destinations as Tel Aviv, Israel; Sydney, Australia; Calgary, Canada; and Seattle! People from all over the world can get access to your online store quickly and easily. Furthermore, you can reach these people for a mere fraction of what it would cost to reach them with other marketing tools like direct mail, television and print advertising, promotions, and even public relations.

Do business with an affluent market

The profile of the average online consumer is very, very positive. According to a study in June 1995 of 13,000 respondents by the Georgia Institute of Technology's Graphics Visualization & Usability Center, http://www.cc.gatech.edu/gvu/user_surveys, showed:

- 82 percent are male, 16 percent are female, and 2 percent did not answer
- Average age is 35
- Average income is $69,000 (45 percent between $50,000 and $200,000)

- 46 percent are single; 50 percent are married; 24 percent have two or more dependents
- 61 percent graduated college
- 34 percent have jobs in professional management, 31 percent are in computers, 24 percent are in education
- 86 percent live in North America, 10 percent are in Europe.

Another source of demographic information is TIC/MIDS Internet Demographic Survey, http://www.tic.com, which was conducted in October 1994. The survey estimated that 27.5 million people used the Internet, while 13.5 million people had access to the World Wide Web, where Internet commerce is conducted.

The Internet can also be reached by members of the major online vendors (CompuServe, America Online, and Prodigy). They report even more affluent consumers, who earn between $60,000 and $75,000 on the average.

Further, these people see the Web as a viable business center, provided they charge prices in line with normal retail channels, according to a report by Simba Information, Inc., of Wilton, Connecticut.

The study predicts a compound Internet user growth rate of 62.4 percent between 1994 and the year 2000. Simba expects total commercial online subscribers to reach 19.7 million by the end of 1995 and grow to 27 million by the end of the decade. Simba believes women will comprise 35–40 percent of the total users of the Internet by the end of 1995. The study also shows that women lean toward personal applications, particularly real-time chat and shopping.

The best news is that more and more people are coming online every day.

Chuck Martin, the publisher of Interactive Week, gave a presentation in May 1995 in which he showed the hockey-stick like growth of the Internet was so sharp, that it if kept growing at the current rate, by 1999 there would be more Internet accounts than people on the face of the earth! I think he was kidding. But only by a little.

No barrier of time zones, you are open twenty-four hours a day

You have to feel sorry for my Uncle Bud. He had a hardware store on the main drag for thirty years. He had to close up shop for twelve to sixteen hours a day, even though he was paying rent twenty-four hours a day. He had to keep an employee in the store on the slowest days and lose money so he would have that person around on Saturday, the busiest day. He closed the store on Sunday so he could get one day of rest. Then he lost all the business to the new superstores in the mall as customers shopped on Sunday.

That is not so on the Internet. Your storefront is open for business twenty-four hours a day. If people are looking for information at 5:05 P.M. or 5:05 A.M., they will be able to find it because your online shop is always open for business. Someone from New Zealand could see your store, browse, and order in the space of a few minutes on Monday morning when you are fast asleep in your bed in your Sunday time zone. It is the neatest feeling to get an e-mail order from Europe late Monday night that is time stamped Tuesday!

Reach consumers when they are ready to buy

Every store has its share of tire kickers who just browse and leave. They are on the Internet as well. However, when they are ready to buy, your store is open for business. As Carol Wallace, a marketing ace at Prodigy says, "You are never going to get more attention from any customer than when they are online. Both their hands are on the keyboard and both their eyes are on the monitor. You are interacting with them. They have pre-selected you. They want to see you. This is a very intimate selling situation."

Memorize those lines. They should form the basis of your business plan!

Appeal to consumers who hate salespeople

If you are in sales, you might find this hard to believe, but many people do not like to buy from salespeople! That is right. They hate the high pressure and power closes. Most people say "just looking" when asked by salespeople if they can merely "help." Because of that, the Internet is the perfect place for the consumer who likes to look around, size things up, draw her own conclusions—and buy. These people do not like to be persuaded or manipulated. That is why they use online services, mail order catalogs, and other sales situations that are not conducted face-to-face. Your Internet store taps this market.

Open a new channel of distribution for your company

Your company might be doing a great job now selling products through a storefront or by mail order. You will also want to use the Internet to open a new channel of distribution for your products. As you will see, for a very low cost of entry, you can reach millions of consumers all around the world for much less than the cost of opening a new store on the other side of town.

The Internet offers established businesses the opportunity to find new markets in their neighborhood or around the world. For the company that is selling a product, like bikes or flowers, the entire world could be a potential market for your products. You will read many examples in the case study section of this book that shows how companies on Main Street are selling products to people in far away places.

... Or sell products only on the Internet

Some companies exist only on the Internet. These include information brokers who sell research information to companies on hard-to-find data, and artists who sell pictures via the Internet but do not have their own gallery on Main Street. These companies exist because of the low barriers of entry in starting a business on the Internet.

Beat competition to new markets because they are not online

If you operate a business on Main Street, you cannot afford not to open a storefront on the Internet. Your competitors might already be there snagging business you didn't even know about.

For example, Thanksgiving Coffee operates an online mall in addition to their stores and mail order business. Frankly, I never had heard of them before I stumbled across them on the Internet. However, many people in my classes had used their coffee and ordered gifts for friends. When I think of coffee, I think of Starbucks. However, they are not online. Now let us take a hypothetical scenario: I am in Sioux City, probably the only place on the planet that does not have a Starbucks store, at least not yet. I want to buy a gift of assorted gourmet coffees for my brother-in-law because he is a caffeine hound. I go online and do a search for coffee stores. The search shows Thanksgiving Coffee, which I have never heard of. It does not show Starbucks, which I have never heard of either since I do not leave Sioux City. Who am I going to buy from? Thanksgiving, of course.

You do not have to operate a mail order business to appreciate this scenario. You can create any business and attract new clients by being listed in directories that show your name to prospects (and other marketing tactics that we will talk about later). Lawyers are getting referrals from other lawyers, authors are selling books, companies are selling flowers, gourmet foods, and even garlic to people all over the world just because they are on the Internet and their competitors are not! You cannot afford not to be on the Internet if you operate a business.

Make additional sales more easily

Research has shown that it is easier to sell to an existing customer than to develop a new one. The Internet can be very helpful with this. Once a customer has bought from you, you can ask to send her more information about the product, product upgrades, and related products. If they were happy with your pea pod seeds, then they just might buy rose plants from you next season.

Create cost-effective catalogs that are long on details

Print catalogs are great marketing tools, but they suffer from a lack of space and the expenses of mailing lists, postage, and printing. They can also become out of date quickly as suppliers raise prices. Online marketers have much greater flexibility with online catalogs. Because space is cheap, they can print descriptions and photos of their entire 10,000-product line, not just the 100 items that the marketing department thinks will sell this year. The descriptions can be full and complete and go on for as much space as is needed. This is important for a company that sells to other businesses. For example, an industrial strength glue might require the reader to analyze complex chemical formulas to ensure the product meets the buyer's specifications. Printing and mailing outbound communications, such as price sheets, catalogs, and brochures, could strain a company's financial resources. However, the cost to publish these materials on the Internet is minimal.

Companies are cutting their printing and mailing costs for catalogs and marketing materials by placing them online. Sun Microsystems announced it has saved more than $1 million in one year by placing its marketing information online. It also saved a ton of money in related costs, such as manpower to mail the materials. Tandem Computers not only saved a great deal of money by placing their marketing materials on the Internet, they also reached five times as many customers!

Online catalogs can also include demonstrations, voice-overs, and other benefits of technology that print catalogs cannot begin to duplicate.

Low cost of doing business

Selling on the Internet can be more efficient and effective for many businesses because of the lowered cost of doing business and of making the sales. Let's look at these factors:

- Low cost of entry
- No or low rent
- No inventory or warehouse costs
- Offer lower costs to online consumers
- Reduced costs of salespeople because customers sell themselves

Low cost of entry

The cost of starting your online store can vary from a few dollars to tens of thousands, much less than the price of opening a physical store.

No or low rent

Unlike a physical store, your cyberstore does not pay a fortune in rent. You might pay a monthly fee of $100 or less to store your site at a Digital Mall or Internet Access Provider, two types of service providers who connect your store to the Internet. The competitive climate is forcing prices way, way down. In 1994, you could pay $250 a month for basic storage. By 1995, the price plummeted to about $100 in the San Francisco Bay Area. If prices are higher in your town, call a few providers in San Francisco.

If you operate a sizable business, you might have the Internet hookup at your office. That will cost about $15,000–150,000 to get started with recurring fees of about $1,000 a month—fees that are much less than remodeling an office.

Offer lower costs to consumers and beat competition

Because online merchants have lower overhead—they do not pay for heating, air-conditioning, water, security, janitorial, and a variety of other fees imposed by landlords—they can pass the savings along to their customers in the form of lower prices. Companies can offer discounts to their online consumers. This tactic might have attracted them to the Internet in the first place and keeps them coming back. They can offer lower prices also because of two additional factors:

Reduced or no inventory, warehouse costs and costs of money—Internet-based businesses can rely on drop-shipping their products to meet their customers' orders. They don't have to stock large supplies or products in expensive warehouses. Instead, they can offer the product for sale on their online catalog and order the products from their suppliers only when they receive payment from their online customers. Since the product is not being bought until needed, the online merchant does not have to tie up money in goods or pay interest on that money. Instead, his money can be earning interest or invested into other profitable ventures.

Reduced costs of salespeople because customers sell themselves—You do not need salespeople online. Your prospects are their own salespeople. They sell themselves! That happens when you place your sales material online and prospects browse. They follow their own line of thinking, find answers to their own questions, and buy when they are ready. In order to construct this kind of sales plan, you must interview your top salespeople and ask them what questions people ask, and how to best answer them. Many online consumers like the fact there are not any pushy salespeople online to harass them into buying a product. Online selling is more immediate and less intrusive than dealing with salespeople.

Interact with customers

Online communications offers merchants the benefits of interacting with consumers, which cannot exist in print or television communications. Using e-mail, infobots (automated e-mail, similar to a fax back system), and other online tools, merchants can create a dialog with consumers that leads to long-term relationships and sales.

Engage the senses by using audio, video, and multimedia to create relationships and sell products

Vendors can showcase their products and services by using the Internet's multimedia capabilities. Using audio, video, and multimedia, merchants can make their products come alive on the Internet. Technology and tools are still immature, but the promise of interactive, multimedia demonstrations is becoming a reality.

Four Additional Marketing Benefits

In addition to increasing sales, companies that are using the Internet are finding they can add value to their businesses by:

- Conducting market research online
- Finding competitive information
- Providing customer support
- Decreasing costs of printing and distributing marketing materials

Conducting market research online

You can find out a lot about your customers simply by seeing which information they select and what appeals to them. For example, on the Saturn Home Page, the potential car buyer can select a picture of four car models. Then he can see the car in a certain color. Does he pick red or white or blue or green? Does he read about the safety statistics, how fast it can go from 0 to 60 mph, or about the luxury features of the interior? By seeing which information is selected, the marketer can adjust the messages in other advertisements!

Finding competitive information

You can use the Internet to find out news and information about your industry by using the many news services available, such as Clari.Net, `http://www.clari.net`. Stock and financial news can also be obtained from Quote.Com, `http:/www.quote.com`. You could also visit your competitor's businesses. To find out their addresses, check out their sales and marketing material, or go to one of the many search engines on the Internet, such as Yahoo, `http://www.yahoo.com` or InfoSeek, `http://www.infoseek.com`.

By typing in a search term, like "bagpipes" or "antiques" you will find all the businesses that offer those products. One additional word about InfoSeek: you can ask it to search through every newsgroup and mailing list, which are online bulletin boards where people leave messages for people who are interested in the same topics. When it finds a match, it sends the note to your mailbox, where you can answer the person's questions. Think of it as an online prospecting tool. You can also use InfoSeek to find out what people are saying about your company, so you can use damage control if they are saying bad things.

Providing customer support

Many companies, especially computer hardware and software companies, are finding the Internet to be a great way to answer customers' questions. They do this by setting up files of Frequently Asked Questions (FAQs) in which every possible customer question is answered. Customers go online and read the file that pertains to their problem. If you would like to do this for your company, here are the steps:

- Interview the customer-support personnel to find the questions and answers
- Create files for each product (e.g., computers, modems, monitors)
- Create sub-files for each product in the line (e.g. computer model 1, computer model 2)
- Place the files on your server in an attractive and easy-to-use menu structure. Companies can save a great deal of money by using this method because they free the human operator to do more important tasks or handle more complex calls.

Six Challenges to Running an Internet Store

The Information Highway is not paved with gold. You will have to invest time, money, and energy into making a success of your business. You cannot just open your store and expect to make a million dollars overnight. It will take work. You will be able to do some of it yourself, but you will have to hire others to do parts for you, just as you would hire a plumber to install a bathroom in your store on Main Street. Here are reasons to be careful in creating an Internet business:

- Standing out from the crowd
- Shifting prices for services
- Buyer reluctance
- Security issues
- Audience size
- Shopping as a participant sport

Standing out from the crowd.

Imagine shopping at your local mall, except the mall has 50,000 stores and not one directory that shows where they are located. Welcome to the Internet. Your first job once you open your cyberstore is to publicize and promote it so it stands out from the others. You will learn many ways to do this in Chapter 3.

Shifting prices for services

Prices for services are all across the board. Providers and suppliers are charging whatever they can get away with. That is the sign of an immature industry, not of price gouging. Skills that are highly sought today, like HTML programming to turn your marketing material into a format the World Wide Web can read, are coming under price attack as more people learn the coding—and automatic conversion programs hit the market and replace humans!

Buyer reluctance

People are wary about ordering products online. A report by Dataquest shows that only 25 percent of the people who bought products online paid with a credit card. This means 75 percent of the people ordered by phone or mail or visited a store after seeing the ad on the Internet. While this statistic should not frighten you away, you should make alternative ordering methods available to all customers.

Security issues

Security of your data and customer records could be subject to attack by hackers who want to destroy things because they think it is fun or to show the world they are smarter than anyone else. Fortunately, there are security devices and business practices that can protect your store most of the time. However, your store on Main Street can be robbed, too.

Audience size

The online audience is small, only about 10 million people on the World Wide Web and 30 million worldwide on the Internet. Your audience might not be online, or only a small part might be. However, as the Internet trend reaches fad and epidemic proportions, the audiences will grow. Experts expect that to happen in a very short time—months, not years.

Shopping as a participant sport

Some people will never buy online because they want to see and touch the product. They might also like the stimulation of going to a store, interacting with live people, and fighting for a parking spot. Hard to believe, but it is true—and they are the majority!

Disclaimer-The Small Print

Here is the paragraph the lawyers want inserted. Not every business will succeed on the Internet or on Main Street. There are many reasons businesses fail, including lack of experience by the operator, lack of investment capital, bad marketing, intense competition, and improper product selection and pricing. Reading this book will not guarantee success. However, by studying this book, you can minimize the risks of failure and increase the chances for success.

The ideas and tips given in this book are not meant to be a comprehensive business guide to starting and running a business. That would be the subject of 101 individual books. We direct you to your local library to read the loose-leaf publications published by Entrepreneur Magazine on how to start a business in general, and for more than a dozen businesses in particular. Those books are comprehensive road maps for providing many insights into starting and running many traditional business. Their sound advice will be helpful in planning your Internet business as well.

Ask the reference librarian for other resources that the library has or can obtain for you. Of course, look for business resources on the Internet (start with the search indexes, like Yahoo, at `http://www.yahoo.com` or ask entrepreneurs and Internet Presence Providers for their advice, if they are willing to give it. Also, join mailing lists and newsgroups that cater to entrepreneurs and business owners in your field. For a list of newsgroups, go to Neosoft at (`http://www.neosoft.com/paml`). For a list of mailing lists, check the newsgroup menu of your Internet software.

You will also notice that many of the businesses profiled in this book did not create business plans. I did not either. However, this is not necessarily a good idea. Maybe we all would be more successful with clearer goals in mind at the beginning of the project and realize that the plan can and will be adjusted along the way. You should have at least a modest idea of what you are doing, how much it will cost, and what you hope to gain from this venture. You definitely need some kind of plan or road map to help you get there.

If you start with this book and then read specialized books in the areas you want to pursue, you will be following a good plan.

Summary

Yes, there are risks to starting a business on the Internet, just as there are risks in starting any new business anywhere in the world. You need to study the facts so that you can make intelligent decisions. Not only do you need to study the businesses and markets, you need to study yourself as well.

DO YOU HAVE WHAT IT TAKES TO BE AN INTERNET ENTREPRENEUR?

We do not mean to present a picture through rose-colored glasses. Not every idea is destined for success. Some people really do not have what it takes to manage themselves, let alone a business.

As a first step, let us take a simple test to see if you have the raw materials to become a successful net entrepreneur.

Do you have discipline?

One of the keys to running a good business is to go to the store every day. Whether you are a corporate executive or a home-based entrepreneur, getting a few extra winks or getting up at the same time every day and going to the desk in the extra bedroom is the difference between success and failure.

Running an online store will take time. It will not run itself. Your main activities will be to check the e-mail to answer questions from prospects and take orders, ship merchandise, order new stock, keep the store looking attractive and fresh, and promote the store. You will see by the case studies in this book that some entrepreneurs spend only a few hours a week online, while others live online. It is up to you. The more time you put in, the more results you will see.

Do you have the support of your family?

Running a business takes time, space, and money—all of which can be scarce resources. Will they give you those resources and support you? Or will they guilt-trip you and sabotage your plans? It is important to get their buy—in and support up front. Perhaps the online store can be a family adventure, with everyone pitching in and making it a fun exercise. It seems that every teenager knows her way around the computer and that every teenager wants a job after school to make some spending money for clothes, dates, and cars. Perhaps they can handle simple e-mail requests for information, process credit card forms and ship products. After all, isn't that task better than a job dishing out yogurt at the mall? Of course, younger children will want your time and won't be fascinated by the inner workings of big business, so you'll want to evaluate your relationships carefully before going online.

Have you been on the Net?

Trying to explain how sales work on the Internet is like trying to explain jazz to someone who's never heard it. You can describe the passion and excitement of music with words, but you will understand it a whole lot more on a more personal level if you listen to a record. Same with the Internet. Get online, see what others are doing, and determine if it could work for you.

Summary

The questions in this section should get you started thinking about whether you should be an online merchant or not. We are here to separate the hype from reality, not to sell you a bill of goods. Running a business is work. It can be fun and financially rewarding, but there are no guarantees. Just because there are 30 million people on the Internet do not mean they will all go to your store and buy everything in sight. This book will show you how many entrepreneurs are succeeding—but you will also read about hard times and heartaches.

WHAT ARE THE HOT BUSINESSES AND PRODUCTS?

When I teach my Internet marketing seminars all over the world, the first question eager entrepreneurs ask is: "What are the hottest businesses to start on the Internet?"

Here are the top answers, according to a study in April 1995 of 13,000 respondents by the Georgia Institute of Technology's Graphics Visualization & Usability Center. The entire survey can be seen at their home page, http://www.cc.gatech.edu/gvu/user_surveys:

- Books
- Computer software
- Computer hardware
- Music
- Casual clothes
- Movies or videos
- Home electronics
- Plays and concerts
- Vacations
- Sunglasses
- Jewelry

According to a survey by the University of Michigan Business School, these items were the most widely purchased on the Internet:

- Computer software
- Books
- Computer hardware
- Music
- Home electronics
- Videos
- Travel services
- Tickets for entertainment events
- Casual clothing and apparel
- Legal services
- Jewelry
- Shoes
- Sunglasses

However, there are at least two other ways to answer that question.

The second way to answer the question is for companies that already have a storefront or catalog operation to seek a new channel to market. If you are successful selling your existing products, then the Internet offers you an opportunity to reach new markets around the corner and around the world for a low cost. You do not have to learn a new business, you simply expand on the knowledge base you already have.

The third way to answer this seemingly simple question is to look straight in the mirror and say: "What would make you happy?"

No, I am not a Zen philosopher or trying to sell a new kind of religion. What I am trying to get you to do is think about what business you want to be in. That is because if you are in the hottest business on earth but it makes you sick or bores you to death, then it is not the right business to be in no matter how much money is involved! So let us use that as a reality check. Ask yourself what kind of business you would like to be in. There are many successful businesses you can start on the Internet. The best one is the one that gets your juices flowing.

What You Have Learned in This Chapter

If you have a great product, or great ideas, the Internet could be the place to help you sell it to an affluent, educated, worldwide audience at a relatively low cost of entry. Good sales and marketing skills—the weak points of most start-up business—are nice, but not required. You must determine if you have what it takes to succeed, like a good idea, the support of your family, and the time and finances to devote to the task. If so, the Internet could be for you.

2 INTERNET BASICS

GETTING UP TO SPEED

Let's get your business online! You probably have some basic questions and fears about the Internet and how to make sense about the technology and how to run a business. This chapter will explore such basic questions as:

- What is the Internet?
- What is the World Wide Web?
- What is a Home Page?
- What is e-mail?
- What equipment do I need?
- How do I connect to the Internet?
- What are the costs to get up and running?
- Do I have to be a programming geek to do this?

We will answer these questions from a decidedly non-technical point of view and give you just the information you need.

What is the Internet?

The Internet is a vast network of computers that gives consumers the ability to see and interact with information on those computers. This means that a consumer in Wichita can read the brochures and sales material of a company based in Portland—in just a few seconds. The implications for marketers is that consumers all around the world can read your material, send e-mail, and order products any time of the day or night.

What Is the World Wide Web?

The area on which merchants can safely conduct business on the Internet is called the World Wide Web (also called WWW or Web). If you imagine the Internet to be a city, then the World Wide Web is zoned for commercial activity. Advertising and commerce cannot be conducted on other parts of the Internet called Mailing Lists and Newsgroups. There aren't any laws that prevent this; however, people go to those areas for nonbiased and noncommercial information. They react very negatively to people who try to conduct business there. It is as if you go to the steam room in your health club to relax and someone sits next to you and tries to sell you life insurance: Sure, there is no law to stop him, but you aren't going to buy from him either. In these cases, everyone wastes their time. So don't do it!

What Is a Home Page?

Merchants can post their sales literature, product information, coupons, sales incentives, press releases, brochures, ads, promotional materials, and take orders in their own space on the Web, which is called a "Home Page," "Web Site," "Site," "Online Presence," or "Cyberstore." More importantly, this place can be thought of as your storefront, billboard, convention center, shopping mall, brochure, newspaper, or magazine where consumers can find out about your products and make a purchase.

Your marketing information can be displayed with color graphics, lively text, and even sound and video files, although the last two are still a bit quirky at this stage of technological development.

Although the term "Home Page" is used, this space is really larger than a single page. In fact, as you look at your computer screen, the page actually can scroll down to allow merchants to post a great deal more material than can fit on a printed page. To tap the full power of the Web, Cyberstore owners can post an unlimited amount of information on "sub pages," which are linked to the Home Page through "hypertext" links that allow consumers to jump from one piece of information to the next immediately. These hypertext links reveal the true power of the Internet because these tools can allow consumers to find information anywhere in your cyberstore. They can pick the information that interests them and helps them make an intelligent sales decision. Through the use of hyperlinks, consumers can transparently connect to computers of other companies and businesses in faraway places.

These tools give consumers the ability to comparison shop in seconds, without having to get into a car and drive to another mall. They can search for the information they need, check prices, warranties, and return policies and then place orders—without leaving their homes.

The beauty of this hypertext material is that customers can create their own sales presentation. They don't have to read a presentation that doesn't appeal to them. For example, if they enter your Home Page where you sell books, they can see options for reading about fiction, non-fiction, self-help, and mystery. They can use their mouse to select a category and see the titles in that section. In other words, they don't have to read a lot of information that doesn't appeal to them. They can read what they want and order when they are ready.

To put your material on the Web, it must be designed in a format that the computer can read. That format is called HTML, which stands for Hyper Text Markup Language. It is a simple programming language that can be mastered in a few hours. In fact, Microsoft Word and WordPerfect can convert your text files to HTML automatically, although you will need to edit them to make them look more attractive. Of the 50 or so people interviewed at length in this book, all but five wrote the HTML codes into their marketing materials—and they wouldn't describe themselves as technicians. Unless you are technically inclined, you will probably want a programmer to handle this task.

Another option is to create a simple Home Page by answering a few basic questions on America Online or Prodigy.

What Is a Cyberstore?

Your Home Page is a cyberstore. It can also be referred to as a Web Site.

What Equipment Do I Need?

Consumers and merchants link up with the Internet by using a computer, a modem, a phone line, and a communications software called a "browser." Larger companies might want to install a server if they plan to house all the equipment at their facility. Let's look at each component:

Computer—Consumers and merchants can access the World Wide Web with virtually any computer built in the last five years. At the very least, an IBM PC compatible computer with a 386 MHz processor and black and white monitor will let people run the software needed to browse your store. However, a faster computer, color monitor, and audio speakers will enhance their experience. Any Macintosh with 8 MB of memory and a modem is capable of connecting to the Internet.

In the not too distant future, a CD-ROM drive will be part of the online advertising and shopping trip. That is because the CD-ROMs can store and display graphics and sound faster than the Internet can deliver over phone lines. Internet merchants will want to use the CD-ROM as a delivery and display mechanism, and the Internet as an order-taking system.

Merchants who want a direct connection to the Internet will need a minimum of a 486/33 MHz processor with 8 MB RAM running Winsock 1.1 compliant TCP/IP stack and the server software of their choice, such as Windows HTTP Deamon or Sir Web. Merchants who favor Macintoshes will want to use an 8150 Workgoup Server or a 9150 Workgroup Server with BB edit and Web Star. Most merchants and startups will do nicely with their desktop PCs and Macintoshes as they connect to the Internet through local Internet Service Providers.

Modem—A modem is an electronic device that allows the computer to transmit and receive data from other computers via the telephone lines. Modems are rated by the speed at which they can do their jobs. The higher the number, the faster the time to transfer data and the less waiting your customers will have to endure. Most modems sold now are in the 14.4 kbps class, which is adequate for use on the Internet. For optimum performance, however, a 28.8 kbps modem is preferred. The slower modems cost about $100, while the faster ones cost about $200, but like most technology tools, prices are falling every day as efficiency increases. Practically every new computer comes equipped with a 14.4 kbps modem.

The type of modem merchants will want to use depends on what kind of service they select and how active they plan to be. They can get by with a 14.4 kbps modem if they outsource the entire activity, use America Online or Prodigy, or rent space from a Digital Mall. If they have a direct connection to the Internet, they will need either a 56K frame relay access drive and high speed serial port, or a T-1 line with router and T-1 CSU/DSU device.

Telephone line—The standard telephone line that connects consumers to their friends and families is the same wire that can connect their computers to the Internet. Nothing needs to be done to modify this cord to conduct business on the Internet. In some parts of the country, telephone companies are offering higher speed phone lines, called ISDN (Integrated Services Digital Network), that allow faster transmission of data—56K. For more information, call your local telephone company, as prices and rates for installation and monthly fees vary widely. Merchants who want to connect directly to the Internet must use a 56K connection at the very least and a T-1 line if traffic to your Home Page is heavy.

Browser Software—A "browser" is a software program that lets consumers use the World Wide Web, the area of the Internet that permits commerce. Browsers let consumers find information on Home Pages simply by allowing users to point and click on the material they want to see. Good browsers have features that make finding and printing information quick and easy. Those tools include bookmarks so you can find desirable stores again. These browsers also have tools that let consumers send and receive e-mail on mailing lists, newsgroups, and to and from merchants; receive and send longer files, such as software programs and pictures; and find many types of information in vast data libraries on the Internet. Currently, the most popular browser is called Netscape Navigator. All are available at computer software stores for PCs and Macintoshes. In addition, CompuServe, Prodigy, America Online, Microsoft Network, eWorld and other popular commercial online services have browsers attached to their systems which consumers can use without buying additional software. Instead, they pay for the time they spend online. Merchants will want to select a browser that has built in security and features for taking orders via forms sent on e-mail. Netscape Commerce Server is the choice of many ISPs.

Under ideal conditions, merchants will want the fastest computer, modem, and telephone line they can afford. While it is possible to upgrade to better hardware in the future, it is best to start out with the best you can afford at the beginning to get the most out of the Internet.

POPULAR BROWSERS

These software programs are available at computer and software stores.

*   Netscape Navigator by Netscape Communications
*   Quarterdeck Mosaic by Quarterdeck Office System
*   Mosaic in a Box by Spry
*   Netcruiser by Netcom
*   Internaut by Pipeline

You can download Netscape Navigator at http://www.netscape.com.

How Do I Connect to the Internet?

Consumers need to subscribe to an Internet Service Provider (ISP) to view the World Wide Web in much in the same way that a couch potato needs to subscribe to a cable TV company to watch Nickelodeon. You can subscribe to the net in a number of ways:

Commercial Online Services—Merchants can put their store online by subscribing to a commercial online network. As mentioned earlier, Prodigy and America Online have space available for merchants. Expect other online services to offer the same.

Direct connections—Merchants can connect their store to the Internet with one of hundreds of local ISPs, either directly (in what is called a SLIP or PPP account) or through a shell account (such as those offered by Netcom, Pipeline, or Hooked). A shell account provides access to your ISP's computer where you can access the Internet. A SLIP or PPP account connects your modem to an Internet Service Provider's terminal server which connects you directly to the Internet. The latter method means you'll see graphics faster. Merchants will want a PPP account. To edit your files online, you will need a SLIP or PPP account.

Sources of Additional Information

Here are the names and phone numbers of companies that provide access to the Internet:

- CompuServe-800-848-8199, 614-457-8600
- America Online-800-827-6364, 703-448-8700
- Prodigy-800-848-8199
- Microsoft Network-206-882-8080
- Netcom-800-501-8649

How do I select an Internet Service Provider?

Most people who read this book will probably want to get onto the Internet via an Internet Service Provider who can provide many technical and marketing services for you, such as those found at a Digital Mall. To select a provider, ask these questions:

What kind of connection do you have to the Internet?

The right answer will be a 56K line, if they have less than a dozen clients who don't generate a lot of online traffic, or a T-1 line if they have a large volume. Under no circumstances do you want to sign up with a company that has a 14.4 kbps or 28.8 kbps connection. It is simply too slow.

What does the service cost per month?

Service charges can range from a flat fee for a minimum amount of space your cyberstore occupies on the computer, such as $100 per month for 50 Mbytes of data. These figures are only samples, as rates range widely from one part of the country to the next, and even within region. Also, prices will continue to go down, as competition goes up.

What are the additional charges?

In addition to "rent," some malls charge you for additional services. Be sure to ask if there are additional charges for:

- Each time a person visits.
- The number of pages each person sees.
- A percentage of sales.
- Editing or changing your data
- Registering your business name with InterNIC (which provides you with a needed domain name.

The answers you are looking for are "none" for the first four questions. It costs about $100-$150 to register a domain name.

Can I edit files from my office?

Select a provider that will let you access and edit your files from your home or office.

Can I connect to the service from anywhere in the country for a local phone call?

Most providers don't have local phone numbers all over the country, although Prodigy, CompuServe, America Online, Netcom, and a few others do. If you do a lot of traveling, this feature can be important as you'll save money if there is a local access number. If you don't travel, then this feature is not relevant.

Other questions to ask

How long have they been in business? Since the Internet's commercial capabilities are relatively new, you won't find many that are older than two years.

How many customers do they have? How fast are they growing? The number of customers can be a bonus, as it shows stability and growth. It could be a minus in that the service might be overloaded with traffic and support needs. Will you get your share of support?

How many people are on staff? This is important as you need to ensure that someone will be on hand to answer questions, or deal with the problems in the computer system in the middle of the night.

Is technical support included? If not, how much will it costs? Check to see how other vendors are charging for support and see how each vendor stacks up.

Summary

Your Internet Service Provider could be the most important ingredient to your success on the Net, if you don't have a T-1 connection at your business. Their technical ability can make or break you. If they are thinly staffed or poorly trained, your cyberstore could suffer. If they charge too much, your profitability will be affected. If they nickel and dime you for every service, you might hesitate before implementing needed changes, or surrender a substantial portion of your fees. You should call several providers and ask these questions. Prepare a chart showing the name of each provider and the costs for each service. By doing this you will be able to find the provider who best meets your needs for the most reasonable fee.

What Is E-mail?

E-mail is short for electronic mail. These are notes of any length you can send from one computer to another. By using e-mail a consumer can ask questions of merchants who can reply to their specific concerns. E-mail on the Internet is free and is provided as part of the normal service from most Internet service providers. E-mail is sent quickly to respondents, usually within a few seconds, although longer files can require more time.

E-mail knows where to go because you give it an address, just as you would a normal piece of mail. Each person who uses a commercial online service has a username, which could be a series of numbers and letters, such as 760046.1046@compuserve.com or a person's real name, or first letter and initials, such as djanal@aol.com, dan.janal@mycompany.com or a non-human mailbox, such as info@mycompany.com. The addressing system looks like this:

`username@service.ext`

In case you are interested, the extension, "ext" tells you what kind of organization the name belongs to, such as:

> .com-commercial
> .edu-educational
> .gov-government
> .mil-military
> .net-network
> .org-organization

People in other countries, such as Germany, would have an additional extension as part of their address, such as:

`Franz.Bruner@mycompany.com.gr`

Other country codes would include:

> au-Australia
> br-Brazil
> ca-Canada
> de-Germany
> ie-Ireland
> il -Israel
> jp-Japan
> kp-Democratic People's Republic of Korea
> se-Sweden

E-mail can be sent to people on different systems. Here is the format:

America Online   `user@aol.com`

AT&T Mail   `user@attmail.com`

CompuServe   `user.number@compuserve.com`

Delphi   `user@delphi.com`

Genie   `user@genie.geis.com`

Microsoft Network   `user@msn.com`

MCI Mail   `user@mcimail.com`

What are Infobots?

You can create an e-mail version of a fax back system with an infobot or mailbot. When people send e-mail to that address, such as info@your-company.com, they will get a pre-written response immediately. This can be an effective marketing tool that can tie in nicely to your print advertising campaign.

Your online image is reflected in your e-mail address. The Internet community perceives an address with your company as being more credible than an address at an Internet Service Provider's address. For example, John Williams at XYZ Company would be better with the first example:

```
john_williams@xyzcompany.com
jwilliams@aol.com.
```

How Do Customers Find My Cyberstore?

Each store on the Web has its own address, just as in the real world. However, where your store address would be 123 Main Street, Anytown, Calif., the Web address looks like this:

```
http://www.mycompany.com
```

You've seen these addresses throughout the book. Here's what it means:

http:// stands for hyper text transfer protocol. It tells the computer to begin looking for something.

www stands for World Wide Web (but you knew that!).

mycompany.com is the name of the company. Many companies choose to call their Home Page by their company name, like Wells Fargo `http://www.wellsfargo.com`. Others do not, like Southwest Airlines, which uses `http://www.iflyswa.com`.

Companies that rent space from a Digital Mall, a type of Internet Service Provider, might have an address like:

```
http://www.digital-mall.com/vendors/yourcompany.html.
```

This looks like a second-class address. You would want to ask your Digital Mall landlord to create an alias that would let users type `http://www.mycompany.com`, but the Digial Mall's computer would know it was really your address.

These groups of words and punctuations are called URL, pronounced "earl" which stands for Uniform Resource Locator. Also, instead of saying, "Let's go to the Mycompany mall." You might see it written in the following manner: "Point your browser to the URL `http://www.mycompany.mall`."

The name of your address is called your domain. Names are assigned by a group called InterNIC, which assigns all business names on a first-come, first-served basis. If you want to protect your company name now—even before you are ready to go online—you can arrange to register a name with any Internet Service Provider, Internet Presence Provider, or Digital Mall. They'll charge a one-time fee of about $100-$150. By the way, don't even think of registering the name of a famous company, like McDonald's or Hertz, in the hopes of selling it to them. InterNIC frowns on this—and so do recent court cases.

Strategies for drawing customers to your store are found in the next chapter.

To find businesses that compete with yours, go to a directory like Yahoo or Webcrawler and type in the keyword that best describes your business (e.g. skiing, baby supplies, clothing). You'll see a list of stores that you can visit for ideas and analysis.

How do I get started and how much does it cost?

Putting your business online involves five major steps:

- Deciding your marketing goals for being online and finding your unique niche.
- Creating the content (marketing message, sales materials, ordering materials, art).
- Converting the content to HTML, the programming language that

allows the Internet to read your content.
- Connecting your finished product to the Internet.
- Promoting your Home Page so people shop.

Each carries its own costs. The following discussion will talk about the activities in general and provide a range of fees.

Deciding your marketing goals for being online

What is your purpose to be online? To sell directly to customers, or to draw customers to your retail location? Different goals will require different messages and content to support the messages. For a complete discussion of the benefits of being online, please see Chapter 1. You can create these messages by yourself for no cost at all. You could retain a marketing person to help you on an hourly basis. The cost could range from $75 to $175 per hour. Five hours should complete the job, although it might take as little as an hour if you are well organized and focused. The marketing person will help you define your goals and your message and propose strategies for creating material that will help you get online, including a storyboard outlining the entire site. As with all steps of marketing, you should constantly be asking yourself, "What makes my business unique?"

Creating the content (marketing message, sales materials, ordering materials, art)

Once you know what you are trying to accomplish by being online, you'll need to create materials that will support your marketing message. Your marketing materials convey your message, describe your products or services, order forms so people can buy from you or know how to get in touch with you both through e-mail and on the phone, and present enticing artwork that makes your storefront attractive and inviting. Fees range from $75 to $175 an hour. A modest site could take at least five to

10 hours for a cost of $375 to $1,750. Pricing is very competitive and varies by region. The advertising agencies on Madison Avenue will build a dandy site for your company for $25,000 minimum. Marketers in San Francisco can build an even better one for you for about $5,000. To get your feet wet and test the waters, you might want to use the templates on Prodigy or America Online and set up your site by yourself, for about $10 a month.

It is important to immerse yourself in the Net and Net culture to see what others are doing. You'll see what's working and what is lame, what was hot yesterday and cold today. You'll be able to integrate the best of what you see with your own materials. You won't waste time creating lame sites.

Converting the content to HTML, the programming language that allows the Internet to read your content

After you or your marketing firm or department has created the content for your site, it must be converted into a file format the Internet can read. The format is called HTML, for Hyper Text Markup Language. It is pretty easy to learn and you could do it yourself if you have the time and feel comfortable with computers. If not, you can hire an HTML artist to prepare your documents. They charge about $75 an hour, but I expect the price to drop rapidly to about $35 an hour as every desktop publisher in the world learns how to perform this task. The costs for the conversions will depend on how many pages of material you have. For a rough estimate, plan on one hour per page.

Connecting your finished product to the Internet

Now that your material has been created and is in the proper format, you must connect to the Internet so that your potential customers can see your storefront. You are basically putting your files onto a computer that is connected to the Internet. There are several ways to do this, with varying costs, ranging from $10 a month to be on Prodigy or America Online to $15,000 startup to renting space from an ISP, to having a direct connection to the Internet from your office. These costs and options will be described in the next section.

How Do I Connect My Business to the Internet?

Merchants have several options to connect to the Internet. Each carries a radically different price. Let's look at these options from easiest and least expensive to most intricate and expensive:

* Prodigy and America
* Digital Malls
* Direct Connection

To find the best vendor, ask for recommendations from a computer user group (lists of groups can be found in Computer Shopper magazine or in local computer newspapers and local papers or libraries) or someone who's already on the Internet. Let's explore the pros and cons of each option.

Prodigy and America Online

Prodigy and America Online are two major commercial online service that connect to the Internet. They allow you to create your own Home Page for about $10 a month. They maintain all the hardware, software, and security for your Home Page. You need to design it, but that's easy with the software they have created. You basically answer a few questions and the computer lays out the material onto templates.

Costs—Prodigy charges about $10 a month for 50 pages on Prodigy. America Online prices are comparable.

Pros—Great price. You can't get online more easily. You don't have to learn about the intricate hardware and software to run a business.

Cons—They don't provide you with order-taking capabilities or forms.

That will come soon, but carry a higher cost, which hasn't been set yet.

Who should use it—Start-ups and people who are getting their feet wet with the Internet. This is the easiest and least expensive way to test the waters to see if your company should be online. Downside risk is limited to less than the price of a meal for a family at a fast food restaurant.

Here are phone numbers of popular commercial services that allow merchants to set up shop:

America Online	800-827-6364
Prodigy	800-776-3449

Digital Mall

A Digital Mall is the electronic version of a suburban strip mall. The Digital Mall hosts your site, provides the equipment and phone lines, and offers general maintenance and security. Good Digital Malls also offer business services, such as marketing, advertising, and promotions to draw people to the mall, accept credit card transactions from consumers, and create the art and text for your Home Page.

Costs—Monthly rental prices vary around the country from several hundred dollars to several thousand dollars. Some Digital Malls also ask for a percentage of your sales, or charge a small fee for each time a consumer visits your site. Marketing costs also are an add-on fee. Some malls also charge a fee for processing credit card transactions.

Pros—A good Digital Mall can be a one-stop shopping solution for merchants hopping onto the Internet. You might benefit from the increased traffic created by associating with other companies hosted on the same mall. For example, when a consumer visits the mall, they see a directory listing of all merchants. A thematic mall, like travel services or financial products might attract the perfect prospects for your travel agency or accounting services.

Cons—You are renting, not owning a system, so it could cost more in the long run. If there are many popular commercial sites on the Digital Mall, the entire system could slow down and annoy consumers. A Digital Mall site can become very expensive to operate if the landlord charges rent and takes a cut of your sales. Also, the shopper who is attracted to another store in the mall and stops by yours as he sees your store's listing on the directly, might not be a qualified prospect. For example, he might have come to visit the ski shop but doesn't have any kids, so he wouldn't be interested in your baby supplies.

Who should use it—Companies that want to pass off all labor relating to their Home Page, including programming, updating material, and marketing.

There are many digital malls. You find them from word of mouth, by reading messages on newsgroups and mailing lists, and from advertising sent by the digital malls themselves.

- Maui.net `http://www.maui.net`
- Aloha.net `http://www.aloha.net`
- Internet Shopping Network `http://www.Internet.net`
- Commerce.net `http://www.commerce.net`
- Teleport `http://www.teleport.com`
- Halcyon `http://www.halcyon.com`
- SF Web `http://www.sftweb.com`
- Branch Mall `http://www.branch.com`
- Clark.net `http://www.clark.net`

Direct Connection

A direct connection to the Internet means your computer hooks through your Internet Service Provider into the network of companies that provide the highest level of service to connect to the Internet, such as Sprint and MCI. If you go this route, you will have all the equipment and telephone connections to the Internet located at your office and operated by your employees. This choice eliminates the middle-man companies like Digital Malls.

Costs—A direct connection to the Internet is expensive. You will need at least $15,000 to purchase computers, modems, and software, another $10,000 to install a T-3 superfast telephone line or about $5,000 for a T-1 line. You'll also pay about $400 a month in telephone charges. You'll also be responsible for creating the pages, maintaining the system and providing security. For large companies with in-house computer departments, this is the way to go because you'll pay less in the long run and have more control over the contents of the Home Page. For mom-and-pop stores and startups, a direct cnnection is an expensive—and possibly unnecessary—alternative.

Pros—You own the shop and can depreciate equipment. This option offers the greatest amount of control and speed, as you are the only tenant on the line.

Cons—You must invest heavily in equipment and manpower to operate the system.

Who should use it—Larger, established companies that want direct control over all aspects of Internet operations, including computer system maintenance and security, marketing,and materials creation.

Addresses of Internet Service Providers (ISPs)

There are hundreds of ISPs throughout the country ranging from one- and two-person companies handling personal accounts in remote areas of the country, to multimillion dollar corporations providing high-end access and programming for large companies. For smaller firms, check advertisements in local computer publications and daily newspapers, or computer magazines. The larger services can be found in the Yellow Pages.

- BBN Planet—617-873-2000
- InterNex—800-595-3333
- PSInet—800-827-7482
- Uunet Technologies—800-488-6384

Do I Have to Be a Programming Geek?

You don't have to be a programming geek to get started on the Internet. There are consultants and agencies of every stripe that will help you every step along the way. As with any business, your time is best spent providing the service and management needed to make the sale and keep customers happy. Don't let all this programming or network connecting stop you from starting your business on the Internet. This section helped you find out what you will need for them to do and the prices you can expect to pay.

What You Learned in This Chapter

There are many ways to connect to the Internet and each method carries a radically different cost—ranging from $10 a month on Prodigy and no additional equipment charges beyond what you have in your office today, to thousands of dollars a month and tens of thousands of dollars in startup costs for equipment, fees and manpower. You learned about the pros and cons of various types of connections and their rates.

Sources of Additional Information

Getting Started on the Information Superhighway, Wally Bock, Crisp.

Internet for Dummies, by John R. Levine and Carol Baroundi, IDG Books.

Managing Internet Information Resources, by Cricket Liu, O'Reilly and Associates.

The Whole Internet User's Guide, by Ed Kroll, O'Reilly & Associates.

Word Wide Web FAQ—

    http://sunsite.unc.edu/boutell/faq/www_faq.html

3 INTERNET BUSINESS PRACTICES

ONLINE MARKETING IN A NUTSHELL

As we've seen, the Internet holds great promise for sales, but only if you know how to speak directly to the consumers in a manner consistent with their online culture. This chapter will discuss:

- Netiquette online marketing strategy
- New paradigms for online marketing
- Steps to take to open your online store
- General business practices

Let's look at these important areas.

Netiquette

Online consumers are a special breed. Unlike couch potatoes who don't mind the barrage of commercials hitting them when they watch TV, online consumers don't like hard-selling, image building, information devoid commercials. They like to read and browse information and content to make an informed buying decision. Also, they are spending their time to be online—time that could be spent on other activities. They are also spending money to be online. With those two factors-time and money-they aren't in a mood to view junk mail.

A code of conduct has developed on the Internet called "Netiquette." This is the Golden Rule of the Internet and must be obeyed before any commerce can be conducted. Some call it the etiquette of the network. I define it simply as "Information and advertising that is *unsolicited is unappreciated.*" If you err on the side of politeness, you won't risk offending people. If you do offend them, you might find your e-mail box full of nasty notes called "flames" which are e-mail notes filled with obscenities or threats to your life and your property. Yes, some people on the Internet can be nasty. They have a right to their privacy. Don't abuse it!

One reason the net has this philosophy can be traced to its roots. Scientists used the net to share information. This sharing remains the overriding rule in the message boards known as mailing lists and newsgroups. People give their time and information freely—knowing they will learn from others along the way. They don't go to these areas for commercial information.

Some people have asked me whether they can post junk mail anyway because the practice isn't illegal and they have thick skins. I tell them not to and then I tell them this story:

Every night between 6 and 9 P.M. I get three to five phone calls. They are all from telemarketers selling newspapers, magazines, and insurance. They have the right to call. However, these calls interrupt my dinner and relaxation time. When I answer the phone only to hear some person mangle my last name, I am most definitely not in the mood to buy. I have gotten so disgusted by these calls that I either turn off the phone during those hours, or don't answer the ring. Yes, I might miss a call from a friend, but that's the choice I make for peace and quiet. In the same manner, if junk mail floods the Internet, people won't go there anymore.

So don't muck up the environment! You'll only hurt yourself in the long run.

New Advertising: Understanding and Using New Paradigms

The Internet is a new medium, much like television was a new medium from radio. When TV first came along, advertisers didn't realize they were dealing with a new media with a whole range of new capabilities. Instead, they did ads the old fashioned way—at first. They put a camera on an announcer who was seen reading a script and talking into a huge microphone, just as on radio. They didn't realize at that time that TV was a visual media that is at its best when it shows action pictures of people and products in action—a car corners a mountain road, a group of young people on the beach play volleyball and drink a soda, a little man stands in a little boat in a toilet bowl. Those are the images TV was meant for. The same is true of the Internet. We are dealing with a new media that uses different tools to evoke different relationships with consumers.

This is especially true in regard to:

- Space
- Time
- Image creation
- Communication direction

Let's explore these concepts to gain a better understanding of how to create a message that will appeal to Internet consumers.

Space

Old Advertising—Space is a commodity you buy. It is expensive and finite. No matter which standard size you buy (a 30-second TV or radio commercial, or a full-page ad in a newspaper or magazine), you have only begun to tell your story. You are forced to leave out so much information because of the limitations and constraints and costs of space.

New Advertising—Space is unlimited and cheap. You can post an encyclopedia's worth of information about your company and its products on the Internet for a modest amount of money. Because of this, you can tailor sales messages to the different kinds of buyers: information seekers, money conscious, value oriented, or the like. If they are visual, you can post pictures and movies. If they are number-oriented, you can post reams of statistics. In fact consumers can create their own sales script as they seek out information that interests them, and avoid information of little interest.

Time

Old Advertising—Time is a commodity you buy on TV and radio. It is expensive and limited. You have a short period of time to convey a message. Advertisers tend to try to create an image about a company or a product through visual means because of these limitations.

New Advertising—Time is what consumers spend. It is a valuable commodity to them for two reasons: they are spending hard dollars to be online and they are spending real time away from other business or personal activities that constantly pull at them. In order to attract them to your store, hold them there, keep them coming back, and tell their friends to stop by. You must add value to their experience at your store.

The first step is to have quality products and information that is displayed in an attractive manner. The second step is to add real value to the consumer's experience—and that might have only tangential reference to your product or sales or advertising as we know it today. For example:

- Wells Fargo Bank allows its customers to find their account balances online.
- Visa lets anyone read free information about how to get out of debt.
- Seattle Film Works lets people retrieve screen-saver software for free.
- Southwest Airlines has free travel information about vacation destinations it flies to.

These experiences help create goodwill with consumers that enriches the time they spend online.

Image creation

Old Advertising—Images are primarily created with static or motion pictures, music, lighting, and action. Information is secondary. For example:

- A cigarette manufacturer shows a film of a cowboy on a horse lighting up and creates the rugged image of the Marlboro Man.
- A sleek sports car door opens, a woman's bare leg emerges and seductive music plays in the background as the announcer says, "The night belongs to Michelob."
- Teenagers are having fun playing volleyball at the beach and drinking Pepsi.

In each of these cases, image is created with words and pictures that trigger emotions. Information and data are not used at all.

New Advertising—Images are created with information. Because the tools for audio and video on the Internet are still fairly crude, the main way to get information across is through the printed word. The Internet takes full advantage of the printed word! Sales scripts and product information can be written in a manner that takes advantage of hypertext, the feature that allows consumers to go from one piece of information to another at will, instead of having to plow through an entire document in a linear format, from top to bottom. For example, lets say you are selling a product that can be understood on several levels, like food. You could have a picture of the piece of chocolate, a seductive paragraph of copy extolling the virtues of the dark, seductive nature of the candy and its smooth, silky texture. However, a health conscious person would want to know about the fat and calorie content of the product. You can write that information as well. You can increase your sales opportunties by then showing gift box options and describing the flavors.

For a more technical product, like phone systems, you could begin by showing the phone and basic information, like features, benefits and price. That would probably be enough information for the owner of a small business. However, people buying large phone systems would have more detailed needs for information, such as will it work with our current system? Will it work with our remote offices? The Internet allows you to create the image needed based on providing as much information as the consumer needs to make a buying decision.

Communication direction

Old Advertising—TV broadcasts images and messages to couch potatoes who sit by passively and either hear or ignore your message. If they have questions, they can not get answered immediately. For example, if they see the picture of the car and want to know how much it costs, they have to turn off the TV and drive to the dealer. If they see the ad for a bottle of beer and want to know how many calories it contains, they have to turn off the TV and go to the supermarket. Some commercials will post a toll-free telephone number to call and begin a relationship in that manner. But that is the exception, rather than the rule (except, of course, for infomercials and shopping programs).

New Advertising—Consumers seek out your message. They choose to be at your cyberstore and read the information. Not only that, they expect communication to be interactive. This means the consumer can establish a line of communication with the company and find out answers to her questions quickly, if not immediately. Right now, the technology allows consumers to find information at your store, and send e-mail to your staff. You must respond as fast as possible to this message to build a relationship. The first step is to create an e-mail tool called an infobot, which is analogous to a fax-back system. In this case, the person hears or reads about your product, possibly from a print ad, and sends a message to an e-mail address. The infobot immediately sends a pre-written note to the consumer that answers most questions they would have. Of course, people will always think of a question your staff didn't think of and send another note. At this point, human intervention is required to answer the question. This is good, as the action begins to build a relationship between the company and consumer. From this, good marketers can create a customer for life.

Summary

The new media requires that you understand the new paradigms for creating relationships with consumers through new uses of time, space, image creation, and communication direction. Once you understand these concepts you can create your online marketing plan.

Defining Your Marketing Mission–Your Success Blueprint

One of the most frequent questions people ask about the Internet is "Is your Home Page a success?" This is a tricky question because most people do not have a definition for the term "success."

For some companies, the goal clearly is to make money by selling products directly. That goal can be measured. For example: We sold 100 doodads last week and are rolling in dough. However, other Home Pages are designed to draw customers to retail outlets. Since store clerks do not usually ask how the customer found out about the store, Internet marketers might not know that their site is actually working! A third group of vendors aren't even interested in selling products; they want to establish a brand image. Consider Silicon Graphics. You and I can not buy their products. They want to sell multimillion dollar animation sequences to Hollywood movie producers who want to create the next Jurassic Park. They use the Web to show the world what they can do in the hopes of reaching the 20 people in the world who can actually sign a contract.

Your first step in determining whether your Home Page is a success is to define in advance what a success is. Is it monetary, market exposure, or reach? For example, specify the amount of money you think it should make and the time it should take to reach this goal. For example, most traditional businesses say they will lose money the first two years and break even the third. Because of lowered costs of getting started and running a business on the Internet, these businesses find they can make money in a few weeks, break even in a few months, and really pull ahead in less than a year! Set your sights early, and adjust them continuously. That way you'll be able to determine if your Home Page is a success.

Clearly then, the prime vehicle for selling your products is your storefront, which is called a Home Page on the World Wide Web. Here are the essential steps in designing a Home Page:

- Define market and product
- Create content
- Create art
- Convert content and art to HTML
- Connect to the Internet
- Drive people to your Home Page (Publicity Techniques)
- Make the sale
- Collect the money

- Send or deliver the product
- Stay connected with your customers on a regular basis

Define market and product

Behind all the cool graphics and clever writing of a Home Page lies a basic business strategy designed to sell. Good Home Pages have a mission to provide information in an entertaining and interactive manner that helps to not only make a sale, but create a customer for life.

For example, one of my clients, Gold Disk, a publisher of Video Director computer software that lets you use your computer to edit home movies, wanted to attract people to its site so they would have good feelings for the company, order additional products andupgrades and tell their friends to use the products. We realized that the first reason people come to a software site is for technical support. Soft-letter, a highly respected industry newsletter, conducted a survey that showed customers have technical support questions during the first 90 days they own the software. After that, they do not have any more questions and can use the product—or they return the product. We wanted to figure out how to get people to come back to the site after the 90th day. I thought about what the customer really wanted. The answer was that they wanted to take better home movies, not become better computer users. My solution was to write and post a series of articles each month such as how to take better videos or how to edit a child's birthday party video. The purpose is to *enhance* the customer's experience at your site. If they feel they are becoming better people, more productive, or saving money, they will come back time and time again. Each time they come back, you have the opportunity to create the bonds that will keep a customer for life.

Because space is cheap on the Internet, and different people make buying decisions based on different factors (price, value, safety, quality, image, brand identity, color, etc.) you have the unique opportunity to finely craft individual sales messages to each type of consumer. You can do this by interviewing your top sales people to find out what line of questions and answers helps to make the sale for each type of consumer. You can also interview your support staff to find out what kinds of questions people have about the product. Place those questions and answers into a file called FAQ (Frequently Asked Questions) and you might be able to overcome objections before the sale, and reduce the number of support calls after the sale.

Create content

Once you have created the marketing plan for your Home Page, you should create a flow chart or storyboard that shows the content and its links. You can use the sample on the following page, which was created by Alan Crofut of Launch Point, a San Francisco Web Farm and Internet Presence Provider (415-995-8535, cpu@1point.com, http://www.sfweb.com). He has graciously given permission for you to copy his storyboard and distribute it freely, in the spirit of giving something back to the Internet community. You can use this story board to capture good pages and ideas you see on pages as you browse the Web.

WEBSITE STORYBOARD

Launch Point Internet Services   221 Main St. Suite #1040
San Francisco, CA 94105 415/995-8535 FAX415/ 995-8548
This design is property of Launch Point Internet Services.

The term "Home Page" is a misleading name. It is really a table of contents or directory to your store. The opening page (commonly called the Home Page) is actually longer than a computer screen and can be quite long. The advantage is that you can display a great deal of information in a precise location. It is important for you to think in screenfuls of content so navigation is easy for consumers. Small companies with one product have only one long page. Companies with more content will use additional pages—"Sub Pages"—that contain additional information about products and ordering capabilities.

The Home Page should contain the following pieces of information, which are displayed as headlines or buttons and link to a page with more detailed information:

- *Name of company*
- *Mission statement*—explains what your business does and the market it serves. The statement should be printed in full on the first home page.
- *What you'll find here*—headlines of the information and products on your site. These headlines will link to descriptions and pictures of products.
- *E-mail response forms*—people can contact you directly and create a one-to-one relationship that can last for life.
- *Contact information*——your company's physical address, telephone, and fax numbers.
- *Date of last update*—so people will know if anything has changed since their last visit.
- *Notice of special events*—entice people to visit your store and explore its contents.
- *Sales*——tells people what the hot buys are this week at a glance. This information should be printed on the first page.
- *What's new*—tells viewers what information has been added or changed. This information should be printed on the first page as headlines, and linked to related pages.

- *Message from the president*—can show the true character and nature of the company that give a personal, as opposed to impersonal, feel to the company. This line links to the actual message.
- *Press Releases*—give people a depth of understanding of the products and the company that might not be contained in sales materials. This line links to the press releases section.
- *Sales materials*—give broad and deep information about the products or services. This line links to the sales materials section.
- *Catalogs*——shows the full range of products in your store, with descriptions, prices, and ordering information as well as transaction capabilities. This line links to the catalog section.
- *Registration forms*—asks people to identify themselves so you can build a relationship with them. Forms should ask only a few questions, such as name, address, e-mail address, and the scantiest of demographic material, as the more questions you ask, the fewer people will answer. Remember that people value their privacy and might not want to reveal their identities. If you require that people identify themselves before you allow them into your store, they might walk on by. This line links to the registration form.
- *Testimonials*—of your products and services by satisfied customers can help convince prospects to invest in your company. This line links to the testimonials section.
- *Employment notices*-—how descriptions of jobs that are available at your company. This line links to the employment section.
- *Links to other sites*-—are listings of information sources on the Internet your readers will find interesting. These links tie into other home pages.
- *Copyright notices*—protects your work.

Create art

This assemblage of content must be presented in an attractive fashion to your customers. You will see various examples throughout the book that show the character and personality of the business and creator. The best ones also show the marketing function in an enjoyable manner.

It is important to note that many stores today look similar to their printed brochures. In this manner, you'll find it easy to jump onto the Internet. However, you will be one of the crowd. To stand out, you need to use cool graphics to make your store look like it is a happening place. As more cyberstores upgrade their graphics away from brochures and into environments that take advantage of multimedia, you will too—or risk looking like your father's Home Page.

Convert content and art to HTML

After you have created your content and art, it must be converted into a format that the World Wide Web can read. That format is called HTML which stands for Hyper Text Markup Language. It is a fairly simple language to understand, as computer languages go. If you are comfortable formatting text with Microsoft Word or WordPerfect, then you can learn how to use HTML in just a few hours. There are a number of good books that can guide you through this process including:

Creating Cool Web Pages with HTML, by Dave Taylor, IDG Books.

HTML for Fun and Profit, by Mary S. Morris, Prentice Hall.

Teach Yourself Web Publishing with HTML in a Week , by Laura LeMay, Sams Publishing.

If you use Microsoft Word, you can get an HTML editor for free by downloading the file MIA (which stands for Microsoft Internet Assistant) from the Microsoft Home Page, http://www.microsoft.com. It is very simple to do the conversion, however, you will need to learn a bit about

HTML to make your page look pretty. Word Perfect users can get Word Perfect Internet Publisher free from Novel Applications Group, 800-861-2554, `http://wp.novell.com/elecpub/intpub.htm`.

There are several good programs that have additional features not found in MIA. I like these:

HTML Assistant Pro Version 1.5-a good editor that is easy to use. FTP to ftp.cs.dal.ca look in the directory /htmlasst/ for the file htmlasst.zip. Brooklyn North Softworks, 902-493-6080, `http://fox.nstn.cal/~harawitz/index.html`. Price: $99.95.

Web Author-another good editor, from noted software publisher Quarterdeck, `http://www.qdeck.com`, info@qdeck.com, 310-314-3222. Price: $149.

SkiSoft's Web Publisher-especially good at converting dozens of files automatically and conforming to style sheets you create. SkiSoft Publishing, `http://www.skisoft.com`, ken@skisoft.com, 617-863-1876. Price: $495.

Hot Dog-another good, all purpose editor that is getting good reviews, from Australia. `http://www.sausage.com`. Price: $195.

Connect to the Internet

Now you are ready to let the world see your work! You will need to connect your pages to the Internet. Please see the discussion in Chapter 2.

Drive people to your Home Page with Publicity and Promotions

Remember the saying "If you build it, they will come." If you believe this will happen to your Home Page, then you are living in a field of dreams. You must actively promote and publicize your Home Pages so people can find it. If you are successful, people will tell their friends so that hundreds and thousands of potential prospects line up at the doorstep of your Home Page. Fortunately, this step doesn't require a lot of money.

However, it does require about five hours to get started and about an hour or two a week to prime the pump.

Here are the six essential steps to promote your Home Page.

- Register with "Yellow Pages" search engines
- Link to complementary Home Pages
- Send press releases to reporters
- Hold contests
- Create a signature (electronic business card) that directs people to your Home Page and answer people's questions in newsgroups and mailing lists, the Internet's electronic bulletin boards
- Post messages in appropriate newsgroups and mailing lists

Let's look at each of them.

Register with Search Engine Directories

The Internet has two problems for consumers and merchants: First, there is no top-down directory on the Internet. That means it is difficult to find vendors. Second, more than 1,000 companies open Home Pages every week, so even if some enterprising company printed a directory, it would be seriously out of date even before the ink dried.

Fortunately, technology provides a simple solution in the form of directories that allow the consumer to type in the product or service she's looking for and find all references. For example, she could type "chocolates" and the computer will show her the URL for Godiva Chocolates and its competitors. The consumer could then connect directly to the Home Page.

There are several competing directories on the Internet and they all will let you list your page for free. You should register your store on each directory. To register your page, you need to do these basic steps:

1. Go to the search engine directory.
2. Go to the menu item that says "register a new site" or something similar.
3. Type in the name of the store, the address, keywords that describe your products or services (e.g. a ski resort might use these keywords: ski, vacation, travel, entertainment, hobbies, sports and romance), your e-mail address, and a paragraph describing your product or services.
4. Click on the "submit" button.

Not only is this service free to merchants, it is free to consumers so there are no barriers to its use.

The most popular engines and their addresses are:

Yahoo	`http://www.yahoo.com`
Web Crawler	`http://webcrawler.com`
Lycos	`http://lycos.com`
EINet Galaxy	`http://einet.com`
NCSA	`http://www.gnn.com/wn/whats-new-form.html`
InfoSeek	`http://www.infoseek.com`

InfoSeek automatically searches for all new Home Pages and list them by keyword and company name. The first time I used InfoSeek, I typed in my company name and found every reference to my Home Pages. I also found every reference of my Home Page on other companies' sites! That was a truly great service.

By listing your Home Page on a search engine directory, customers will be able to find you quickly and easily–and for free!

If you have a product, you can get a free listing in Dave Taylor's Internet Mall, `http://www.mecklerweb.com/imall`. For registration information, send e-mail to taylor@netcom.com. In the subject box, type send mall.

Link to complementary Home Pages

You can attract new audiences to your Home Page if you create a link to a complementary Home Page. You can understand this concept easily if you have ever been to a pharmacy. My local pharmacy has a spot near the prescription counter where doctors, nurses, infant-care providers, and other health-related professionals place their business cards. They assume that people who go to a pharmacy are concerned with their health and might be in the market for a care giver. This tactic works well for the merchant who spends the price of a few business cards, as well as for the pharmacy which builds good will with merchants and customers by providing a service. Further, these merchants do not steal sales from the pharmacy because they do not provide the same products. Everyone wins.

The same can be true with your Home Page. You can expose your site to a new set of customers by creating links with other merchants' pages. For example, if you conduct eating tours of New York City, you can create a link to the Home Page of dozens of travel agencies. If their customers are going to New York and want to take a tour of the best ethnic restaurants in town, they will know who to call. Good business sense requires you to create a link to those travel agencies. In this way, their customers can find out about your service, while your customers learn about theirs.

To create a link, follow these steps:

- Go to a search engine directory and find complementary sites. Our travel guide might type in the following keywords "travel, tourism, New York, restaurants, vacations, adventure, and guided tours." Be creative! Think of all possible people who would be interested in your service and where they would hang out on the Internet.

- Send a note to the Webmaster, the person who oversees the Home Page, of each site asking for permission to link to her site and for her to link to your site. Common courtesy requires this step. For example:

    Hi!

    I operate the Janal Communications Home Page, which contains important and interesting information for marketers. Your readers would be interested in this page, and my readers would be interested in yours as well. If I put a link to your page, will you put a link to mine? The address is `http://www.janal-communications.com`.

    Thanks!

- When you get permission, add the link to your Home Page in section with a catchy name, like "Related Sites," "Additional Information," "Related Reading," "Links to Other Home Pages," "Cool Web Sites," or "Our Favorite Home Pages." You can probably think of something more catchy than these, but they'll work!

Search for new sites every couple of weeks and send out new requests, as hundreds of new Home Pages go online each week.

Write a press release and send it to reporters

We live in an exciting time because the media considers the act of opening a Home Page to be news, just as a local newspaper considers the opening of a new store on Main Street to be news. Since cyberspace is national and international, major periodicals like USA Today and Adverting Age list new Home Pages quite frequently.

The best way to reach reporters is to send them a press release announcing the opening of your site. Here are the basic questions a press release should answer:

- What is the name of the store and its address (URL)?
- Who will the site appeal to?
- How will they benefit?
- What information, sales, and contests are at the site?
- What else makes the site special?
- What is the name, phone number and e-mail address of the contact person so the reporter can ask for more information?
- The finished press release could look like this:

For Immediate Release

Contact: Daniel Janal, 510-831-0900

Janal Communications Opens Cyberstore on World Wide Web

Danville, CA, August 1, 1994—Janal Communications, a leading provider of marketing services on the Internet, announced today it has opened its virtual storefront on the World Wide Web. The address (URL) is `http://www.janal-communications.com`.

The Home Page contains free articles about how large and small companies can market their products and services on the Internet, such as The Fool-Proof Positioning Statement. A free copy of the Online Marketing Update newsletter is also available.

Readers can also participate in a monthly joke contest in which the person with the best joke will receive a canvas tote bag from a computer show.

Viewers can also find information about Dan Janal's speaking and consulting services as well as his books and software, which include the Online Marketing Handbook, How to Publicize High Tech Products and Services, and the Publicity Builder software program.

The site also includes links to other marketing Home Pages.

Founded in 1986, Janal Communications is a leading marketing and public relations agency.

Here's a template that you can use to write your own press release. Just fill in the blanks.

Your Company Opens Cyberstore on World Wide Web

Your City, State, Date- Your Company, short description, today announced it has opened its virtual storefront on the World Wide Web. The address (URL) is http://your address.

The Home Page contains .... Readers can also participate in a .... contest in which the winner receives .... prize.

Viewers can also find information about ....The site also includes links to .... Founded in ...., (long positioning statement).

One of the best ways to distribute press releases inexpensively is to use a service called PR Newswire, 800-832-5522. For about $75, you can send a 400-word press release to all the reporters in a major metropolitan area, like Chicago or New York, as well as to reporters who write about a specific industry, such as computers or automobiles.

Best yet, consumers can read these press releases via the Internet's clipping services, like InfoSeek, and through other sites that print all these press releases. Using this tactic, you can tell reporters and consumers about your new site.

Hold contests

Contests are a great way to attract people to your Home Page. By having a chance to win a cash prize or merchandise, people will want to come to your site. While they participate in the contest, they learn about your products and services. They just might buy something as well!

Contests serve a secondary function: you learn who is visiting your store. People who come to your store are anonymous. You do not know who they are or their e-mail address so you can not follow up with them. By holding a contest, these faceless consumers MUST tell you who they are so you can send the prize to them if they win! There you have it. You've gotten their IDs!

What ideas make good contests? Lots. Here are a few ideas: name this site, design a logo, and fill out a form that can only be completed by searching for clues on the Home Page (which means the consumer will learn about your company).

Prizes can be a few dollars, such as $25, although some sites offer $1,000! You can also offer sample merchandise.

To promote your contest, you can send out press releases, as described above. You should also see what other companies are doing. For a list of current contests, go to the Yahoo directory `http://www.yahoo.com` and search for contests.

Create a signature (electronic business card)

A signature is a four-to-eight-line message that appears at the end of an e-mail message. It can be thought of as an electronic business card. The signature is a marketing tool that directs people to your Home Page or retail location. It contains such basic information as your name, address, e-mail number, phone number, and mission statement. Here is an example of my signature.

```
========================================================
```
Daniel Janal * Author, Speaker, Online Marketing Consultant *
Janal Communications * update@janalpr.com * 510-831-0900
Info: http://www.janal-communications.com
Author of:
 "101 Businesses You Can Start on the Internet"
 "Online Marketing Handbook"
 "How to Publicize High Tech Products and Services"
```
========================================================
```

This signature is attached to the end of each message you send, whether it be to a newsgroup, mailing list, or private e-mail. This can be a very valuable tool as you participate in discussions the Internet's bulletin boards, which are called USENET newsgroups, and mailing lists. There are more than 10,000 groups that discuss everything under the sun, from parenting to computers to Melrose Place. They can be good places to prospect for new customers. The next topic shows you how to use the groups effectively.

Post messages in appropriate newsgroups and mailing lists

Netiquette, the etiquette of the Internet, dictates that you can not post ads in newsgroups and mailing lists. Instead, you can only answer people's questions, raise your own questions and contribute free information to the discussion. This is a vital rule for publicizing your Home Page.

These restrictions are necessary because these message areas would be filled with commercials otherwise. Then no one would go there!

In this marketing strategy, you find appropriate newsgroups that would be interested in your Home Page and place a notice about it. Here is an example that a travel destination might place into a travel or sports recreation forum.

Check out my new Home Page. There's lots of information about windsurfing!

==

Awesome Windsurfing Trips, Inc. "California's Best Windsurfing Vacations"

`http://www.windsurfers.com`   `info@windsurf.com`

800-555-1212

==

The key word in the previous message was "information." If you point people to information and not advertising, your message will be accepted as being positive.

Please avoid hype and overselling. Internet consumers have seen enough junk to last a lifetime. Using headlines like "get rich quick" will evoke disdain rather than interest.

You can also promote free reports and white papers in the appropriate groups. Again, be sure you back up your message with information that is truly worthwhile.

You can find groups of people who could be potential clients by visiting various newsgroups and mailing lists. You can get a directory of mailing lists by pointing your browser to `http://www.neosoft.com/Internet/paml`. You can find newgroups by searching the newsgroups listed with your ISP, or from Newsgroup Index, `http://www.tile.net/tile/news/index.html`.

Because the names of some groups can be vague or misleading, remember to read messages for several days before posting a message. You might find that the group really doesn't meet your needs at all. For example, the multi-level marketing (MLM) list doesn't want to learn of new MLM programs; they want to learn how to sell more effectively. You do not want to run the risk of being flamed by the group members.

The next step is to contribute information to the people on the newsgroup. For example, if someone asks a question that you can answer intelligently, you should do so. So if you operate an herbal pharmacy and someone in the hiking newsgroup asks about the treatment for poison ivy, you can offer your advice. People will see in your signature that your store sells herbal remedies. Your signature will contain all the advertising that is allowed. Your message will stay visible for several days, so you could reach a large audience by contributing to the community.

If you use these tactics, you will not get stung, or worse–flamed.

Summary

If you implement these publicity and marketing strategies, you'll help increase the traffic to your site. Many of these publicity and promotion methods are inexpensive. You can perform most tasks without the help of expensive consultants.

Make the Sale

The next step is to make the sale. You must ask for the order and make it easy for people to say "yes." Three options are:

- Displaying your traditional ordering numbers.
- Creating an e-mail form.
- Creating an online ordering form.

Let's look at these methods.

Display your traditional ordering numbers

Some people want to order the old-fashioned way—on the telephone or by sending a check in the mail. To accommodate these conservative, safety minded folks, you will need to place your address, phone number, and fax number on your Home Page and on ordering pages.

E-mail form

Others will want to ask you questions or send their credit card information via e-mail. Your HTML programmer can put in a "mailto" command onto your page easily. When the customer clicks on the highlighted text, a mail window will open up, already addressed to you.

For More Information

For information about our services, or to order products, please send e-mail to 76004.1046@compuserve.com, or call 510-831 0900.

Figure 3-1. Clicking on the highlighted information can lead to a "mail-to" command which opens an e-mail form below. Courtesy of Janal Communications.

```
┌──────────────────────────────────────────────────────────────┐
│ ▬         Send Internet E-Mail Message                         │
├──────────────────────────────────────────────────────────────┤
│  From:  VXYM62A@prodigy.com                    ┌────────────┐  │
│                                                │    Send     │  │
│    To: │76004.1046@compuserve.com           │  └────────────┘  │
│                                                ┌────────────┐  │
│ Subject: │test messge                       │  │   Cancel    │  │
│                                                └────────────┘  │
│   Text: │Hi!                                               │▲  │
│         │                                                  │   │
│         │Please send me 10,000 copies of your book. I will send you │
│         │a check by overnight courier.                     │   │
│         │                                                  │   │
│         │A fan                                             │   │
│         │                                                  │▼  │
└──────────────────────────────────────────────────────────────┘
```

Figure 3-2. Consumers can write an order or question in the emial from. Courtesy of Janal Communications.

They can type onto the page. You'll see it appear in your mailbox. I received an order from Germany in this manner, complete with credit card information.

Order forms

Your entire catalog of products can be on your Home Page. At the end of each description, you should place an "order" icon after each product description. (Figure 3-3).

Figure 3-3. A sample order button. Actual size shown here.

When they click on the icon, they will see a fill-in-the-blank order form, which they can complete and submit for processing. This form can be created and linked properly by any competent HTML artist, or Digital Mall (Figure 3-4).

VIRGINIA DINER
PEANUT · CAPITAL · OF · THE · WORLD

Online Ordering

To Order from the catalog, simply fill in this easy to use order form.
Ordering Information

Bill To:
Name:

Address:

City: State: Zip:

Figure 3-4. The top part of the order form asks for basic mailing information. Courtesy of the Virginia Diner, Inc.

Optional - Approximate delivery date requested: _____

If a gift, enter message for card: _____

Email Address: _____

Daytime Telephone: _____

Evening Telephone: _____

Credit Card Number: _____ [MasterCard ▼]

Exp. Date: _____

Qty	Catalog Number	Description		Item Price	Total Price

Figure 3-5. The form continues with the address of the recipient. Courtesy of the Virginia Diner, Inc.

```
┌─────────┐ ┌Subtotal
│         │ └4.5% Sales Tax (Virginia Residents Only*)
│         │ └Shipping -see chart below
│         │ └Total Order
├─────────┤
│ submit  │ your order
└─────────┘
*Sales tax required by order of the Virginia State Attorney General
Shipping rates are charged per ship-to address:


                 Ground |    2nd Day  |  Next Day
$0-$14.99         4.10       8.55        19.75
$15-$24.99        4.70      13.25        27.50
$25-$34.99        5.70      20.75        36.35
$35-$49.99        6.75      24.95        40.50
$50-$74.99        7.75      30.40        44.65
$75-$99.99        9.35      36.35        51.95
$100-$124.99     12.45    .....Call for rates
$125-$149.99     15.55    .....Call for rates
$150.00 or over          ..........Call for rates

Copyright © 1995, Virginia Diner & InfiNet, L.C.
```

Figure 3-6. The smart form can add the total for the order. Courtesy of the Virginia Diner, Inc.

Collect the money

Collecting money on the Internet can be a thorny issue today, but should be cleared up in a few months. A report by Dataquest, a leading computer industry research firm, shows that only 25 percent of people who have bought products on the Internet are comfortable sending their credit card information via the Internet. That means that 75 percent of those people will not purchase products in this manner. This doesn't mean they won't order products, it just shows you have to provide customers with other means of ordering products. Here are several ways to collect money:

Print your address, phone, and fax numbers—on your Home Page. People will contact you in the manner they feel most comfortable.

Here are several electronic commerce methods of taking orders:

Registration numbers—In this method, the customer gives you his credit card number over the phone line. You check out his information before he can order. If the information is correct, you supply him with a registration number, such as R1234. When he orders, he sends the registration number—not the credit card number—via e-mail or your order form.

As an added security feature, you could send e-mail to his account verifying his order. For example, "We are confirming your order for a yellow ski parka. To receive this product, please send an e-mail. Thank you for helping us protect you from fraud."

If the person responds affirmatively, you can ship the order. If someone stole his registration number, the true owner, not the thief, would receive the confirmation note. If a fraudulent order was placed, the true owner would be able to cancel the order.

Deposits-You could ask people to send a check to you which you would place in their account. As they order products, you could deduct the transaction amount from the account.

Other methods for securing transactions are becoming available from such companies as Visa and Mastercard, Microsoft and RSA. Be sure to check other Home Pages to see what other merchants are using, as well as visit the sites of the producers of this kind of software and service. As these security procedures are introduced and become more widely accepted, people will drop their reluctance to pay for their orders online. Companies engaged in this business include:

Company	Internet address
CyberCash	`http:/www.cybercash.com`
Digicash	`http://www.digicash.com`
First Data/ Netscape Communications	`http://www.netscape.com`

First Vitual Holdings Holdings, Inc.	`http://www.fv.coml`
Mastercard	`http:/www.mastercard.com`
Visa	`http://www.visa.com`

Send or deliver the product

After you have verified the credit card information, or waited for the check to clear, you can feel confident about delivering the product. To protect yourself, you should send the product via a carrier that requires a signature from the recipient. That way, the customer cannot claim the product was never received and demand their money back. You can get a free account from Federal Express or Airborne. UPS actually charges people an annual fee in addition to the per package charge, so I do not recommend using them. The U.S. Post Office's Express Mail Service will also get a signature from a customer. If you send a great deal of product, you can ask for discounts or lower prices from Federal Express, Airborne, and UPS.

This step can be cost-prohibitive for inexpensive items so you might want to limit this action to expensive products. In either case, you can pass along the costs of shipping and handling to the consumer.

If you have an information product (like a newsletter, report, or online research) or software program, you might want to deliver your product to the customer over the Internet to a person's e-mail box. That way you'll save the printing and postage costs, although you won't have a signature proving delivery. In a short while, several companies will have a "digital notary service" that gives you proof that information was sent and received via e-mail.

Stay in touch with the customer

It is easier to sell products to existing customers than hunt for new ones.

Therefore, try to stay in regular contact with your customers. Consider offering them a newsletter or place them on a mailing list so they can see your new products or learn about your sales. Be sure to ask their permission first, as netiquette dictates. If you do so, you'll be able to build a customer for life.

General Business Practices

This section will discuss the general business practices you need to follow to operate a successful business. Because these topics can be covered in full-length books, it will also steer you to other resources to get a full understanding of operating a business.

Get appropriate permits

To start any business you will need to get the appropriate business permits required by your state, county and municipality. A good place to start is city hall or the county clerk's office. These offices usually have easy-to-follow information on what you need to do to comply with the law.

Consult a lawyer

General business lawyers can save you a great deal of time, money, and hassle by advising you on how to start your business. They can alert you on local and state requirements that you might not be aware of. They can work to protect your assets. You'll want to use a general business attorney. Ask for references to find a good one.

All the advice in this book is presented openly and honestly. However, not every situation is the same. Before adopting any business strategy presented in this book, consult with an attorney specializing in business operations.

Consult an accountant

Accountants can set up your financial records books and tell you how to operate your business efficiently. They can advise you on how to save money with financial planning and might be able to show you ways to shelter income from taxes

Do your research

The best information for starting a business might be close at hand. Check out classes at the local universities and community colleges. The Small Business Administration might be able to offer you a great deal of information for free.The local branch of SCORE (Service Corps of Retired Executives) might be able to provide you with a braintrust of experienced people who are willing to give advice to entrepreneurs for free.

What you've learned in this chapter

In this chapter you've gained an appreciation for netiquette, the etiquette of the Internet. You also learned how new advertising on the Internet differs from traditional advertising. We discussed the essential steps a marketer must take to create a plan for success on the Internet, important facts to list on a Home Page, and how to promote your store on the Internet. You also learned how to create relationships with consumers, make the sale, get the money, and deliver the product.

Sources for Additional Information

Doing More Business on the Internet, by Mary Cronin, Van Nostrand Reinhold.

Getting Business to Come To You by Paul and Sarah Edwards and Laura Clampitt Douglas, Jeremy Tarcher.

Launching a Business on the Web, by David Cook and Deborah Sellers, Que, 1995.

Making It On Your Own: Surviving and Thriving on the Ups and Downs of Being Self-Employed, by Paul and Sarah Edwards, Jeremy Tarcher.

Marketing on a Shoestring, by Jeff Davidson, John Wiley and Sons.

Online Marketing Handbook, by Daniel S. Janal, Van Nostrand Reinhold, 1995.

Marketing Primer: The Basics of Online Marketing, by Wally Bock, Cyberpower (tape series).

The Entrepreneur Magazine Small Business Advisor, John Wiley and Sons.

Publicity Builder Software, JIAN Tools for Sales.

Working from Home: Everything You Need to Know about Living and Working Under the Same Roof, by Paul and Sarah Edwards, Jeremy Tarcher.

Working Solo, by Terri Lonier, Portico Press, 1994.

Working Solo Sourcebook, by Terri Lonier, Portico Press, 1995.

SECTION 2

This section will show you 101 good ideas for businesses on the Internet. You will gain valuable insight into how the owners began these businesses and discover the financial and personal costs involved in starting a business on the Internet.

4 KILLER BUSINESS MODELS

OVERVIEW

Now that you have an overview of why you should open a business on the Internet, how to think like an online marketer, and have the basic tools to promote your business, it is time to explore the large number of enterprises you can create on the Internet.

This chapter and the ones that follow present the highlights of 101 businesses you can start on the Internet. These businesses include:

- Businesses that exist only on the Internet, like software.net, an online software retailer.
- Offshoots of existing businesses, like Lobster Direct, which sells crustaceans and lox by mail and Internet.
- Companies that use the Internet to draw customers to their off-line store, such as Nine Lives Clothing.
- Professions and careers that serve the Internet community, like HTML programmers and Webmasters

Each business profile will contain such information as:

- *Overview*—what this business entails and the background you need to get started.
- *Rewards*—pros of starting this kind of business.
- *Risks*—cons of starting this kind of business.
- *Special marketing elements for the Home Page*—insightful tips that can make the cyberstore a success.
- *Practical examples and links to Home Pages*—see what works on Home Pages of stores that lead the way of online commerce.

More than 40 businesses are profiled at length, with pictures of their Home Pages for illustrative purposes. Another 20 businesses and professions are described in short interviews, in a question-and-answer format. These episodes will help give you a clear impression of the joys and sorrows of starting a business on the Internet.

ABOUT THE INTERVIEWS

The businesses profiled in this book were found through online searches and recommendations from online surfers. No one was paid to be in this book and no one received compensation of any sort.

I wrote the questionnaire, sent it to the business people, who answered via e-mail. This is truly a virtual book that happens to be printed on paper. All the online addresses appear on my Home Page, so you can review the interview subjects' Home Pages easily. My Home Page address is http://www.janal-communications.com.

The veracity of the answers are the responsibility of the business owners. I have trusted them to be honest and open. All respondents gave their permission to have information included in the book.

I asked all business persons how much money they made on the Internet. Some people were naturally hesitant to reveal this information for a variety of reasons: they do not want their competitors to know how much money they are making and encourage competition; they do not want their spouses to know how much money they are losing; they just plain aren't comfortable talking about their finances in a world full of kidnappers and weirdos.

In order for the personality, enthusiasm, and emotions of the entrepreneurs to come alive, we did not edit the interviews, except for light changes to protect them from their own typos.

The voices that come through are those of the writers, so you will experience a dynamic, earthy, conversational tone. This could be the new media version of Studs Terkel's Working book—an oral history of working in cyberspace.

I have included their own smileys and emoticons, those funny keyboard characters that convey emotion in an otherwise silent and faceless world. Here's the short course on smileys. Tilt your head to the left and you will see the emotion displayed in text in the left-hand column and as a smiley in the right-hand column.

> *smile* :-)
> wink ;-)
> sad, frown   :(

Another key emoticon is the grin, which appears as <g>.

Additionally, several online abbreviations are used:

TIA   Thanks in advance
IMHO   In my humble opinion

People gave freely of their time and information, knowing that someone could come out of the woodwork and compete with them. These are true Internet entrepreneurs who believe in the code of contributing to the community.

Browse through the other interviews, as they contain a wealth of information about how to start, run, and market a business on the Internet, or how to integrate work with your personal life. All these stories are fascinating! They offer you practical tips, even if you do not plan to start that particular business.

Where Are All the Millionaires?

As you read the case studies and interviews, you might notice that not everyone is making a million dollars. The fact is that no one I spoke with has gotten rich quick. The media might have portrayed several flower, wine, and T-shirt Web businesses as leading the way, but the vast majority of businesses seem to be getting by and waiting for the rest of the world to realize that they should be online and buy from online merchants. In this way, the Web seems to be a place where people can make a business, but not a killing, at this time. Many people interviewed are looking to make a modest sum, or increase business in their traditional stores and offices. I have decided to include these stories because they can inspire you to continue working away on your online store for the big payoff when more and more consumers use the Internet as a preferred shopping vehicle.

KILLER INTERNET BUSINESS MODELS

Certainly the first and foremost goal for most readers is either to sell products directly from the Internet, or convince prospects to visit your store in person. However, there are several ways to generate additional income from your site.

BUSINESS MODEL-MAGAZINE PUBLISHER

You can attain additional revenue by selling advertising space on your

Home Page to merchants who want to reach the same market as you.

Let's say your store sells ski equipment. Your customers are also prime buyers of clothing, music, liquor, cars, and the like. If you can demonstrate to potential advertisers that you have a large number of qualified people coming to your site on a regular basis, you can make money either selling an ad to them, or charging them for a link to their Home Page. Here's how it works.

Your hot shot business attracts 10,000 highly affluent ski bums each week. You have verified these numbers with an independent accounting service, like Internet Profiles. You might even have registration forms completed that show the person's age, income, marital status, and hobbies. Now you are ready to present this information to advertisers.

You can sell them a button about the size of a postage stamp that appears on your Home Page. The fee can range from hundreds to thousands of dollars depending on the size of your audience and the length of time the ad runs. For example, the Mercury Web Center, an online version of the San Jose Mercury News, charges $3,000 a month for an ad that reaches an Internet audience estimated at 7.2 million readers. Advertisers included Coldwell Banker, Ameritech, Del Monte, IBM, and Wells Fargo. The advertiser benefits from the increased exposure to your target audience.

If people click on the postage stamp ad, three things can happen:

- *Nothing*—advertisers benefit merely by the exposure, much as a billboard along the highway allows a one-way advertising message with minimal information. This button-sized message can contain a company logo or a short sales notice.
- *Readers see a simple ad*—This can be a page of information and pictures about the product. Readers are still in your store, and they return to your Home Page after seeing the ad.
- *Readers are transported to the advertiser's site*—They can have an interactive experience with advertiser, who exposes readers to as much information as readers want.

Each activity can carry a different price point.

Your upside potential for income is unlimited. You can make as much money as you like based on your ability to convince potential advertisers that you can help them sell.

To ensure that your site attracts repeat visits and new customers, you will need to create editorial and entertainment value. For example, the Ragu company, which manufactures sauces for pasta, offers their customers cooking recipes, Italian lessons, and e-mail from a too-good-to-be-true vision of everyone's favorite Italian grandmother. Ragu has created a fun space for a product that is suitable for a mass market audience. The URL is http://www.eat.com.

BUSINESS MODEL-DROP SHIPPING MERCHANDISE

The dream business of any merchant is to make money without having to carry an inventory. This is the drop-ship business.

In this model, you do not carry one bit of inventory. You create a Home Page for a line of products, such as clothing, crafts, or books. Each product is described and has a picture. When you get the order and verify the customer ordering data, call your suppliers and have them send the products directly to the customer.

Your costs are only for the creation, advertising, and promotion of the Home Page, as well as for the time you spend finding interesting products. You pass along the costs of the merchandise and transaction fees to the consumer, along with a tidy profit. Good items to sell on the Internet include clothing, records, videos, and books.

BUSINESS MODEL—CATEGORY

Nearly everyone has received a catalog in the mail. However, you might not know how many catalogs make money. They sell ads on each page to vendors. It's like a magazine with ads and no articles.

The model works for other Internet retailers as well. If you can convince other merchants to advertise their products for sale in your store, then you can make an unlimited amount of money. Here are the essential steps:

1.   Create the page.
2.   Draw consumers.
3.   Sell ads, brochures, links to other sites.
4.   Take the order.

Let's look at the case study of software.net, which sells software online, but also sells advertising space to the software publishers as well. This business model would work for almost any product sold at the retail level in the real world. Software.net (that's pronounced software dot net, and spelled in lower case) http://software.net 800-617-SOFT pubinfo@software.net. Software.net is also profiled in depth in Chapter 17, Software.

CASE STUDY—SOFTWARE.NET

Software.net is an online store where consumers and businesses can order software. According to company literature, the company's modest goals are to "revolutionize the distribution of software and related information by eliminating the inefficiencies of physical distribution for the software publisher and consumer."

As of March 1995, software.net offered 8,200 products from leading vendors on virtually every platform, from Windows and DOS to Apple System 7 and UNIX. The products are available in retail packages that can be sent by overnight services. Many products can be downloaded for those who seek instant gratification.

"Electronic fulfillment is preferable for both the software publisher and customer. Publishers benefit from lower distribution and marketing costs. Customers benefit from the reduced transaction costs," the company says.

Software.net "aggressively pursues" customers through ads on sites like the NCSA What's New Page, Yahoo, NetSurfer, Netscape Communications, and others. As a result of this advertising, traffic on the site has grown to over 150,000 hits per week generated by over 35,000 customers. The company also has reciprocal links with its partners and sources such as the Software Publishers Association to make it easier for customers to find the site.

Merchandising plays a critical role in generating repeat traffic. Software.net uses such merchandising techniques as special offers, bundles, free promotions, and surveys to build repeat customer visits.

The company uses the same business model as the traditional retail channel. Margin is based on the difference between cost to the company from the publisher, and sale price. Software.net reports to the publisher within 20 days of the end of each month the quantity of licenses or products sold, amount due and registration information. Payment is made to the publisher within 30 days of the end of each month.

Publishers benefit in these ways:

- Lowered cost of goods by eliminating packaging and mailing expenses
- Reduced marketing and distribution costs
- Increased upgrade revenue as a result of 100 percent registration
- No inventory or obsolescence risk
- Immediate access to international markets

Consumers benefit from:

- Convenience and immediate gratification
- No back-orders
- Try-before-you-buy option via free trials
- Large product selection with current versions
- Competitive pricing

What makes this business model interesting for vendors of any product is that the company charges the software publishers differing fees for different levels of exposure. Here are sample prices:

Standard Product Merchandising ($395 per product) includes product conversion and packaging for electronic fulfillment, quality assurance testing, product listing (name, part number, and price) HTML brochure, and guaranteed customer registration.

Enhanced Product Merchandising ($765 per product) includes Standard package plus color product photo image, reviews and awards, business partner directory listing and link.

Publisher Showroom ($2,495 per product) includes all of the above plus faxable scanned product specification sheets, two weeks of Level 2 advertising (see below), and a trail program.

Advertising is available on the Home Page (Level 1, $1,500 per item/week), What's New (Level 2, $1,000 per item/week), Free Stuff (Level 2, $1,000 per item/week), and the Product Catalog (Level 2, $1,000 per item/week). Advertisers can purchase advertising on a separate private page for $2,500 per item/week.

The company reports income of $15,000 per week as of July 1995, and expects to gross $3 million in its first year.

This is a good marketing strategy as it provides a new sales channel for software companies. It is an especially good plan for publishers who have difficulty getting into traditional distribution or meeting the hefty MDF (marketing distribution funds) required to play in the big leagues. Small publishers and business-to-business publishers, who couldn't or would not want to be in retail distribution can gain access to new customers with this method. To software.net's credit, the fees are reasonable, especially when compared to advertising in national computer magazines or as part of the chain's advertising programs.

This business model can be used for virtually any industry selling consumer products, business-to-business products, or information.

BUSINESS MODEL-STARTING POINT HOME PAGE

Another way to generate revenue from advertising is to create a starting point Home Page. This is a page that is dedicated to a single topic, like finance or travel. If you publicize and promote the site properly, you will attract people who are interested in those topics. You would need to supply fresh links to Web sites and information resources on the Internet to draw people on a continual basis. As you verify these numbers and the demographics of the shoppers, you will be able to sell advertising space on this page. Yahoo, the directory service, sells ads for $20,000 a month, even though they do not have any demographics on their users. Imagine what a service could charge for a page that reaches a defined market! Entrepreneurs can create starting pages for people with special interests, such as cooking, skiing, travel, or finance.

The Internet Mall is a good example of how to create a directory that provides a starting off point for people who are shopping for products and services. If you visit this mall, which lists stores for free, you will find hundreds of stores, old and new, that can be browsed on the Internet. Of course, you would not want to take his idea and compete with him, you would take the same idea and do it for a topic of interest to your target customers, so that your page is known as the source for links to information, entertainment or resources of interest.

CASE STUDY—THE INTERNET MALL

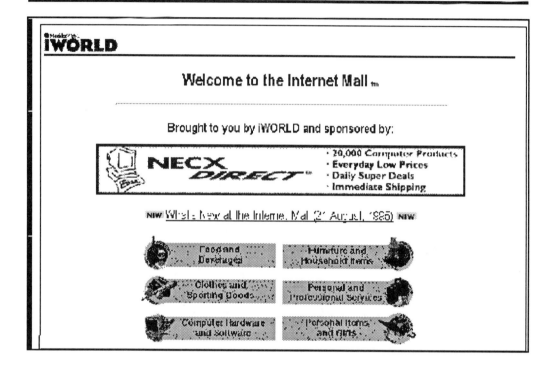

Figure 4-1: Internet Mall describes thousands of businesses. Copyright 1995, Intutitive Systems.

Dave Taylor   http://www.mecklerweb.com/ imall

Intuitive Systems   taylor@netcom.com

P.O. Box 368   415-361-8400

Menlo Park, CA 94026   Home Page for Intuitive Systems:

                                   http://www.mecklerweb.com/~taylor

Background

Who is your primary audience?

We seek to offer a central spot for consumers to find fun and interesting places to shop on the Internet. With over 2,500 stores listed, we're a lot more fun to visit than even the biggest cybermall, yet we include all the shops in all those malls too!

How does your product or service differ from others?

The Internet Mall is the only mall on the net that offers free listings for all, and at a growth rate of about 75+ new stores each week, it's also the fastest growing spot for shopping on the Internet. Also, since we focus on just legitimate shops and services, we allow users to focus on their own interests without worrying about whether the listings they're finding are shopping related or not.

Finally, the Internet Mall is also a lot more encompassing than those sites that naively believe that the World Wide Web is the beginning and the end of the Internet. We list shops with Gopher addresses, e-mail addresses only, and even those with representatives on AOL, CompuServe, eWorld, and other Internet-accessible systems. The Internet Mall information is also quite widely available, with versions accessible on Gopher, via e-mail, on Usenet through bi-monthly postings, and even uploaded in ASCII format to all of the major commercial services.

Does this business exist only on the Internet?

Essentially the Internet Mall only exists on the Internet. The purpose of the Internet Mall was philanthropic: commercialism is colliding with the Internet, like it or not, so I thought that something like the Mall could offer a central spot where people would be less compelled to "spam" the network (flood the mailing lists and newsgroups with notices) to build a presence, yet still not have to spend hundreds or thousands to succeed.

Where is your work place?

Separate, attached, office space.

What is your background and training?

Bachelors degree, computer science. Masters degree, education. I have worked at HP Labs, edited the Reviews section of SunWorld Magazine, and written a variety of books and hundreds of articles.

When did you start your business?

I started consulting in 1988. The Internet Mall began in 1994.

How much has your company made?

The Internet Mall has paid out about $7,500 in direct billings, and much more indirectly (e.g., speaking gigs, interviews, credibility for consulting jobs, etc.).

Getting started

Did you create a business plan before going online?
Nope.

How much did time did it take to get up and running?

I had a first version of the Internet Mall up and cruisin' within a few days, because I started out with a non-Web version and gradually expanded to include other Internet services.

Did you create the pages yourself?

I did the pages myself. Indeed, the pages are all automatically generated through some custom C programs I have written that take the output of my actual database (tab separated fields) and build the over 200 HTML pages that comprise the Internet Mall you see today. This includes automatically generating all floor and department indices, and building the index of companies by company name too. It's about 1200 lines of C code.

How much did it cost to get started?

Nothing: My account with Netcom was free for some consulting work I did earlier in their corporate history, and I signed a cooperative agreement with Mecklermedia so that they'd pay for the necessary space on the IBM Advantis system where the Internet Mall currently resides (e.g., MecklerWeb) in return for a percentage of the gross revenues on the Mall project itself.

Did you need to go to an outside source for startup capital?

I did not.

What mistakes did you make that you wish you hadn't made?

Best not to comment in print on this one. :-)

What advice would you give someone starting a business?

Scope out the competition, assume it'll take you twice as long to get going as you think, and make double, no triple sure that you have a unique slant that will help produce a fun and unusual Internet site.

What skills would a person need?

Excellent written and presentation skills.

What special qualitites are needed to run your site?

An understanding of the legalities of promoting a business that you know nothing about, and a sufficient level of professional decorum to be able to enjoy the adults and ignore the juvenile folk on the net that send hostile e-mail.

How did you promote your site?

Listings, articles in magazines, personal correspondence with book and magazine authors, pamphlets and brochures at trade conferences.

How much did it cost to promote your site?

About $200 total, probably.

How long did it take until you got your first sale?

Almost immediately.

How did the startup phase affect your personal life?

What personal life? :-) Seriously, not too much at all; as a freelance consultant I just integrated the project into the daily workload.

My day

What does your average day look like?

I work from about 8:30 A.M. to 5 P.M. with lots of breaks to play with my dogs, hang out with my SO (significant other), etc.

What does your job entail?

Varies dramatically; lots of travel, lots of talks at conferences, and lots of on-site client visits.

How many hours a week do you spend working on your site?

I spend no more than fifty hours each week working and answering mail, though frankly I spend too MUCH time answering e-mail: I'm hiring someone to start filtering Internet Mall related e-mail so that I see only the more obscure requests.

What percentages of time are spent on each task?

N/A

What was the hardest aspect of the work in the beginning?

Keeping up with e-mail.

How long did it take to get established?

N/A

What do you like most about your work?

Freedom, independence, publicity, travel.

What do you like the least?

Varied time constraints.

What was your greatest moment?

Getting e-mail from you to invite me to be in this book. :-) Seriously, it's all been great fun.

How much time do you spend upgrading your site?

Probably one hour per day or more.

Are there any hazards to running your site?

Legal: I am anxious that I will help promote a scam.

How much money do you expect to make?

$25,000.

General

Are you glad you are on the Web on personal and business reasons?

Absolutely. It's 95% hype, but 100% fun.

Given what you know now, would you do it again?

Definitely.

Where can people look for more advice?

The Internet Business Guide by Rosalind Resnick & Dave Taylor, SAMS.net Macmillan Publishing, 1995 (2nd edition)

Creating Cool Web Pages with HTML, by Dave Taylor, IDG Books, 1995

The future

What is your next venture?

Who knows?

BUSINESS MODEL-STARTING PAGE & HOME PAGE

Entrepreneurs can create another business in which they create a starting page and create Home Pages for the companies that seek to reach that audience. This business is similar to the previous one, but adds the ability to make money by creating and selling Home Pages. Companies benefit from the traffic you create by attracting a rich variety of companies as well as a reasonable amount of editorial content that adds value to everyone associated with the page—consumer and company alike. For an example of this type of business, read about Internet Health Resources.

CASE STUDY—INTERNET HEALTH RESOURCES

Providing access to practical health and fitness information

Developed and maintained by Internet Health Resources

Welcome to the Internet Health Resources (IHR) Web site. It is important for us, as individuals, to take more responsibility for our healthcare. In order to do so, we need access to reliable and practical information. This Web site's goal is to provide just that. This Home Page allows you to access both Internet-wide health information (useful wherever you live) and local health information (for the San Francisco Bay Area). Please feel free to sign our guest book.

Figure 4-2. Internet Health Resources provides information that draws readers to its Home Page and potential customers for its health-care provider clients. Copyright 1995, Internet Health Resources.

Cliff Bernstein, Ph.D.

Internet Health Resources
1845 Franklin Street #503
San Francisco, CA 94109

http://www.ihr.com/index.html

cliffb@hooked.net

BACKGROUND

Internet Health Resources is a firm that creates web sites for companies involved in the health care industry in San Francisco. This case study is a good example of a web site designer who specializes in a niche market.

Who is your primary audience?

Internet Health Resources (IHR) has two audiences. First, IHR provides health and fitness information to Internet users who want to take more responsibility for their healthcare. Secondly, IHR builds Web sites for healthcare organizations who want to deliver well-organized, user-friendly information.

How will they benefit from your product or service?

Internet users can gain practical health information for both their general interest and for effective healthcare decisions. Healthcare organizations can gain a low-cost medium for effectively distributing service and product information to the rapidly-growing Internet market.

How does your product or service differ from others?

IHR provides one of the only Web sites devoted exclusively to a wide range of healthcare topics. And IHR builds Web sites exclusively for the healthcare industry. We understand the needs of healthcare organizations.

Is this business an offshoot of your existing business, or does it exist only on the Internet?

Exists only on the Internet.

Where does your business operate?

I operate from my home office and from my Web service provider.

What is your background and training?

I worked nine years in healthcare as a psychotherapist and evaluation consultant. The work settings were in hospital psychiatry departments, Community Mental Health, and private practice. I also worked nine years as a computer systems analyst, including two and a half years on a medical cost containment system. My current work as president of IHR is an opportunity to bring together my healthcare and computer science interests.

When did you start your business?

November 1994.

How much money has your company made?

N/A

Getting started

Did you create a business plan before going online?

I did not create a formal business plan before getting started. However, I did have a clear business model of what I intended to do.

How much time did it take to get up and running?

It took about one month from the time I thought of the project until I finally put the IHR Web site online in December 1994.

Did you create the pages yourself?

I created all the pages myself.

How much did it cost to get started?

The initial start-up cost very little. In November/December 1994 I did all the HTML using my existing hardware and software. However, since that time, as I have obtained customers, I have had to beef up my hardware and software. I purchased a gigabyte hard drive (@ $400), a tape back-up system (@ $260), and a computer to serve as my Web server (@ $760). There are also hidden costs, such as the time I now take off from my previously full-time job. This results in a loss of one fifth of my salary income.

Did you need to go to an outside source for startup capital?

No, I did not need this.

What mistakes did you make that you wish you hadn't made?

One early mistake was to not establish a Domain Name as early as possible. My previous Web service provider said they could provide a Domain Name, but then was unable to do so. Because I was unable to establish my Domain Name upfront, I did not want to market my site with an address that was "hardwired" to my Web service provider.

What advice would you give someone starting a business?

First, if you are serious about growing a business on the Internet, I think it is very important to get a Domain Name. This serves two major purposes: It shows the Internet community that you are serious about what you are doing and it gives you portability. That portability allows you to move to another Web service provider, if you need to, with no disruption in your URL.

Second, I would advise finding competent people to work with, whose compensation requirements fit with your budget. It is impossible to do all the work by yourself; you cannot develop all the skills to do everything well. You may need to work with Web site administrators, graphic artists, CGI experts, database specialists, marketing people, etc. By being creative, you can work within a start-up budget. Think about advertising for students who are graphic artists or database specialists, then make sure that the work you give them is within their sphere of competency.

Third, because the Net offers so many possibilities for developing a Web site or providing services, it is easy to get lost or spend time in non-productive activities. I recommend always asking yourself "How will this activity further my short-term or long-term business goals?"

What skills would a person need?

Developing an Internet business requires many skills, including computer software (HTML authoring, graphics, etc.) and hardware, graphic design, sales and marketing, project management, finance, and overall business savvy.

What kind of education is necessary to run your site?

I do not believe someone would need a formal education, however they would need the skills listed above.

What special qualities are needed to run your site?

I think the main qualities for me are vision, persistence, and sticking-to-my-business-model. Vision allows me to develop a road-map of where I am headed, and lets me know when I am off-course. I constantly have to move from the details of my work back to the vision. Persistence keeps me moving forward in the face of the inevitable frustrations and difficulties. I have to keep reminding myself why I got started in this in the first place. And sticking to my business model helps me to stay on course. Staying on course can be tough in the face of the awesome number of possibilities and distractions there are on the Internet. I try to keep things simple, focus on the business, and not get too caught up with all of the new technology.

How did you promote your site?

I requested to be listed on large directories such as Yahoo, GNN, and CityNet. Also, I have been fortunate, in that the June 1995 issue of CompuServe magazine selected the IHR Web site as one of the three notable health Web sites on the Internet. Other print publications have also listed the IHR Web site.

How much did it cost to promote your site?

I hired a marketing person to promote the IHR Web site on the Internet. That work is projected to cost $200 to $300.

How long did it take until you got your first sale?

It took about four months from the time my site was up in December 1994 to the first sales agreement from a customer.

How did the startup phase affect your personal life?

IHR has very much affected my life. Basically, although it does not cost a lot of money, it takes considerable time and attention. This means little time with my wife and friends, very little time enjoying weekends, and no personal time. I often sit indoors on sunny weekend days. It is a major sacrifice of my personal life. This is the biggest cost in developing the business. Additionally, I am earning less money now, due to cutting back in my salaried computer systems work.

My day

What does your average day look like?

I work four weekdays as a salaried systems analyst, leaving one weekday to devote to IHR. I also devote most evenings and weekends to IHR. My one IHR weekday consists of sales demos in the morning and then dozens of phone calls in the afternoon. In the evenings and weekends I answer e-mail, build customers' and IHR's Web sites, and do administrative work.

What does your job entail?

The job entails lots of phone calling, HTML authoring, e-mailing, Net surfing, demos, meetings, doing financials (billing, etc.).

How many hours a week do you spend working on your site?

About 40 hours a week.

- Phone calling-17%
- Demos-8%
- HTML authoring-15%
- E-mail (including reading e-mail newsletters)-30%
- Net surfing (for business objective)-10%
- Miscellaneous administration (meetings, financial)-20%

What was the hardest aspect of the work in the beginning?

Putting all the pieces together (i.e., building the infrastructure), marketing, building the Web site, learning all the new software and HTML, administrative work, demos, etc.

How long did it take to get established?

I cannot say that I am yet established but I do feel more confident that the pieces are falling together and that I am working with the right business plan.

What do you like most about your work?

I enjoy building the Web sites, doing demos, being a pioneer in new technology and business processes, and making sales calls to tell people about the IHR services.

What do you like the least?

The frustrations of dealing with technology that is not always consistent or plug-and-play. For example, my backup tape drive software did not work, my Web server TCP/IP stack kept crashing, and getting a dial-up script to work correctly was difficult.

Health Resources for Consumers

- Health Topics
- Healthcare Providers and Clinics With a National Scope
- Healthcare Publications
- Internet Health Newsgroups and Listserver Groups
- State and National Healthcare Organizations
- Healthcare Policy and Legislation

Local Health Resources for Consumers

- San Francisco Bay Area Health Resources
- San Diego County HealthCare Resources Guide

Health Resources for Healthcare Providers

- Health Topics
- Healthcare Schools
- Healthcare Publications

Figure 4-3. The Home Page divides contents into areas for consumers and providers.

Online Health Topics

Developed and maintained by Internet Health Resources

This Internet Health Resources page contains pointers to online health information, arranged in alphabetical order, by topic.

Allergies

- Allergies: What They Are, What You Can Do About Them.

Alternative/Holistic Medicine

- Natural News Wire Digest(tm) contains articles on natural health and healing.
- Alternative Medicine Information Resource describes the NIH Office of Alternative Medicine (OAM).

Anxiety

- "Attacking Anxiety" booklets . The "Attacking Anxiety" booklets are a set of booklets that equip readers with the information they need to find expert, professional help.

Figure 4-4. Selecting a menu option a page with information titles that will lead to a provider's Home Page.

What was your greatest moment?

My first sale.

Are there any hazards to running your site?

There are potential legal liabilities when operating a Web site devoted to healthcare resources. I do not, though, give medical advice.

How much money do you expect to make?

I expect to make over $70,000 a year.

General

Are you glad you are on the Web for personal and business reasons?

I enjoy the excitement of the business. I do not like the time away from my personal life.

Given what you know now, would you do it again?

Definitely yes.

The future

What is your next venture?

This is it for now.

What else would you like to say?

The Internet affords exciting opportunities both for business potential and for operating on the cutting edge. However, anyone getting into this should know up-front that this requires a lot of time and attention to do it right. Thanks for the opportunity to share some of my thoughts. I hope others will find this helpful.

BUSINESS MODEL—AUCTION

Going once, going twice, sold to the entrepreneur in the first row who knows how to bring buyers and sellers together. Yes, you can create an auction business!

Auctions can be run on the Internet in much the same way they are run in the real world. You gather merchandise on consignment and offer the items for sale to an interested public that bids on the merchandise. When the last, highest bid is received, that person has bought the product at a 10 percent override from the high price, which the auctioneer keeps as his fee.

This business model can work for almost any product, such as art, collectibles, antiques, jewelry, books, furniture, real estate, business furnishings and computers.

An online auction can work this way: you post pictures and descriptions of the merchandise, as well as bidding minimums and deadlines for bids. People send their bids via e-mail, along with their credit card information and address, which gives you time to verify their authenticity and spending limits. By the way, this is exactly what auctioneers in the real world do. They even accept phone bids during the auction from customers who have been pre-approved.

Practical examples and links to Home Pages

The Rock and Roll Save the Earth Art Auction is a fund-raiser for the

Save the Earth Foundation-http://www.commerce.com:80/save_earth

BUSINESS MODEL—NETWORKING GROUP

You do not have to be a computer consultant to start a networking group. This business is not to be confused with people who install computer network systems for a living. Instead, it is a group of people who share a common interest and trade new business leads, business advice, and camaraderie. They exist in the real world as Le Tips, and other similar businesses. In the real world, people get together for lunch or breakfast once a week or once a month and discuss items of common concern and network with one another. In the online world, you could create a group that includes these people:

In your profession (like Realtors or computer programmers or travel agents) to share news of general interest; such as business trends.

In your community—to find vendors and consultants who you can refer business to—and get business from. For example, a community based networking group could include a photographer, painter, Realtor, caterer, and the like who could use each other's services or refer business to one another.

You can make money doing this by charging a fee for membership. In the off-line world, memberships can run $300 a year plus the costs of the meal and room rental. In the online world, your costs include running your home page and marketing. People would network at virtual meetings held in a chat session, using Internet Relay Chat, or commercial programs that allow for messages to be typed to one another and read by everyone at the same time, like WebChat (http://www.irsociety.com), or with a voice system, like RealAudio (http://www.realaudio.com) or VocalTel (http://www.vocaltel.com).

BUSINESS MODELS—DIGITAL MALL, FLEA MARKET, ONLINE EXPO, PROFESSIONAL SUITES

These four business models share a common theme—the entrepreneur creates an environment (Home Page) that attracts business people who want to sell products and services to a defined market. In some ways, you might think these are the same business, but targeted toward different markets:

*   Digital mall appeals to businesses that sell products on the Internet or on Main Street. It also provides a marketing venue for service providers, consultants, and professionals.
*   Flea markets will draw vendors who sell home-made jewelry, art, crafts, surplus products, clothing, tools, hardware, close-out merchandise, bric-a-brac, toys, books, records, and the like.
*   Online Expos are virtual trade shows that will attract people who would normally attend a conference, Expo, trade show to see vendors' booths, who sell services and products aimed at a highly targeted audience, such as health care professionals, corporate computer users, lawyers, and accountants.
*   Professional Suites are digital malls promote professionals' services, like accountants, doctors, architects, designers, and marketers.

Entrepreneurs make money selling space to merchants under several levels of service and fees:

*   Free listing of company name, description, and phone number. This basic listing helps the mall begin to attract customers. The mall operator benefits by having a mall that looks like it contains a lot of businesses. Merchants benefit from seeing if an online presence helps their business. If they get leads and sales, they might increase their advertising commitment on the Internet.

- E-mail services. This listing allows prospects to send mail directly to the merchant, who can form a relationship and sell products and services.
- Link to Home Page. Consumers can click on the listing and connect to the merchant's Home Page.

Fees can range from a few dollars to hundreds or thousands of dollars depending on the number of qualified people who visit. For example, if you can attract hard-to-reach consumers in a specialized field, you will be paid more for those leads.

Online providers can also make money creating Home Pages for merchants. Some digital mall providers charge merchants a small fee for each person who visits, which can become a large amount of money given the number of people on the Internet.

Entrepreneurs who operate these services should be able to promote and market the site to appropriate audiences using online and traditional methods in the real world.

CLASSIFIED ADVERTISEMENTS

Entrepreneurs can create a Home Page of classified advertisements that sell everything from cars, boats, sporting goods and other merchandise to listings for travel, houses, and other products and services seen in daily newspapers. Online bulletin boards have been providing this kind of service for years. The Internet is a natural medium for this service.

Ad publishers will make money by selling advertisements. Additional income can be made by handling inquiries, forwarding mail, and running a blind response box (in which the buyer doesn't know who the seller is). Ad publishers can also sell links to the advertiser's Home Page.

Summary

These business models can be used to create cyberstores for hundreds, if not thousands, of traditional Main Street businesses.

5 CONSUMER PRODUCTS

There are literally thousands of companies selling products in every conceivable category on the Internet. Yet there are opportunities for entrepreneurs to enter the field. You can sell different kinds of products to different segments of the market. For example, although there are jewelry stores on the Internet, an entrepreneur working from her house might find an eager market by specializing in modern designs, while others sell more traditional wares.

You should not be scared off by big companies that are online because on the Internet, no one knows if you are a big company or a small one. Consumers know you by the quality of your products and the advantages and skills you bring to their design, creation, and marketing. You probably would not want to sell chocolates head-to-head against Godiva, but you could outflank them by selling chocolates in the shape of company logos or toys, which Godiva does not do.

This chapter looks at entrepreneurs who use the Internet to create new customers for the products they sell in stores on Main Street or from their mail-order catalogs. Through case studies and interviews, you'll see how companies sell a variety of products to diverse markets including jewelry, clothing, teddy bears, boats, bicycles, collectibles, condoms, flowers, and T-shirts.

Internet entrepreneurs should be aware of the business model for drop shopping products as described in Chapter 4, in which they merely advertise and promote the need for these products and then fill orders. Because many of these businesses follow the same models, the introductions will be briefer than those in succeeding chapters, so as not to be repetitive.

SELLING PRODUCTS ON THE INTERNET

Overview—If you create earrings, bracelets, belt buckles and the like, you can find a ready market on the Internet, which is home to dozens of companies selling these kinds of products. You can differentiate your products by specializing in regional flavors, such as Southwestern, Appalachian, Western, modern, traditional, and avant garde, to name a few.

Rewards—Selling products could be the perfect entry point for the wannabe Internet entrepreneur, the part-time worker, and the full-time corporate executive who create products as part of their hobbies, such as jewelry, knit goods, candles, or calligraphy. They can keep their day jobs and ship products as the orders come in.

For companies on Main Street, the Internet provides an additional channel of distribution to reach new customers around the world. You will read about Milne Jewelry of Salt Lake City, Utah, selling its fine products to people in Japan, as well as the Virginia Diner selling peanuts and gift baskets to people around the world.

Risks—Selling products online involves certain risks that can be minimized with proper planning. For example, there are hustlers and frauds in the off-line world who will prey on companies that are on the Internet. Therefore, it is a good idea to verify credit card orders and check the address against the clearing house's records. When you send products you should use a service that requires a signature showing receipt of the product, such as Federal Express, Airborne, UPS, and U.S. Post Office Express Mail. In the near future, you'll be able to charge people by debiting their digital bank accounts. You can also join a digital mall that uses a registration number system, which asks customers for their credit card numbers and provides them with a registration number in which they can order products. This step can thwart criminals.

Special marketing considerations for cyber stores—Home Pages should make browsing for products fun. This is an important consideration on the Internet, which delivers graphics slowly. Merchants should be careful to design pages that have thumbnail pictures of products instead of full-screen views, because of the time needed to display art.

Browsing should be done by categories that lead to more and more levels in information and detail. For example, a store that sell books, music, and videos should have those three options listed first. Consumers would select music and see a menu offering a search by title or artist or type of music. In this manner, they can easily find the products they seek. The less desirable alternative is to present a laundry list of all products, which could frustrate and confuse consumers who will run to another site if you make their shopping experience less than desirable.

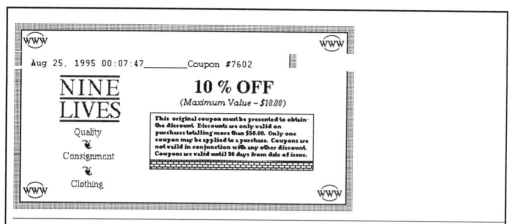

Aug 25, 1995 00:07:47_____ Coupon #7602

NINE LIVES

Quality

Consignment

Clothing

10 % OFF
(Maximum Value – $10.00)

This original coupon must be presented to obtain the discount. Discounts are only valid on purchases totalling more than $50.00. Only one coupon may be applied to a purchase. Coupons are not vaild in conjunction with any other discount Coupons are valid until 30 days from date of issue.

This **original** coupon must be presented to obtain the discount. Discounts are only valid on purchases totalling more than $50.00. Only one coupon may be applied to a purchase. Coupons are not valid in conjunction with any other discount. Only one coupon per person per day may be applied towards purchases. Coupons are valid until 30 days from the date of issue.

Figure 5-1. Nine Lives offers Internet consumers a coupon that can be redeemed at their clothing store in Los Gatos, Calif. Copyright 1995, Nine Lives Quality Consignment Clothing.

Merchants can use the tools of the traditional world, such as coupons, sales, and promotions, to attract customers to their cyber stores and traditional outlets.

All product cyber stores should be listed on as many directories as possible. See Chapter 3 for a list of directories and instructions for using them. Store owners should also try to link their store to as many digital malls and complementary sites as possible.

CASE STUDY-MILNE JEWLERY

Figure 5-2. Because the Internet reaches a worldwide audience, merchants should offer their home pages in several languages.

Milne Jewelry Company

P.O. Box 58958

Salt Lake City, Utah 84158-0958

`http://www.xmission.com/~turq`

`turq@xmission.com`

Voice /Fax: 1-801-486-1618

Background

What is your company's background?

Milne Jewelry Company was established in St. George, Utah in January 1951 and has maintained an exceptional reputation for high quality merchandise and service to clients for over 40 years. As a family business, Milne Jewelry Company is founded on the principles of honesty and integrity that are the trademark of founder, Wes Milne.

As a wholesaler of Native American Indian silver and turquoise jewelry and jewelry of the American Southwest, our product lines are featured in fine gift shops throughout the United States ófrom the bright lights and glamour of the casino cities to the rustic western grandeur of several National Parks. Many international airport, hotel, and resort gift shops all delight tourists and collectors alike with the authentic quality and beauty of Milne Jewelry Company designs.

One of the prime objectives of Milne Jewelry Company has been to promote the talents of Native American Indian artists and craftsmen, currently using the talents of over 300 silversmithsórepresentatives of the highest quality artisans making jewelry today.

What was your purpose in putting a home page on the Web?

As one of the first 300 Web sites making an entrance on the Internet, and not knowing what to expect, we mainly just wanted to test the waters and get our feet wet. We wanted to see what kind of opportunities might be available with this new medium of advertising and selling. The first Web site we saw was Grants Floral on the Branch Mall. Our assumption was, "If they can sell flowers, we can sell turquoise!" (You may be aware that as of Spring 1994, there was no information available on commercialism on the Internet and WWW.) Our main goals were to reach new markets and build name identification. Customer support and product knowledge is of high priority to Milne Jewelry Company. Including the internet in our communication systems seemed to be an effective and low-cost way to meet a wider variety of needs of our domestic and international customers through Web sites, ftp, and e-mail. We have been extremely pleased with the results so far.

How has the Home Page helped your business?

A good example might be our entrance into the Japanese market.

For years, Japanese visitors to the United States have been delighted with the quality and beauty of our truly "authentic American product." We get many requests from these customers asking how they can get additional pieces of jewelry once they get home to Japan. (The Japanese like to buy our products in the United Statesónot Japan.) We are now able to make our products readily available to our retail friends in Japan with a Japanese version of our catalog - and they can still say they purchased their jewelry in the United States.

Some stats you may be interested in:

Percentage of sales from Web site domestic and internationally:
United States-56%
Japan-18%
All other countries-26%

Percentage of International Sales Only:
Japan-40%
All other countries-60% (average 4% per country)

Average Order:
United States-$54.25

Japan-$122.00
All other countries-$69.50

The strong sales to Japan are not accidental. Years of watching our retailers and tracking their sales showed us the Japanese were our best customers. This market was specifically targeted.

What advice would you offer a business on the Web?

To have no great expectations. Building a business on the Internet takes time and effort.

CASE STUDY-NINE LIVES, CLOTHING STORE

Welcome to Nine Lives!

New! We are now accepting **menswear**. View the consignor's <u>brochure</u> before you call to make an appointment.

Special Promotion: For a limited time you can obtain a free <u>coupon good for 10% off</u> your (over $50) purchases at Nine Lives. Have your printer ready!

Enjoy yourself

Figure 5-3. Nine Lives uses its cyber store to lead people to its store in Los Gatos, Calif. Copyright 1995, Nine Lives Quality Consignment Clothing.

Mary Jane Nesbitt

Nine Lives Quality Consignment

Clothing

9 Montebello Way

Los Gatos, CA 95030

http://www.los-gatos.ca.us/nine.html

mmers@chezhal.slip.netcom.com

408-354-9169

Background

Who is your primary audience?

Professional women and men who are looking for top quality clothing and accessories in like-new condition at 1/3 retail price (or lower!!).

How will they benefit from your product?

Customers will be able to dress up to a level they could not otherwise afford, or save money on the items they would ordinarily buy at full retail prices. The Internet (Web) page is "out there" to make it easy to see what is inventory, what the consignment policies of the store are, and to provide business and contact information.

Does your product differ from others?

No, but making the inventory of the store available on the Internet through the WorldWide Web is unique. The Personal Shopping Assistants, which store profiles and e-mail against them, are also extremely rare on the Web. They are unheard of in stores the size of Nine Lives.

Is this business an offshoot of your existing business, or does it exist only on the Internet?

The Web is definitely an offshoot of the real business. We cannot sell our products through the Web. People demand a chance to try the clothes on before they buy, and the margins are too slim to offer a return policy through the mail.

Was the Internet store meant to generate income on its own or to steer people to your other outlets?

The Internet storefront is 100% designed to steer people to the real store. Every aspect of the pages is focused on getting the customers to visit the physical store.

Where is your workplace?

The server is at home (converted dining room) but the inventory is maintained from the store (through the Internet) by dialing the server.

What is your background and training?

I have a masters in management. No retail or computer experience to speak of, except as a user (word processing). My husband, the Webmaster, has worked as a UNIX instructor for the past ten years, and has an MBA.

Getting started

When did you start your business?

Nine Lives (the real store) opened in February 1993. The Virtual Storefront opened in January 1994.

Did you create a business plan before going online?

No. It was done incrementally in spare time, with no real plan. Each feature was added as the Web evolved.

How much time did it take to get up and running?

The initial pages and inventory search took about a week. Personal Shopping Assistants took a weekend to create and have taken months to fine-tune.

Did you create the pages yourself or did you get help?

We did it all.

How much did it cost to get started?

The computer was already part of the family and my husband was on-line quite a bit with Prodigy, so we had modems and a second phone line. No software was needed (UNIX has everything we need) so the only initial cost was the Internet Account ($100 startup) and then monthly fees.

Did you need to go to an outside source for startup capital?

No.

How did you promote your site?

We listed it on every index in the world :-O We also put the URL on our flyers, our store signs, and Nine Lives business cards.

How much did it cost to promote your site?

No $$ - just time to look for new indexes and get it listed.

How long did it take until you got your first sale?

Visitors appeared immediately through the Web. Five to ten from the very first day.

How much has your company made?

$100/week of new business, saving of $100/week from advertising we do not have to do, costs of $50 a week for the site, net $150/week. It's a small site.

How much money do you expect to make?

Another $200-300/week.

What mistakes did you make that you wish you hadn't made?

We are happy with things as they have progressed.

What advice would you give someone starting a business?

Concentrate on providing service. Save people time, trouble, or $$$. There is no other long-term reason to be there, unless you count entertainment.

What skills would a person need to be a success?

Infinite patience, the ability to redesign Web pages based solely on log file audit trails, an extremely organized approach to managing a business.

What special qualities are needed to run your site?

Programming, business organization, and communication.

Your day

What does your average day look like?

I work in the store five days a week, where I do all the inventory maintenance through normal POS (point of sale, the displays you see at the check out counter) activities.

My husband works a normal job, then comes home and works on the Website in the evenings.

What does your job entail?

Entering 800 items and selling 800 items every three months. The rest is completely automated. The whole inventory presentation and query system on the Website is automated.

How many hours a week do you spend working on your site?

Myself, none to one hour/week. My husband, one to twenty hours a week depending on whether we are stable or adding/debugging a new feature. My delightful husband usually spends about ten hours a week on the site, answering mail, checking the inventory system, and adding little touches here and there. I do not have to do anything except enter all the inventory. Lucky for me this is not extra work. The POS terminal in the store is connected to the Web server, so entering the intake items for the purpose of printing labels and entering sales serves to keep the inventory up to date.

What was the hardest aspect of the work in the beginning?

Learning the correct answers to technical questions asked by customers and reporters. My husband says writing the Personal Shopping Assistant part of the software was a challenge.

What do you like most about your work?

The feeling we are doing something new, exciting, and truly valuable with this new technology.

What do you like the least?

Major changes to the software right before month-end. (Are you listening, dear??)

What was your greatest moment?

The greatest moment was when the CNN Camera Crew said "That's It! We're Done."

How did the startup phase affect your personal life?

Ha! For both of us, the startup phase neatly replaced our personal lives.

Are you glad your store is on the Web?

Yes. We have tremendous exposure through the Web. There is no way Nine Lives could afford that much publicity using traditional marketing. In addition, my husband landed his most recent job partly due to the strength of the site.

Given what you know now, would you do it again?

Yes. The publicity from the Web page has been tremendous. Nine Lives has been on CNN, written up in Women's Day and Smart Money, and has appeared in numerous other publications.

The future

What is your next venture?

The menswear section just opened, after being in the planning phase for months. Next: who knows?

CASE STUDY-FLOWER STOP MARKETING CORP.

Chuck Haley

Flower Stop Marketing Corp.

P.O. Box 7070

Colorado Springs, CO 80933

http://www.flowerstop.com/fstop

800-L-D-ROSES (800-537-6737)

Background

Who is your primary audience?

We're still trying to figure that out. Outside of the normal demographics of the net, which are changing all the time, we do not have specific demos on our customers. The demos of the net seem to parallel those of the traditional flower buying public. Consequently there appear to be more florists on the net than any other industry.

How will they benefit from your product?

It can be easier to order flowers on the net than from a local florist or an 800 number. Often times customers do not have all the information needed by the florist in order to process the order and when it comes time to verbalize to an operator what they would like to say on the enclosure card, they become tongue-tied. When they place their order on the net, they can take their time to complete all the information needed and compose the appropriate card for the occasion. Another benefit is that the accuracy is not dependent on the operators' spelling skills or ability to understand unique voices on the phone or decipher handwriting. The order comes through exactly how the customer wishes in typed format.

How does your product differ from others?

Along with being in the top 300 FTD florists in the country, Flower Stop also features a product line unique in the flower industry. Flower Stop's parent company is Pikes Peak Greenhouses and we ship our famous Long Distance Roses AE, and Long Distance Flowers AE direct from our own greenhouses by FedEx AE to the lucky recipient.

Is this business an offshoot of your existing business, or does it exist only on the Internet?

Flower Stop and Long Distance Roses started in 1983. They have been marketing through 800-L-D-ROSES (Long Distance Roses) and 800-GIVE-FTD since their opening. Long Distance Roses has been marketing on CompuServe, GEnie, and Delphi for six to eight years.

If it is an offshoot, was it meant to generate income on its own or to steer people to your other outlets?

Flower Stop on the Internet was designed from the beginning to take orders. By providing customers full graphics and description of the products and having a complete order entry form Flower Stop has one of the easiest ordering systems on the net. We prefer to get orders over the net because of the accuracy of spelling which makes it easier for us to enter the order into our system.

Where is your office?

All our Internet operations are run from our Long Distance Roses headquarters.

What is your background and training?

Born and raised in the flower business, I have spent years in all facets of the industry from growing, wholesaling, retailing, and direct marketing.

I started working on the Internet a year ago.

When did you start your business?

This is a family business thath my brother and I purchased ten years ago.

How much has your company made?

In the past five months Flower Stop has received 400 orders for $18,000.

Getting started

Did you create a business plan before going online?

Not really. Our experience with online shopping from CompuServe et. al. was a good indicator of what we could expect. We looked at it as being able to open another location for the cost of a good ad campaign.

How much time did it take to get up and running?

We made the decision to go online in July 1994 and were up and running by the first of October 1994.

Did you create the pages yourself or did you get help?

We hired two outside firms to put our site together. First, we hired a programmer to write all the HTML and set up the order entry form. We also hired a commercial artist to design the Home Page graphics and scan in the transparencies of the products.

How much did it cost to get started?

It cost about $20,000 to get the site up. From then on it has cost another $20,000 for things like upgrades to the site, fees to get listed in electronic malls throughout the net, fees for our access provider, and advertising to get exposure.

Did you need to go to an outside source for startup capital?

We used funds from inside the company and redirected some of our ad budget to the Internet store.

What mistakes did you make that you wish you hadn't made?

Since this is largely experimental still, I'm not sure what of the things we have done will turn out to be mistakes. The cost of getting on-line is so reasonable, it's hard to believe that any mistake can cost enough to worry about.

What advice would you give someone starting a business?

Getting online at this point is so easy I can't imagine why a company wouldn't do it just for the exposure. (Down the road someone is going to have to foot the bill and it will be the commercial element. After all, they stand to gain the most.) The next decision is to determine your purpose and level of involvement. If it's more for advertising (like Zima) then you will approach the Internet with that objective and go for the information and exposure to build product and/or company recognition. If you're going for on-line sales, then you need to build your store for taking orders and providing the information that the customer needs to make an informed buying decision.

What skills would a person need to conduct business?

My advice is to determine the aspect of online marketing that interests you and spend your efforts in that area. Then you can hire people to fill in the gaps. There is no shortage of displaced programmers that would be anxious to serve you.

What education is necessary to run your site?

It's more important to have someone in charge of the content of the site. In this case, marketing is still the key. If you want to be a do-it-yourself-er, you will need to start by learning how to get all the latest versions of software needed to get online and learning how all of them interact. Since there are programs to do just about anything you need done, the real challenge is finding them and installing them. Once they are installed, any bozo can operate them. This is where good programmers will earn their pay.

How did you promote your site?

The first decision we made was to develop a Home Page that was graphically superior to anything on the net at the time. By doing that, we were able to get exposure in the likes of *PC Magazine 2/7/95, Computerworld,* and several local newspapers throughout the country. We were featured by IBM in their introduction of Warp/2 at the Comdex show last year. We were featured in another book and we have received a lot of attention from the Internet community itself. Our next decision was to get listed in all the search engines, which is an ongoing project. And finally, we have a link in more malls than any other florist on the net.

How much did it cost to promote your site?

Some listings are free, especially in the search engines. But the price for exposure ranges from $50/year to $2,700/week. We lean toward the lower cost options.

How long did it take until you got your first sale?

We got our first sale on the third day. It was a birthday arrangement from a customer in Hong Kong to a recipient in Manchester, England. Another lesson is to be prepared for international interaction.

How did the startup phase affect your personal life?

The whole computer experience was new to me. Since my children had all left home, the time was right for a new adventure. I now have parallel systems at home and at work.

My day

What does your average day look like?

There is no average day when you own you own business.

What does your job entail?

Just about everything. Mostly, I'm involved in the retail divisions.

How many hours a week do you spend working on your site?

Not much really, 10 to 20 hours. A lot of it is spent answering question-naires like this.

What percentages of time are spent on each task?

Conducting Business - 60%
Marketing - 10%
Selling - 10%
Upgrading Site - 10%

What was the hardest aspect of the work in the beginning?

Getting a comfortable work station. Hours at the computer can cause a lot of back pain if your station doesn't fit.

How long did it take to get established?

N/A

What do you like most about your work?

It's a new adventure and I'm learning new skills.

What do you like the least?

N/A

What was your greatest moment?

N/A

Are there any hazards to running your site?

I haven't found any yet.

How much money do you expect to make?

Lots!

General

Are customers concerned about security for their credit cards?

We installed PGP (Pretty Good Protection, an encryption program) and less than 1% use it. Their other choice is "call me for credit card information." Less that 1% use that. Judging from the orders we get with their credit card information, I would say that there is no concern. Afterall, everyone knows that the merchant takes all the risks of the transaction.

How do you process orders via credit cards?

We transmit the credit card number electronically to our bank from our computer and get an approval number. Any order not approved is canceled.

Are you glad your store is on the Web?

Definitely. I believe that although home computers will not take over our lives, they will become a communications tool as common as the telephone.

Given what you know now, would you do it again?

We are so far away from where we will be in the next five years, the question is premature.

Where can people find advice about running a site like yours?

Books like yours are being written and published on a regular basis. Due to the changing nature of the Internet, more books will be written just to keep up with these changes. Also, there is a lot of information on the Internet itself.

The future

What is your next venture?

We need to make money at this one first.

What else would you like to say?

 I gotta go. Just visit our site and you'll see what I have been talking about.

Thanks!

Thank you,

Chuck > > >=01=01 >

CASE STUDY-WORLDWEB SUPPLIES & ACCESSORIES, INC.

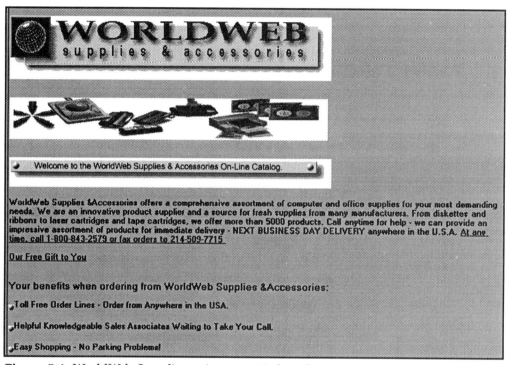

Figure 5-4. WorldWeb Supplies points out it's benefits on the opening screen of the Home Page. Copyright 1995 WorldWeb Supplies and Accessories, Inc.

Michael A. Berger   http://www.wsa-supplies.com

WorldWeb Supplies & Accessories, Inc   mberger@intex.net

1103 High Vista Lane   214-437-2538

Richardson, TX 75080

Background

Who is your primary audience?

Computer, fax, and printer owners—both business and personal.

How will they benefit from your product?

They can shop online. We have large ($30 million) inventory. The prices are discounted. Delivery is next day, anywhere in the USA—at discount shipping rates.

How does your product differ from others?

The large inventory, next day shipping, and VERY experienced sales personnel at the 800 number.

Is this business an offshoot of your existing business, or does it exist only on the Internet?

Only on the Internet.

Where is your office?

Home office.

What is your background and training?

Physicist with 30+ years computer training and twenty years computer supply experience.

Getting started

When did you start your business?

March 1995.

Did you create a business plan before going online?

Yes.

How much time did it take to get up and running?

Four months.

Did you create the pages yourself or did you get help?

I got help.

How much did it cost to get started?

About $12,000 for getting online (pages, graphics, etc.) Setup of inventory (consigned) and administration was about $20,000.

Did you need to go to an outside source for startup capital?

Outside source. Wrote and presented business plan.

How did you promote your site?

Search engines.

How much did it cost to promote your site?

Not done yet. About $20,000 over six months.

How long did it take until you got your first sale?

One week after site up.

How much has your company made?

First order, $90.

How much money do you expect to make?

About $300,000 first year sales.

What mistakes did you make that you wish you hadn't made?

Bad site and programmers.

What advice would you give someone starting a similar business?

Hire your own people or contractors.

What skills would a person need to conduct business?

Marketing and technical.

What special qualities are needed to run your site?

MBA would help!

My day

What does your average day look like?

Check site.

Write checks.

Devote about two hours to marketing (plans, etc.).

What does your job entail?

Everything (one-man company) .

How much time do you spend conducting business, marketing, selling, upgrading your site?

40 hours per week. Administration 25%, Marketing 25%, Dealing with vendors 15%, Working on site programming, etc. 15%, Other (?) 20%.

What was the hardest aspect of the work in the beginning?

Getting the initial site running properly.

What do you like most about your work?

Selling!

What do you like the least?

Dealing with incompetent programmers, etc.

What was your greatest moment?

The first sale.

How did the startup phase affect your personal life?

No personal life!

Are you glad your store is on the Web?

Yes.. cutting edge...

Given what you know now, would you do it again?

Yes.

The future

What is your next venture?

Expand product line. More fully automate sales process.

What else would you like to say?

The most important part of doing this if you want to keep employees to a minimum is to systematize and automate the process from order taking to shipping to payments for inventory.

CASE STUDY-BEARS BY THE SEA

Figure 5-5. Since many consumer are afraid to send credit card information over the Internet, merchants must provide traditional methods of order taking. Copyright 1995, Bears by the Sea.

Bears By The Sea

Kitty Wilde

680 Cypress Street

Pismo Beach, CA 93449

Fax: 805-773-5869

http://webmill.com/bears

bears@callamer.com

bears_ca@ppp.callamer.com

Voice: 805-773-1952

Background

Who is your primary audience?

Teddy bear collectors.

Is this business an offshoot of your existing business, or does it exist only on the Internet?

Offshoot of our retail store—generates income as well as funnels people to store Storefront.

What is your background and training?

BA in education. Registered nurse. Have started several businesses.

When did you start your business?

Bears by the Sea began in 1992.

Getting started

Did you create a business plan before going online?

Business plan was created before going on line.

How much did time did it take to get up and running?

Ninety hours.

Did you create the pages yourself or did you get help?

Got help creating pages.

How much did it cost to get started?

Cost of creating WWW pages, storage on line, maintenance—complete package for one year, $1,500.

What advice would you give someone starting a business?

Shop around. Pay attention to potential hidden charges. Get an all inclusive package. Make sure you are listed in the right directories.

What skills would a person need to operate a business?

Open mind. Willing to learn new technology. Patienceóit takes time.

What special qualities are needed to operate the store?

Artistic and business.

How did you promote the site?

URL on business cards and literature. Word of mouth.

How long did it take to get your first sale?

Two weeks.

Your day

How many hours a week do you spend working on your site?

Four hours a day.

What was the hardest aspect of the work in the beginning?

Time to get established: two weeks.

How much time do you spend marketing the site:

One hour per day.

What do you like most about your work?

Challenge of new ideas.

What do you like the least?

Time spent.

What was your greatest moment?

Seeing it all come together online and having people respond.

How did the startup phase affect your personal life?

You do not have one while you are setting this up!

The future

What else would you like to say?

We are helping other people put their businesses on the Internet. It is a great innovative, inexpensive way to do business. Every business needs an Internet presence to be competitive in this changing world.

CASE STUDY-BIKE PEDALERS

Rich Rodenburg

Bike Pedalers and The Walton

Trail Company

3340 S 29th

Lincoln, NE 68510

http://www.inetnebr.com/bikeped/

bikeped@inetnebr.com

402-474-7000

Background

Who is your primary audience?

Bicycle enthusiasts.

How will they benefit from your product?

We have included maintenance tips, local interest, links to other cycling sites, calendars, etc.

How does your product differ from others?

We are a (regular) bike shop, and offer our services online as well. We were one of the first, if not the first, to do so.

Is this business an offshoot of your existing business, or does it exist only on the Internet?

We are primarily a walk (or ride) in bike shop. The Web site is a very small percentage of our business.

If it is an offshoot, was it meant to generate income on its own or to steer people to your other outlets?

This Home Page was set up originally to create local interest and some out-of-town recognition, but has grown into an international thing.

Where is your workplace?

In the beginning, just out of my home office, but now we have Internet access at the shop.

What is your background and training?

In cycling: avid cyclist, and shop proprietor and mechanic for 13 years. Computers: hobbyist.

When did you start your business?

1982 off-line, June 1995 online.

How much money has your company made online?

(Retail) We have grossed 1.5 million a year for several years.

(Online) There was a long dry spell, with only a couple of bikes and a few minor accessories for the first six weeks, but last week I sent about $3,000 out, with more ready to ship. It is too early in the game to make predictions.

Getting started

Did you create a business plan before going online?

It follows our retail business plan.

How much time did it take to get up and running?

About a month.

Did you create the pages yourself?

This was the idea and baby of my former partner who is now setting up Websites as a business.

How much did it cost to get started?

A couple thousand over the course of a year. That also includes full Internet access and some hardware.

How did you obtain your startup capital?

Wrote it off as advertising.

What mistakes did you make that you wish you hadn't made?

I should have appealed more to the top of the line buyer instead of the beginner.

What advice would you give to a similar startup?

do not count on a get rich quick venture.

What skills are needed to run this business?

Basic computer knowledge, and expertise in your own field.

What education is needed to run your site?

Trial and error, and have a guru to help dig you out.

What special qualities are needed to run your site?

Marketing and sales. You've got to know what will get people to read.

How did you promote your Home Page?

Mostly by getting the links included in other sites. I also included the URL in local advertising, and business cards, etc.

How much did it cost to promote your site?

No extra budget, but already have a pretty good advertising plan.

How long did it take until you made your first sale?

Several weeks.

How did the startup phase affect your personal life?

I am spending an additional hour a day responding to questions and updating the site, answering questionnaires like this, etc.

My day

What does your average day look like?

I am Mr. Mom until noon (my wife has her own business at home). Then off to the shop noon-8:00 P.M. Then after the kids are in bed, I hit the computer for a couple.

What does your job entail?

Retail sales, personnel management, (fourty employees), ordering, trouble shooting, etc.

How many hours a week do you spend working on your site?

Probably about twelve hours (total).

Answering mail = nine hours, Researching questions = one hour, filling orders = two hours.

What was the hardest part of the job in the beginning?

Lots and lots of responses and compliments with little or no orders.

How long did it take to get established?

Still growing on the net. Established as a shop in about five years.

What do you like most about your work?

I sell FUN !

What do you like least?

Dealing with the problem customers that do not want to be happy.

What was your greatest moment?

Hearing 3,000 kids yelling my name.

Are there any hazards to running your site?

Yes. I am taking Visa numbers and sending product. UPS damages some product. The extra time I spend, though enjoyable, is at a sacrifice to other projects, and personal time.

How much money do you hope to make?

Eventually, $20,000 extra a year.... hopefully more, probably less.

General

Are customers concerned about security for their credit cards?

Not too much.

How do you process orders via credit cards?

Already had the machine. The bank gave it to me to use.

Was it easy or hard to get a machine?

It was easy. I had all sorts of sales people trying to sell me a machine. I had been doing it by hand. The bank brought one down the next day when they learned that I was about to purchase a machine that would have routed the money though a different bank.

Given what you know now, would you do it again?

This has been time consuming, frustrating, and has cost me more than I have made, but I think it has been worth the expense and trouble, and will just get better. Yes, I will do it again.

Where can people find advice?

They can contact my buddy, Randy, at randy@zyzzyva.com.

The future

What is your next venture?

I wish to have my own products on the Web instead of retailing the same thing other people have.

What else would you like to say?

It is difficult to keep up with changing and dated material. Even now I have a contest that is expired. I should be changing the dates instead of responding to this.

CASE STUDY-MARINEMART, BOATS AND ACCESSORIES

Figure 5-6. MarineMart proves you can advertise high ticket products to a consumer audience via the Internet. Courtesy of S.B. Edan Ltd.

Albert Silverman

MarineMart

P.O. Box 472

Lexington, MA 02173

http://www.marinemart.com/users/
marine/mart.html

silvermn@marinemart.com

617-862-6507

Background

MarineMart proves you can sell big-ticket items on the Internet, such as the boats offered at his mall. The company provides a virtual mall for vendors to sells products of interest to consumers who love the water world.

Who is your primary audience?

Boaters and people interested in boating.

How will they benefit from your product?

They will receive a better understanding of what is available in the sense of products and services.

How does your product differ from others?

Our mall is run by people with a marine background. We have a better understanding of the needs of both the marine industry and the boating public, having been in the pleasure boat industry for over a quarter of a century as a marine distributor selling globally.

Is this business an offshoot of your existing business, or does it exist only on the Internet?

It is a new venture based on our past experience and exists only in the Internet, but we are tying this in with the varied marketing approaches of our clients, so that the varied marketing approaches augment each other. It is driven as a business to be revenue generating.

Where is your business located?

Home and office.

What is your background and training?

Education is four years in graduate school. Work experience is twenty-five-odd years in the marine business as a manufacturer and distributor of pleasure boat marine products and three years as an independent marketing consultant.

When did you start your business?

1995.

How much money has your company made online?

Confidential.

Getting started

Did you create a business plan before going online?

Yes.

How much time did it take to get up and running?

This is an evolving process. It took a short period of time to get on the Net, but our business is evolving to meet the needs of our customers and viewers, the marine providers, and the boating public. Every viable business, if it is to grow, must constantly reinvent itself.

Did you create the pages yourself?

Initially I got help, but later on we did our own creating. I had done marine catalogues and fliers for some fifteen years prior to this.

How much did it cost to get started?

Since this is a service industry there are no merchandise costs. This evolved and is still part of our consulting business so that start up costs were shared by both, i.e. computer hardware and software costs, office, salaries, etc. Estimation for startup just for this would be $25,000 for just capital investment, no salaries.

How did you obtain your startup capital?

Self-financed.

What mistakes did you make that you wish you hadn't made?

Too early to tell, but I try to learn from my mistakes, and so they become an education tool. If you do not try and fail, you do not learn and cannot succeed.

What advice would you give to a similar startup?

The Net is a new medium and not everyone understands or is comfortable with it. Use it in conjunction with more conventional types of marketing approaches. Too many people think of it as an end in itself, and see how far they can go with it as a means to its own end, i.e., technology for its own sake.

What skills are necessary to run a business?

Understand business concepts, your customer, and your marketplace.

What education is needed to run your site?

A background in business especially from the experience side, with experience in marketing and advertising.

What special qualities are needed to run your site?

An understanding of the industry and the boating consumer, from having worked in the industry and having been a boating consumer oneself; the ability to create your own structure and to adapt the old to new and innovative approaches.

How did you promote your Home Page?

Directories, links from other sites, and having customers promote their own presence, which brings people to the mall in general; press releases in general and trade specific publications.

How much did it cost to promote your site?

Time and more time.

How long did it take until you made your first sale?

Immediately to get first commitment, but process is slow in getting people prepared to enter Cyberspace. First commitment still not on, but later commitments are up and running.

How did the startup phase affect your personal life?

I have always worked for myself, so this is not new. We were always doing things differently than the pack and looking at old positions through a different mind set. Although starting up can be frustrating, trying to convince someone to see something that is obvious to you but hidden to them when finally accomplished can be very exhilarating.

My day

What does your average day look like?

Work 6:30 A.M. to 10 P.M., but my day was always like that.

What does your job entail?

Everything, marketing, graphic arts, sales, reading, etc.

How many hours a week do you spend working on your site?

70-80.

What percentages of time are spent on each task?

It varies, since we do not fill orders we have other job requirements like prospecting for marine providers to join our mall.

What was the hardest part of the job in the beginning?

Getting someone to accept your concept as being viable and willing to buy into it, through a sale.

How long did it take to get established?

I am never established, because I always create new goals.

What do you like most about your work?

Exciting trying to sell a new concept.

What do you like least?

It is hard trying to sell a new concept to people who do not see it.

What was your greatest moment?

When someone sees what you see for the first time, "the aha concept."

Are there any hazards to running your site?

The hazard of failing because I didn't do something that someone else did and I failed and they succeeded. Legal, financial, and other hazards are not a major concern to me now.

How much money do you hope to make?

Now, break even or a small profit, and later a larger profit commensurate with other industries.

Where can people find advice for running a business?

Talk to people who are doing it, read about it, work for one.

General

Are you glad to be on the Web?

Yes.

Given what you know now, would you do it again?

Yes.

The future

What is your next venture?

Write another novel.

CASE STUDY-COLLECTIBLES

Jack Stern

World-Wide Collectors Digest, Inc.

2 Railroad Ave Suite 203

Glyndon, MD 21071

`http://wwcd.com`

`market@wwcd.com`

Background

Who is your primary audience?

Hobby and collectibles. Ages 10-60.

How will they benefit from your product?

One stop for collectibles.

How does your product differ from others?

Complete digest, not just dealers and manufacturers.

Is this business an offshoot of your existing business, or does it exist only on the Internet?

Offshoot.

If it is an offshoot, was it meant to generate income on its own or to steer people to your other outlets?

On its own.

Where is your workplace?

Office.

What is your background and training?

College graduate.

When did you start your business?

February 1990.

How much money has your company made online?

N/A

Getting started

Did you create a business plan before going online?

Yes.

How much time did it take to get up and running?

Three months.

Did you create the pages yourself?

Many graphic artists (contributed to their creation).

How much did it cost to get started?

$60,000.

How did you obtain your startup capital?

N/A

What mistakes did you make that you wish you hadn't made?

None so far.

What advice would you give to a similar startup?

Lots of preparation and money. Get the best people.

What skills are necessary to run a business?

Business, marketing, computer, telecommunications experience.

What education is needed to run your site?

College.

What special qualities are needed to run your site?

Business, marketing, legal, artistic.

How did you promote your Home Page?

On the net and in trade magazines.

How much did it cost to promote your site?

$10,000-$20,000.

How long did it take until you made your first sale?

Two weeks.

How did the startup phase affect your personal life?

What personal life?

My day

What does your average day look like?

In at 9 A.M. Answer questions from everyone till 6 P.M.

What does your job entail?

Everything. Overseeing the operation.

How many hours a week do you spend working on your site?

On your site, fifty hours.

Answering mail, three hours.

What was the hardest part of the job in the beginning?

Turning the picture into reality.

How long did it take to get established?

Three or four months.

What do you like most about your work?

Taking part in the creating of new accounts.

What do you like least?

Answering e-mail.

What was your greatest moment?

Our first account.

Are there any hazards to running your site?

Not anymore. There were personal.

How much money do you hope to make?

Millions!

General

Are customers concerned about security for their credit cards?

Yes.

Are you glad your company is on the Web?

YES.

Given what you know now, would you do it again?

YES.

Where can people find advice for running a business like yours?

Hire the successful people that have done it.

The future

What is your next venture?

Building this, then building this, then .....

What else would you like to say?

This is FUN!

CASE STUDY-CONDOM COUNTRY

Figure 5-7. Condom Country tries to inject humor into its cyber store. Copyright 1995. New Frontiers Information Corporation.

Andrew Heitner
Condom Country
New Frontiers Information
Corporation
843 Massachusetts Avenue,
Suite 2
Cambridge, MA 02139

http://www.ag.com/condom/country
  aheitner@nfic.com

617-497-6811
New Frontiers Information Corp.,
Parent company:
http://www.nfic.com/ info@nfic.com

Background

Who is your primary audience?

Anyone and everyone. Our original thought was to reach college students (single, liberal, on the Web) and those people who live in small towns/remote places and do not have close access to novelty or unique condoms, but it has grown to basically everyone and anyone.

How will they benefit from your product?

Privacy. No embarrassment for some; convenience and access to products they normally wouldn't have access to in others.

How does your product differ from others?

There aren't too many others on the Web. Our product line is far more varied and extensive than the others. Furthermore, we've taken a very funny approach to selling condoms, with witty dialog and a cartoony mascot.

Is this business an off-shoot of your existing business, or does it exist only on the Internet?

Only on the Web.

Where is your office located?

Office.

What is your background and training?

Four founders of the company, with eight total degrees from MIT. We've since hired three other computer programmers from MIT and one non-MIT employee as well.

When did you start your business?

Condom Country went online September 1994.

How much money has your company made online?

Unfortunately, we cannot release the exact sales figures. Sales have been good, certainly more than enough to justify owning and operating the catalog. Ad revenue from condom manufacturers is actually expected to be larger than the actual sales of product.

We get just below 4,000 people per day, representing about 68,000 hits/day (17-18 hits per unique user). This puts us at 120,000 people through the catalog every month.

Getting started

Did you create a business plan before going online?

No.

How much time did it take to get up and running?

Four months of development to develop the database-integrated catalog software that runs Condom Country (and forms the basis for our business). Probably a total of four weeks to put together the product line and write the copy. Add another two-to-three man weeks to set up the credit card merchant status, fulfillment warehouse, overnight shipping contract, inbound telemarketing center, etc.

Did you create the pages yourself?

We developed the content and the software ourselves.

How much did it cost to get started?

For us, a $10k Sparc20 server, $1k/month net connection, plus roughly $5k of inventory to start. But, of course, our primary business was in the software, not necessarily in the condom sales.

How did you obtain your startup capital?

N/A

What mistakes did you wish you hadn't made?

I think the Condom Country catalog has been a big success for a lot of reasons. There's not much I would change.

What advice would you give to a similar startup?

Address the Internet medium, i.e. do not just take a radio or TV ad and put it on the Net; rotate your content frequently, so as to keep people interested.

What skills are needed to run a business like yours?

A good sense of humor, a good feel for the medium and the way to sell using information content. To operate our software also requires reasonable computer proficiency.

What education is needed to run your site?

N/A

What special qualities are needed to run your site?

A good sense of humor. We have included a lot of information and humor content. This is what people are surfing the Web looking for. They do not just want to see selling, they want to learn and/or be entertained.

How did you promote your Home Page?

We pushed it a little in the beginning, mainly with posts to newsgroups. We also sent out press releases to a number of newspapers and magazines. After that, publicity took care of itself. People put it on their hotlists, and it got lots of write-ups, even up to *Forbes* magazine.

How much did it cost to promote your site?

Dollars out: $0. Time: one-to-two man-weeks.

How long did it take until you made your first sale?

First day it was released.

How did the startup phase affect your personal life?

N/A

My day

What does your average day look like?

We spend about one-two man-hours a day on Condom Country filling orders, keeping the books, tracking down lost shipments, etc. Then probably an extra four-to-five man-hours a month sending out reminder e-mails, changing the content, etc. (We should spend more on the content if we could).

What does your job entail?

 N/A

How many hours a week do you spend working on your site?

Running Condom Country takes one person approximately two hours per day. The most amount of time goes into answering customers' questions about the catalog or about specific products.

What was the hardest part of the job in the beginning?

There were no real hardships in starting up the site. The most tedious part was scanning in the photos of all the products. Writing the copy was long, but lots of fun.

What do you like most about your work?

It's very funny and people's extremely positive comments are a big boost. It makes you feel like you've really put together something good and worthwhile. Seeing nice write-ups in the press are great as well.

What do you like least?

The fact that we do not have enough time to keep it as fresh and up-to-date as we'd like.

What was your greatest moment?

Probably getting a small feature in Forbes magazine. Also, there was an editorial in On-line Access in which the author was mentioning what he thought were good and bad ways to address the online medium. He used MCI as an example of the bad and Condom Country as an example of the good. It was kind of funny and triumphant at the same time to be compared in this way to MCI.

Are there any hazards to running your site?

We were worried at the beginning about the possibility of selling condoms to minors. Even though there is no law against it, we thought that parents might complain. This hasn't been a problem, though. I guess there's always the potential for people to get offended by sex talk or condom talk, but we have made a real conscious attempt to keep the tone of the site light and funny and not offensive. I think we've succeeded.

How much money do you hope to make?

Hard to say. Again, this store is really secondary to our software/services business (i.e. building catalogs for other people).

General

Are customers concerned about security for credit cards?

Not really. We recently started using the Netsite (Secure) Commerce Server and have not seen a significant increase in orders. We give customers the option to send in a cc number online, send us PGP e-mail, or call the number into our answering service. I'd guess that 80% of the cards come in on-line (either secure or insecure, depending on the customer's browser), and 20% of the cards come in off-line.

How do you process orders via credit cards?

We tie into the verification network via a modem and run a batch of credit cards through each morning.

Was it easy or hard to get a credit card machine?

It was tough. At the time we started, there was no such thing as a company who did not exist anywhere but in cyberspace.

Does age or sex make a difference in running your site?

Sex makes a difference ;-)

The Future

What is your next venture?

We have a lot of ideas, but not a lot of time. Again, most of our efforts are focused on developing our software and services.

What else would you like to say?

The future is really upon us as far as the Internet is concerned. I'm glad we're in this business.

T-SHIRT BUSINESS

Overview—Because of the large number of college students who have free Internet accounts, vendors of T-shirts have reported brisk sales since the Web first began to be used as a commercial medium. The general public also has adopted the T-shirt as an acceptable garment for vacation and weekend-wear.

Rewards—T-shirt makers face a very low entry to the marketplace. A high quality T-shirt can cost a merchants about $2 and can sell for $16 or more. Sweatshirts also can be sold at even greater margins. You can even get a free software program called T-shirt Maker from Austin-Brett. The files can be downloaded for free from CompuServe's Graphics Forum (Go Graphics) or America Online's Software Section (search for "T-shirt"). You will have the ability to design T-shirts, import artwork, add text that can be rotated, print on the front and back, and add color. The artwork is sent to a factory via modem or a disk via the mail. The factory sends the high-quality T-shirt to you or your customer. While anyone can get into this business because of the low overhead, the field remains wide open to people who have good ideas, funny sayings and intriguing art work.

Risks—Merchants must be aware of rip-offs of their ideas so they should copyright their works. They also must constantly market their products.

Special marketing elements for the Home Page—T-shirts need to be seen to be ordered. You will have to take photos of the products, scan them and attach them to the Home Page. Because photos take a long time to display on the screen, great care must be taken when deciding how many pictures to place on a page. A good menu structure will help here, as you can ask customers to select T-shirts by category.

Links to Home Pages

Please see the case study on the on the Official Bubba Bullmash Collection. `http://www.com/bubba`.

CASE STUDY-OFFICIAL BUBBA BULLMASH COLLECTION, T-SHIRTS

GET IN TOUCH WITH YOUR INNER BUBBA

The creator of THE OFFICIAL BUBBA BULMASH COLLECTION was born and raised in the South. As a young man he moved from the country to the big city. His sophistication and savoir faire grew in time, yet there was always something missing. He consulted with therapists, gurus, shamans and the like and still could not find the answer. Then one day it all became clear, he was suffering from "BUBBA DENIAL". It's easy to fix once you can accept that "LIL-BIT-OF-BUBBA" that's a part of you. He did, and he created this collection in hopes that when you wear this shirt you too can get in touch with your "INNER BUBBA".

Order an Official Bubba Bulmash Collection

Figure 5-8. T-Shirts are big sellers on the Internet. Copyright 1995, J.Dyer Animation.

Ilene Dyer

The Official Bubba Bullmash Collection

J. Dyer Animation Studio

P.O. Box 420589

Atlanta, GA 30342

http://www.com/bubba

e-mail jdyer@atlanta.com.

Background

My audience is Bubbas from the South and people from all over the world who plan to come to Atlanta for the '96 Olympics. My product is unique, as my character, Bubba, is unique. He represents the humorous side of Southern culture which I feel will be seen over and over again as the media tries to give the flavor of the region. I only sell these shirts on the Internet. It is meant to generate money on its own.

I started this Web site at the end of March 1995. First year stats are unavailable but I hope to make at least $10,000 the first year. My reason for selling this on the Internet is the fact that I do not have the time to go from store to store to try to get buyers to buy my shirts. I have a full time job and this is something I have to do on the side. I spend approximately 15-20 hours a week on the Internet trying to get listings and trying to reach people via newsgroups and/or individually whom I think would be interested in my product.

Getting started

I did not create a business plan before going online. I saw it as an experiment that was going to require a lot of patience and perseverance but the cost was minimal and worth the risk. I created all the artwork and the text and put it into compressed form so I could save time and money from the designers of my Web pages who converted my layout to the language of the Internet. I believe they did an excellent job because I have a lot of pictures but they come up rather fast (in Internet terms). I think it is very important for anyone creating Web presence to try to bring up their graphics and text as quickly as possible or you will lose viewers if you make them wait too long to see your page. I am constantly printing my T-shirts as demand is created for my fourteen 14 designs. I have a good inventory on hand that I was able to finance personally. The site cost me approximately $1,000 to design and put up.

Cost of promoting varies....you need to set your budget and go from there.

Since I had no budget, I looked for any free promotion I could find. It is important to try and register your site with every possible commercial index and then you have to be creative. You need to find people who you think could use your product and contact them individually or through newsgroups that allow a commercial plug... or even listserves if you think your product would enhance their lives. I got my first sale after three weeks on the Internet... they are still slow coming, but that is where continued marketing and promoting come into play. I also use traditional media through press releases to reach people.

My day

My average day is spent working as an executive producer and marketer for my animation studio. I use time at night to promote The Official Bubba Collection. I generally spend 15 -20 hours in this pursuit. I am quite taken with the Internet for its ability to reach so many people across so many borders. I feel the commercial aspects of the Internet are in their infancy and it will be trial and error for all entrepreneurs for some time to come. Credit card usage is still iffy and needs to be worked on for consumers to feel confident using their numbers over the Internet.

Alternatives are being tried but there is no standard and the traditional banking industry has so far stood on the side lines. At my site I use a standard mail order procedure where I just take checks or money orders and you have to print my form and mail it to me. I am researching having my form on line and setting up an account such as First Virtual for having people use their credit cards to make purchases.... this I will have worked out in the next six months.

The on-line consuming of products that are not computer related is also in its infancy.

People who like to find different products than what's available in the mall... and department stores will appreciate shopping online where there is definitely different merchandise.

People like myself who have found traditional outlets like department stores and are afraid to try new and different, funny and crazy stuff, have a chance to let people at least view the product. Usually when one person buys your product and likes it and shows it to a friend you get your next order. You must have a quality product or your chances of word of mouth are lost.

My recommendation for people who are thinking of setting up a web site is do not give up your main job yet. The Internet allows you to get your feet wet and work at home to promote your new product... counting on sales for your livelihood could be a problem your first year.

I definitely believe that in the year 2000 we all will be shopping on the Internet and hopefully little guys as well as the big guys will have their site on the web as it is now.

I would hate for the Internet to be bought out by the huge congloms and limited to people like me. I think the vitality of the Internet is because the sharing of information freely across borders is not in the hands of a private corporation but in universities and governments and not for profit institutions.

Another important tidbit... if you are dealing in original art like my product make sure you have all your material copyrighted and on file before you post it on the Internet.

INTERVIEW-WHIFFLE TREE QUILTS

Figure 5-9 Whiffle Tree Quilts prints a newsletter on the Net and gets orders from around the world. Courtesy of Whiffle Tree Quilts.

Marsha Burdick and Louise Horkey

Whiffle Tree Quilts

10261 S. De Anza Boulevard

Cupertino, CA 95014

408-255-5270

http://www.danish.com/wtq

wtq@aol.com

Background

What were you hoping to accomplish on the Web?

We sell 100% cotton fabric, books, patterns, notions, have classes relating to making quilts, garments, dolls, etc. It is part of the "soft craft" industry. Quilting is a very large segment of the craft and art market.

We wanted to go on the Internet because I had experience using e-mail when I worked at Lockheed, knew many people used e-mail and internet, and wanted to differentiate ourselves from the other quilt shops around. It is a way to make ourselves known to others, and also project the "user-friendly" and modern image—not just country crafts, as often associated with quilting.

How has being on the Internet helped you?

It has gotten us noticed by people around the world who have written to say they liked our home page, and customers who have come in the store because they discovered our home page and read our newsletters. It gained us respect and appreciation that we are "avant guard" as one customer's husband put it (a tourist from Asia).

ARTS AND CRAFTS

Overview——Arts and Crafts companies can find a market full of hobbysts of one sort or another.
Rewards——You can turn a hobby into a source of income.
Risks——Usual business risks.
Special marketing considerations for home pages——Pictures of products must be shown so people can see what they are getting. See other portions of this chapter for advice.

INTERVIEW-ARTS AND CRAFTS

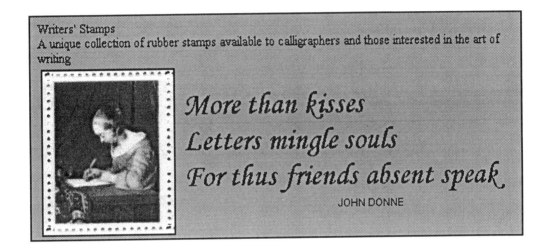

Writers' Stamps
A unique collection of rubber stamps available to calligraphers and those interested in the art of writing

More than kisses
Letters mingle souls
For thus friends absent speak

JOHN DONNE

Figure 5-10. High tech meets high touch at this Home Page. Courtesy of Rubber Stamp Queen.

Moira Collins
The Rubberstamp Queen/Ace
Stampworks
320 S. Jefferson
Chicago, IL 60661

URL: http://www.dol.com/queen

e:mail RSQueen@ aol.com
800-998-2627 for brochures
800-239-9328 for orders & queries

Background

What are you hoping to accomplish by being on the Web?

We sell beautifully designed quality rubberstamp art stamps along with practical useful custom stock stamps and logos. Because of the visual nature of our artistic stampsóeverything from dancing frogs and unicorns to beautifully rendered Japanese crests and calligraphy stampsówe felt the world wide web was the perfect medium to show the joys of rubberstamping.

We are a Chicago-based company that is easily able to handle a lot of business and being on the net gives us access to retail and wholesale orders simultaneously.

How has being on the Internet helped you?

We have not been on the web long in our finished format only about two months. We have not yet really started to advertise the site (because we are still working on pages), but it's clear we have started to be noticed— we get requests for our brochure daily from our 800 number as well as e-mail requests. The response is building so we are planning to print our catalog a couple of months earlier than we intended as we view this as potentially a financially rewarding environment with little effort. It seems like every time we are posted somewhere, perhaps we are recommended, a flurry of requests follows. For example, a week or two ago we received a notice from Prodigy that we had been listed in their arts and crafts section and in sample interviews with customers. We seem to be hitting a responsive chord-that encourages us to continue to invest in this area. We are beginning to receive wholesale requests from states our city reps would not reach.

What advice would you give an entrepreneur?

John Nesbitt wrote some years ago in Megatrends that "the higher the tech-the higher the touch." In other words, in a high tech world, as it becomes increasingly technical, high touch-human products become valuable as a balance and antidote. If you have a service that is high-touch, consider how you might translate that into a high tech environment like the net. Think of the orders that you expect as orders you would normally never get. At the start, do not expect to pay your mortgage or even your office rent by launching your new business on the net but if you are an established business orders over the internet in a sense are "gravy." They are orders that come with little cost of advertising aside from set up costs and if your site becomes popular you may want to learn how to market directly to this global market you are only beginning to tap into. If you are a company that actually is able to handle personal requests and phone calls believe me, you are a rarity in today's world. Take advantage of it! Advertise yourself on the net. Business might be slow in a particularly area locally however in a sense your business may be booming in another town or hamlet in the country where people do not have access to what you offer. It helps if you have a product you already know that people have wanted or a service people already requested, and believe it or not, word of mouth can work in the global neighborhood of cyberspace. It helps to have supporting printed materials until the "ordering potential" via master card/ visa becomes easy, probably early in 1996. Not everyone is comfortable with ordering by e-mail. Although fax orders are perhaps the norm, many net newbies are more comfortable ordering by snail mail. Clearly it's easier to do business internationally if you take master card visa. It also helps to offer information that you do not sell and offer a deal on the net that you might not offer elsewhere to encourage orders on this new medium. And do not be afraid to add a little humanness in your offering. "The higher the tech....the higher the touch."

What else would you like to say?

Perhaps you have discovered that many people aren't interested in panning for gold until it's proven to be a mother lode. However, those of us with a pioneer attitude in keeping with the gold rush mentality that shaped our country. "Go west, young man. Go west." It's kinda fun to be exploring this cyberspace.

6   **REAL ESTATE**

Real Estate professionals–brokers, listing services, and mortgage brokers–are rapidly moving onto the Internet. They see a growing market spurred by demand from the vast number of corporate relocations in America today. People need to know about homes in other parts of the country. Various Internet sites are being used to list homes, vacation sales, and timeshares.

"Mostly, they are using it for self promotion, putting up their resumes, a little information about the homes," said Mark Angolia, editor, *Update* magazine, a magazine for Realtors in Virginia, 703-527-8837, `http://www.nvar.com`. "I do see it becoming a multiple listing service on the Internet so anyone who has access to the Internet can search for a home in any part of the country, see a picture of the home, and call the Realtor associated with it."

This chapter covers roommate rentals, listing services, Realtors, mortgage brokers, and real estate service providers, such as pest control, house inspection, and painters.

ROOMMATE REFERRALS BUSINESS

Overview—Stretching money is a key point for many recent college grads, as well as others. Sharing an apartment is a fact of life for undergrads, as well as the recently graduated. You can start a business to find roommates for people. Of course, this type of service can help people of any age. In fact, you could specialize the service to target specific audiences, such as gays, non-smokers and single parents. You can make money charging fees to landlords and renters.

The Web site is essentially a database of information regarding the apartments and the potential roommates. Your main tasks will be data entry, marketing, and keeping track of the finances. You do not need a Realtor's license to start this business.

Rewards—Unlimited income is yours if you can sell well and show that the site is being visited by qualified buyers.

Risks—There aren't any risks beyond those of a normal business. However, check with your lawyer to make sure you can't get sued for pairing someone with the roommate from hell.

Special marketing elements for the Home Page—To look substantial, the Home Page must show that you have a wide variety of properties and people.

The site is essentially a database of information and pictures of apartments and roommates. It must be easy to search for houses by geographic location and personality traits of roommates (such as smoker, night person, heavy metal music).

Links to Home Pages

Homebuyers Fair– `http://www.homebuyers.com`

REAL ESTATE BUSINESS

Overview—Realtors all over the country can show property without leaving the office. They can show the properties online. Using the Home Page as a starting point, home buyers can search for homes based on location or price. As they find the houses that meet their needs, they can see pictures and detailed descriptions of the home. Moreover, consumers can see these databases from the comfort of their homes before calling on a Realtor. After they have explored the databases of various Realtors, they can call to set appointments for the ones they like.

Rewards and risk——Realtors will benefit as consumers come to them and ask to see specific houses that they have selected. There might be more real prospects who know what they want and make up their minds faster than the walk-in trade.

Special marketing elements for the Home Page—Many sites do not show pictures, but the good ones do. The best ones offer a video walk through of the house, although this can take a lot of time for consumers to download. It is not necessary today, but in the future, as hardware gets better and less expensive, videos will be the norm. However, most people can not view these files easily on today's computers.

To draw attention to specific properties and make an ordinary listing come alive, list properties under enticing buttons, such as "House of the Week," or "Best of the Lot."

Links to Home Pages

Serkes Real Estate Search Engine–http://www.home-buy-sell.com/Realtor

Holiday Resales–http://www.halcyon.com/golfer

INTERVIEW—HOLIDAY RESALES

Don Boehm, golfer@halcyon.com, uses the Internet to sell time shares and holiday properties in the Washington State area. "For now, it allows interested parties to find out about us. It has paid for itself," he says. To be a success on the Internet, "Have a product which lends itself to multimedia advertising and link yourself to as many sites as possible."

CASE STUDY-SERKES REAL ESTATE ENGINE SEARCH

The Serkes Real Estate Search Engine

New & Noteworthy

A story by Ira's Mom, Adele Serkes (now in her 80's) written in her spry 60's - A Day In The Life of Two Ladies over 65 going on 25 Years Of Age.

Figure 6-1. Serkes Real Estate Search Engine helps people find homes–and Ira Serkes. Courtesy of Ira and Carol Serkes Re/Max Bay Area.

Ira & Carol Serkes   `http://www.home-buy-sell.com/Realtor`

RE/MAX Bay Area   `Realtor@home-buy-sell.com`

Serkes Real Estate Search   800/887-6668 510/526-6668

Engine

1758 Solano Avenue

Berkeley, CA 94707

Background

Who is your primary audience?

Home buyers, sellers, Realtors, corporate relocation groups, people who need referrals of great Realtors in the cities they're moving to or moving from.

How will they benefit from your service?

Buyers who use a buyer's broker generally pay about 3.5% lower prices than a buyer who uses a conventional agent.

Our seller clients received higher sales prices, in less time, than sellers who hired other agents to sell their homes.

How does your service differ from others?

We're very organized and computerized and provide a high level of service and follow up. In the past few years our sales (as measured by number of closed transactions as well as total closed dollar volume of sales) have been in the top 1% of Realtors in our market area.

We provide more than just information on homes. Our site has lots of links to local communities, sightseeing, radio and TV stations, personal interests, local history and architecture.

Is this business an offshoot of your existing business, or does it exist only on the Internet?

We earn our living as Realtors.

Our Web site–The Serkes Real Estate Search Engine–is an offshoot of our existing real estate business. We help people buy and sell homes in Berkeley, Albany, Kensington, El Cerrito, and nearby communities, and offer referrals to other highly qualified Realtors all over the United States and Canada.

Was it meant to generate income on its own or to steer people to your office?

It should generate income on its own. I hope to have more people decide to hire us after seeing the kind of service they receive from us. We also hope to help buyers and sellers by referring them to top Realtors all over the nation.

Where do you operate your business?

Back rear bedroom of a two bedroom house facing the garden and watching the cats stroll by.

What is your background and training?

Chemical engineer with two patents in research. I've been using computers for almost 30 years, and the Internet/World Wide Web is the most exciting thing I've ever seen. I once programmed in Octal on a PDP 8 Digital Equipment computer, had an Osborne for many years, and now use a Quadra 840AV Macintosh.

Getting started

When did you start your business?

Realtor: September 1986. Online: June 1995.

Did you create a business plan before going online?

A business plan for real estate business, not Web business.

How much time did it take to get up and running?

I first saw the World Wide Web in mid-February, and hired someone to get me online. I was online within about a week.

Did you create the pages yourself or did you get help?

Initial pages were done by someone else. I had some very good leads at the beginning, and then had very little response. That's when I decided to rework the page. I spent several months surfing over to other pages to see what I liked, and what I didn't like. I also set up a basic template for our page design. Then one Saturday morning, I woke up early and by the end of the day, had our Web pages up and running.

How much did it cost to get started?

It cost about $240 for the initial Web page. Once I went online, it cost me about $25/month for 75 hours/month and 5 megabytes of storage. It cost about $100 to register my domain name "home-buy-sell.com" with the InterNIC.

Did you need to go to an outside source for startup capital?

No.

How did you promote your site?

I registered the site with Yahoo, and with another search engine called "Submit It," which takes the information and distributes it to about 15-20 other search engines! We "cross link" our site to as many places as possible. I've several links to local radio stations. They have our URL on their listener's Web site.

We put our Web site URL on every piece of e-mail we send.

I put our Web page on our business cards, on every property flyer, and on open house ads.

I plan to make a "sign rider" for our For Sale signs so people will see our e-mail and web address as they drive by.

We're sending out a mailing to about 3,500 people in our database (past clients, neighbors in our "farm") attorneys, CPAs, newspaper and TV reporters, etc. This will be distributed the first week of August 1995.

How much did it cost to promote your site?

Except for the mailing, everything else was practically free.

How long did it take until you got your first sale?

Haven't had any sales yet.

How much money do you expect to make?

$10,000—$150,000 a year.

What mistakes did you make that you wish you hadn't made?

I started with a different Internet Service Provider (ISP) than I am with now. I'd chosen an ISP which had no minimum charges, and relatively low $2—4/hour online charges. I didn't realize how much time I'd be spending online.

What advice would you give someone starting a business?

Ira's Tips On Setting Up A World Wide Web Page

- Use a Home Page which is easy to navigate. Make it easy to return to the Home Page. For each page I used a "template" which has a place for someone to e-mail me, a return to the Home Page, and our toll free number and name. I think I'll also be adding the Home Page "address" i.e. `http://www.dnai.com/Realtor` so people will know how to return to the page if they happen to print it out.
- Keep graphics small so they load quickly and easily. Consider using small "thumbnail" graphics to get people interested, and use a larger graphic on the next page.
- Make sure that you do not need to use graphics to navigate around. Whenever you have a graphic, be sure to use text to describe what the graphic does.

- It's much faster to navigate when you only have text, and no or few graphics.
- Put the date and time on each page and keep them up to date and fresh. Make each page about one screen's worth of information. It's easier to click on another page than it is to page down.
- Make it wide and shallow. What this means is set up your Home Page to reach to three to eight other pages, then have each of these second level pages point to several other pages. Think of it like a bamboo plant with wide roots that go out 10-20 feet, but the roots only go down six to 12 inches. That way, it's easy to navigate up and down the web pages. It's very difficult when you have to go down for to 12 levels to find something.
- Make your site interesting! Include something about yourself, your interests, your neighborhood, city, community. Give someone a reason to return to your site.
- Internet Service Provider. Some tips on selecting a provider: Local phone number for calling in. Lots of online time for low cost. My provider gives me 75 hours for $25/month.
- Reasonable free storage. I have five megabytes of storage, which should be more than enough for awhile.
- Decent tech service. It's very confusing to set up your account for the first time, so be sure you've someone who you can ask questions of Domain Name Registration. Make sure you can register your domain. We registered home-buy-sell.com as our domain, which means you can send e-mail to Realtor@home-buy-sell.com and it will come to us.
- TEST TEST TEST. Upload your pages, and check all the links. It's easiest to play with one or two pages or links, get familiar with the concepts, and then charge ahead. If you're a Mac user and have a CD-ROM, purchase the excellent CD Roadside Resources from BMUG–Berkeley Macintosh User Group, 1442A Walnut Street #62 Berkeley, CA 94709 510-540-1029.

What skills are needed?

For real estate: Curiosity, willingness to prospect for new business, and contact with past clients.

What special qualities are needed to run your site?

Curiosity. The language of the Web, HTML, is very similar to the Wordstar word processing program. I'd recommend just surfing around, identifying the web sites you like the best, and then viewing the source code to see how they did it.

My day

What does your average day look like?

Up at 6:30-8:00 A.M.

Search the MLS database for "expired" listings.

Determine what to do for the day. Doing it.

What does your job entail?

Helping people buy or sell real estate, solving the many problems which arise, and offering referrals for people who wish to move to other communities.

How many hours a week do you spend working on your site?

About one hour a day. I often tweak the site, add more links, and add forms.

What percentages of time are spent on each task?

I don't know. Most of the online time is spent writing/reading e-mail.

What was the hardest aspect of the work in the beginning?

Real estate–The frustrations of working on a transaction and having it fall through because of problems with the house.

What do you like most about your work?

Getting paid for our services.

What do you like the least?

Frustration and unsteady income.

What was your greatest moment?

When I was selected to be coauthor of the Nolo Press book How to Buy a House in California, which has now sold over 35,000 copies.

How did the startup phase affect your personal life?

Not much.

Are you glad you are on the Web on personal and business reasons?

Delighted.

Given what you know now, would you do it again?

For sure, only faster.

The future

What is your next venture?

Giving seminars on how business people can use the Internet and World Wide Web to build their business. Letting people know how exciting it is.

What else would you like to say?

Well done survey–lots of good questions.

MORTGAGE BROKER

Overview—As people buy real estate online they will need to find sources of funding. Mortgage brokers come to the rescue. Not only can they get clients from house buyers, but they can promote their services to Realtors as well.

Rewards—The Internet can increase sales and build a network of new professional contacts.

Risks—Normal business risks.

Special marketing elements for the Home Page—Build credibility by showing a resume, awards, professional designations and testimonials from clients. Create a sense of purpose by adding articles about home buying, refinancing and the like. Perhaps you can add a mortgage calculator software program that people can download, or fill out online to see if they might qualify for a house.

Links to Home Pages

See the case study for Mortgage Market Information Services- –http://www.interest.com/mmis.html

MORTGAGE MARKET INFORMATION SERVICES

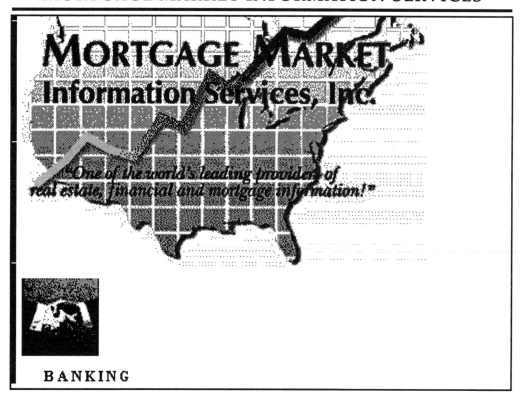

Figure 6-2. Mortgage Market provides links to financial information to brokers and consumers. Copyright 1995, Mortgage Market Information Services, Inc.

Mortgage Market Information Services
Daniel Eaton Interactive
53 E. St. Charles Road
800-509-4636
Villa Park, IL 60181

`http://www.interest.com/`
`mmis.html`
`eaton@banking.interest.com`

Background

Mortgage Market is one of the nation's largest suppliers of mortgage, real estate, and financial information and provides these services to 300 of the top newspapers.

Who is your primary audience?

Consumers.

How will they benefit from your product or service?

By educating consumers on available mortgage products and services, they are able to make a more educated decision that has the potential to save them thousands of dollars in interest payments.

How does your service differ from others?

The information we offer is presented in simple to understand terms, relevant to the existing market conditions.

Is this business an offshoot of your existing business, or does it exist only on the Internet?

The Internet projects compliment our mortgage rate guides that appear in over 300 newspapers across the country.

Was it meant to generate income on its own or to steer people to your other outlets?

This project has several goals.

1. Increase company exposure.
2. Promote company products.
3. Generate revenue from ad space for lending institutions.
4. Promote our client customers.

Where is your office located?

Corporate office.

What is your background and training?

I have been involved in the Real Estate Industry for the past 15 years, educated at the University of Wisconsin, former president of Realty Data Systems, Inc.

When did you start your business?

Mortgage Market Information Services, Inc. was founded by James R. De Both, a former telecommunications and computer planning consultant for Arthur Young & Co. In 1987, De Both acted on his perception that the midwest needed a consumer assisted mortgage information service. He viewed the telephone as the ideal vehicle for providing timely, comprehensive, and comprehensible mortgage rate information to consumers, loan officers, and real estate agents. Expanding on this, he developed specialized mortgage rate directories which are featured in newspapers' real estate sections.

How much money has your company made online?

N/A

Getting started

Did you create a business plan before going online?

Mortgage Market Information Services has operated a public BBS, Mortgage Market ONLINE, 708-834-1450, over the past four years. We were able to build on this experience for an effective Web site.

How much time did it take to get up and running?

I was encouraging management to invest in the project for about six months. Then management saw the light with all of the hoopla and press regarding the Internet and they decided to invest.

Did you create the pages yourself?

I created all of the pages myself with the assistance of our in-house graphics department, and the Multimedia Graphics Network.

How much did it cost to get started?

We incurred capital equipment costs of approximately $15k

How did you obtain your startup capital?

The project was funded internally.

What mistakes did you make that you wish you hadn't made?

Talk to networking experts and people that have already made the mistakes.

What advice would you give to a similar startup?

Use a turnkey solution such as Sun Microsystems Netra or SGI Indy. It will cost you more, however, it will save you time and aggravation in the future. Your time to live will also be shorted dramatically.

What skills are necessary to run a business?

VISION. The ability to see the potentialófor any application.

What education is needed to run your site?

Once it is up and running, you need skills and education similar to a publisher.

What special qualities are needed to run your site?

Unique business perspective.

How did you promote your Home Page?

Our URL is published on our newspaper rate guides that appear in some of the nations largest newspapers.

How much did it cost to promote your site?

Promoting costs were merely incorporated into projects we are already doing. This includes newspaper advertising, trade magazine advertising, and industry trade shows.

How long did it take until you made your first sale?

About six weeks.

How did the startup phase affect your personal life?

You can't help but get excited over this new technology.

My day

What does your average day look like?

Check Systems (Internet, FAX broadcast, Online Services). Review work from previous day, answer mail, review market research, build reports, distribute reports to clients, check marketing projects, check status of graphics in process, check Satellite news feeds.

What does your job entail?

All phases of management.

How many hours a week do you spend working on your site?

At least 30 hours.

Updating–20%
Marketing–20%
Creating new features–40%
Administrative–15%
Need coffee–65%

What was the hardest part of the job in the beginning?

Selling new technologies.

We recently had a visit by some bankers (our customers). They found the demonstration interesting; however, their first question was, "How is this going to make me money?" and, "What kind of results can I expect?"

The questions where reasonable and understandable; however, my observation was that they REALLY scrutinized the entire idea.

The reaction is totally different with our print product. The paper has a circulation of 100,000 and it costs $10 to advertise. They say, "Where do I sign?"

The print product is tangible. People like to touch and feel. They can deal with a paper product.

The comfort level just wasn't there. It is going to take time to convert business people on the benefits and time to build a track record of success.

How long did it take to get established?

This thing has a life of its own. I do not think one will ever get truly "established" because of its dynamic nature. "Recognized" may be a more appropriate aphorism. Users need to find you either by traditional advertising or through an index.

What do you like most about your work?

The creative nature of the media. The ability to help people in their home buying process.

What do you like least?

The difficulty in educating close-minded business people.

What was your greatest moment?

Every day when I read my mail, the comments from consumers on how much they like the service. The day a lender called and stated how many calls they received from the posting.

Are there any hazards to running your site?

Know your market. Know your product and how it fits in that market. You must do your homework. Writing HTML is only a small portion of the big picture.

Compare what you do with a magazine or newspaper. They have editorial departments, sales departments, production departments, etc. Successful publishers rely upon a team of professionals to produce their final product.

How much money do you hope to make?

N/A

General

Given what you know now, would you do it again?

Absolutely.

REAL ESTATE SERVICE PROVIDERS REFERRAL BUSINESS

Overview—Realtors need a lot of support services to close the deal. Buyers depend on Realtors to refer them to home inspectors, pest control companies, painters, plumbers, carpenters, moving companies, and a lot of other service providers.

You can create a referral business for these service providers. Create a home page and list the providers for free or a nominal fee. Charge them more for a link to their home page, or charge them to create a Home Page. You can also sell advertisements to companies that want to reach these service providers.

You can specialize in your city or region, or set up a national referral service.

Rewards—You will receive income from the sale of links, Home Pages and ads.

Risks—Normal business risks.

Special marketing elements for the Home Page—In addition to nice graphics, consider adding timely information of interest to Realtors, such as mortgage rate updates, home construction figures, or the like.

Links to Home Pages

I haven't seen this done yet. Be the first! Use the Internet Health Resources case study as your example (See Chapter 4).

7 CAREERS

The Internet is becoming a resource center for employers seeking new workers, and for employees to find new jobs. Millions of people look for work every year. You can benefit starting businesses that match them up! This chapter will examine a job resource center and a resume writer.

JOB RESOURCE CENTER

Overview—Headhunters have come online! Career centers, headhunters, placement offices, and the like are on the Internet. The Internet is increasingly being used by professionals in the technology and education fields as resource center for job seekers. Many technology companies place employment ads on their Web sites.

Entrepreneurs can start their own placement centers. These sites contain information for both the employer and employees. Job hunters can see a list of jobs with qualifications and pay scales. Employers can see resumes of candidates.

The site can charge job hunters a small fee for placing their resume online. At the same time these centers can sell their services to corporations to conduct job searches. They can find candidates by searching the Web, newsgroups, and mailing lists (in a manner consistent with good netiquette). Hiring companies typically pay 30 percent or more of the first year's salary of a candidate, so the money can be very, very good.

This kind of business can make a lot of sense to college entrepreneurs, as they come across hundreds of their classmates looking for work each day. You could create a career center at your university that has resumes from the general class, MBA students, and/or legal students.

You can select a market and dominate it. Consider creating a site that caters to a specific market, like computer programmers, or a geographic region, like Boston. By going deep, you can become known and develop a following among employers and employees in that industry or area.

Rewards—This business can yield income several sourcesófrom companies placing ads, from job seekers placing ads, and from links to related sites that offer high end counseling and outplacement services to corporations off-line. You should be a good sales person to make this site work, as you will need to prove that you can attract seekers and become sought after. To protect your advertisers, you could offer an exclusive to a company so that it would be the only one of its kind represented on your page.

There are lots of opportunities for local markets and niches. Every town or region can have its own job bank. Every vertical market industry can have its own local, regional, or national job bank as well.

Risks—Competition could heat up, thus driving prices down, or forcing you to sell better, smarter, and harder.

Special marketing elements for the Home Page—Placement center should be able to use the home page to build credibility for itself by issuing a mission statement, noting that it makes reference checks on candidates, and has expertise in handling these matters.

Employers and employees can be attracted to the site with solid editorial information on job hiring, interview strategies, and links to related sites.

Links to Home Pages

Cascade Technical Staffing–http://www.teleport.com/~castech
Intellimatch–http://www.intellimatch.com
America's Job Ban–http://www.ajb.dni.us/index.html
Career Magazine–http://www.careermag.com/careermag/
Career Mosaic–http://www.careermosaic.com:80/cm/cm1.html

Resume Writing Business

Overview—With people being laid off, excuse meódownsizedóin large numbers, resume writers should have a large base of customers on the Internet. Entrepreneurs can start businesses that target select markets, like graduating students, teachers and professors, and college administrators.

Rewards and risks—Most resume writers I talked to for this book didn't want to talk, so things must be good. After all, they don't want their competitors to enter this field. Let's face it, the barriers to entry aren't high! If you can write your own resume, you can pick up money writing resumes for other people. Because of the intense competition in this area, you will need to position yourself as being different from the rest and be up on the latest resume formats and buzzwords. Nothing reads worse than last year's buzzwords! Prices for writing resumes can range from $25 to $150 per resume.

Special marketing elements for the Home Page—Differentiation is the key here. There are lots of people getting into this field, so the consumer must be able to see how your services differ from competitors. At the very least, you should have your own resume online, as well as samples of work you have done. Testimonials from satisfied clients would help too. Articles about job hunting and interview tactics would be a bonus, as would links to companies that offer jobs on their Home Pages. You can also consider offering a free critique of a person's resume. This can help get the ball rolling.

Links to Home Pages

Shawn's Internet Resume Center–http://www.inpursuit.com/sirc

Intellimatch–http://www.intellimatch.com

8 INFORMATION INDUSTRIES

In this age of information, being able to find information is almost as important as creating the information or analyzing it! Information Services People who have information or know how to locate facts provide a valuable service to a corporation or a home-based business.

Entrepreneurs who are computer literate and have a good feel for search engines, online databases, and imaginative querying can do well in this industry.

This chapter explores businesses you can start as information brokers, speakers, speaker bureaus, analysts, financial aid services, advice, astrology charts and review services.

INFORMATION BROKER BUSINESS

Overview—With the vast amount of data available on the Internet and the commercial online services like CompuServe, Prodigy, and America Online, as well as business-to-business services, it is not surprising that a new breed of online librarian has come to the fore. Called "Information Brokers," these researchers find information requested by their clients, which can include large corporations that need voluminous material to support their marketing programs or financial analyses; or home-businesses that must have statistics to bolster a new business proposal. This business can be a good part-time job for a full-time employee in a related field, or a college student.

You must have good research skills, work well under a deadline, have an extensive knowledge of resources on the Internet and other online services. Not only must you be able to understand the client's requests, but you must be able to add value to the search by brainstorming and articulating possible avenues of research the client has not thought about because you knew they existed and the client did not. To get started, read a good book about this field, such as Information Brokers' Handbook, by Linda Rugge and Alfred Glossbrenner

Rewards—Prices for services can vary widely depending on the scope of the project, deadline, or part of the country you live in, as well as your background. Fees generally range from $25 to $125 an hour. A rush job can demand higher fees. Someone starting out or doing this part time can charge less. We've seen prices as low at $10 an hour from a retired librarian. Entrepreneurs can start this type business either full-time or part-time and can subcontract work as demand for services increases.

Risks—Normal business risks.

Special marketing elements for the Home Page—The Home Page can contain credibility building devices, like resume, testimonials from clients, and articles you've written about trends in an industry you want to prospect for clients. As a way to build relationships with clients, search newsgroups and mailing lists for people who ask questions that you can find the answers to. Post the answers and let people know about your services through your signature file. You'll build credibility with them immediately. Consider offering a free proposal that outlines what you would do.

PROFESSIONAL SPEAKERS AND TRAINERS

Overview—Speakers inform and entertain people at conventions, conferences, and dinners. Often, the highlight of a meeting is the address by the keynote speaker. Topics can range from inspiration, business advice, practical information, and humor. Speakers also provide consulting services for corporations that seek outside experts and a fresh way of thinking.

Rewards—Not only can speakers make $3,000 for a one-hour talk, they also generate income from sales of books and tapes they have produced, and by acting as a consultant for audience members who retain their services.

Risks—Competition for these lucrative positions is intense. Program chairmen, who hire speakers, can be flooded with slick materials from hundreds of speakers and dozens of agents representing even more. Speakers must possess all the qualities of actors and entertainers to keep audiences at the edges of their seats. To learn more about the speaking business, read Secrets of Successful Speakers, by Dottie Walters, McGraw Hill.

Special marketing elements for the Home Page—Credibility is a key factor in selecting a speaker, so your Home Page should reflect your expertise by containing articles you've written, overviews of books, tapes and instructional videos you've produced, as well as your speaking schedule, testimonials, mission statement, and topic list. Audio files will be crucial for success, as will videos. Consider adding an audio file of your best five minutes, or a short video, both of which can be downloaded by potential clients who have powerful computers.

Links to Home Pages

David Arnold–http://www.infosight.com
Kim Bayne–http://www.bayne.com/wolfBayne/wB/interview.html
Wally Bock–http://www.expertcenter.com/members/wbock/
Daniel Janal–http://www.janal-communications.com

Interview: David Arnold, Speaker

Welcome to InfoSight, where David O. Arnold, Ph.D. and Gail Rutman, C.P.A. show how to tap the power of the information age to communicate with customers, clients, and prospects.

- The InfoSight Team: Who We Are
  - David O. Arnold, Ph.D
  - Gail Rutman, C.P.A.

- David Arnold's Speeches and Seminars
  - A sampling of David's programs
  - David's upcoming speaking schedule

- InfoSight Articles
  - Using Information Age Tools to Build Your Network
  - Newsletters for the Information Age
  - High Touch Marketing on the World Wide Web

Contact us at:

InfoSight
541 Willamette St., Suite 214
Eugene, OR 97401

Figure 8-1. InfoSight's Home Page lists information about the speaker's background, topics, seminar dates, and articles. Copyright 1995, InfoSight.

David Arnold
InfoSight
541 Willamette St., Suite 214
Eugene, OR 97401-2694

http://www.infosight.com/~speaker
darnold@infosight.com

Background

What was your purpose in putting a home page on the Web?

The Web offers incredible opportunities for reaching out to current and prospective clients. It allows us to establish a progressive, graphic image to appeal to businesses, and organizations who want to learn how to take advantage of computers and other information age tools for marketing and networking.

Since we can modify and add to our Web site almost instantly, we can continually freshen and update the information we offer with little expense to our business. Web marketing is more time efficient and cost effective than more traditional print methods, such as direct mail.

How has the Home Page helped your business?

We're establishing credibility as information providers, which is the essence of our business. We're also providing a model for what we talk about: doing business in the information age, which includes marketing on the World Wide Web.

What advice would you give to a business starting on the Web?

Think through what you want to accomplish on the Web, and design your site to accomplish your goals. Be aware that the Web is different from any other medium you may have used in the past for promotion and dissemination of information. You shouldn't, for example, just slap the design and content of your printed brochure into your Web site. A design that attracts on paper might repel on a computer screen. In addition, the Web culture demands more value and subtlety than other marketing environments.

SPEAKING BUREAU BUSINESS

This model also applies to–talent agencies (models, actors, singers, performers, etc.).

Overview—Speaking bureaus help match the sponsor of the event with a talented speaker who could fill the bill.

Rewards—Agents can make as much as 25 percent of the fee, which can range from $1,000 to $25,000 and even higher for a top speaker like former President George Bush or Colin Powell. Bureaus can also charge speakers for space on their pages.

Risks—None beyond time, effort, and start-up capital.

Special marketing elements for the Home Page—Like the ideas for speakers' pages in the preceding job overview, bureau pages can contain the basic information about speakers. Because they represent many speakers, the Home Page should have an easy search mechanism to find speakers in various categories, geographic regions, and price ranges. Consider adding links to related industries. For example, if a speaker's topic is job interviewing skills, link to the Home Page of a career development and resource center.

Links to Home Pages

ExpertCenter–http://www.expertcenter.com
Can * Speak Presentations–
http://speakers.starbolt.com/pub/speakers/web/speakers.html
Speakers Bureau–www.mcanet.com/speakers.html
Speakers Online–http://speakers.starbolt.com/pub/speakers/web/speakers.html

CASE STUDY– CAN * SPEAK PRESENTATIONS, LTD.

Figure 8-2. Home Pages must tell people what they will find at the site. Courtesy of Speakers OnLine and Can*Speak Presentations.

Tina Boudreau and Linda Davidson

Can*Speak Presentations Limited

318 Stewart Street

1-800-665-7376

Peterborough, ON K9J 3N1

1-800-561-3591

Canada

http://speakers.starbolt.com/pub/

speakers/web/speakers.html

tboudreau@oncomdis.on.ca

lindad@canspeak.com

Background

Who is your primary audience?

Meeting planners.

How will they benefit from your product or service?

We make meeting planning easy! When looking for speakers—often the most important part of a meeting—the match-making ability is what ensures success. We have speakers in many budget ranges that cover every topic from motivation to pathological waste to burnout.

How does your product or service differ from others?

We offer the most fun!

When we send out kits or packages they are often lumpy. When we send out a demo video, we include popcorn. We giftwrap audio cassettes. Stick in candy. Use wacky stickers for letters and envelopes. We try to capture people's imagination.

Is this business an offshoot of your existing business, or does it exist only on the Internet?

This is just an added marketing arm to the existing business.

If it is an offshoot, was it meant to generate income on its own or to steer people to your other outlets?

It is primarily to make us a multimedia company, to find new markets to raise our level of service.

Where is your workplace?

Office.

What is your background and training?

Linda Davidson has sold Mary Kay and was in occupational therapy. Tina is still a Registered Practical Nurse with sales, publishing, and computer expertise. Sheree McGarrity worked in a bank. They didn't totally appreciate her sense of humour or dedication to the client.

When did you start your business?

Eight years ago, Vancouver, four years Ontario.

How much money has your company made online?

After four months on the Web, we booked a speaker, Lauren J. Woodhouse, for a university. This first booking netted us our upfront costs for our placement.

We have made money from participating in different newsgroups, sent packages to more than five new clients, and are now using e-mail for the same number of existing clients.

Getting started

Did you create a business plan before going online?

No.

How much time did it take to get up and running?

About two weeks.

Did you create the pages yourself?

Speakers Online did all the work! We simply used our current one-sheets that go out on our speakers.

How much did it cost to get started?

We pay $100 /speaker/year in $US.

How did you obtain your startup capital?

N/A

What mistakes did you make that you wish you hadn't made?

Taking so long to figure out how to find resources and places to be in the Net.

What advice would you give to a similar startup?

Take your time, but hurry! Realize you probably won't make buckets of money right away, but we do believe it will come. Right now, we do it just so we can say we do!

What skills are necessary to run a business?

With a great provider, we simply have to answer e-mail and check regarding updated material.

What education is needed to run your site?

Nil.

What special qualities are needed to run your site?

Nil

How did you promote your Home Page?

We mention it on all of our promotional material, including signatures on e-mail.

How much did it cost to promote your site?

Nothing right now.

How did the startup phase affect your personal life?

Nil.

My day

What does your average day look like?

First thing in morning, check site and e-mail, then get on the phone, computer, and files.

What does your job entail?

Sales, customer service, computer usage.

How many hours a week do you spend working on your site?

Check site, 20 minutes/day.

E-mail, 20 minutes/day.

What was the hardest part of the job in the beginning?

Figuring out the system and finding a service provider that was reliable.

How long did it take to get established?

Six months before we felt comfortable in newsgroups and were able to surf to find a suitable site, such as Speakers Online.

What do you like most about your work?

The variety, the global feelings, and participation.

What do you like least?

My lack of knowledge and unsureness of what works or doesn't work.

What was your greatest moment?

It will be the first sale!

How much time do you spend upgrading your site?

Not much, as we don't run the site.

Are there any hazards to running your site?

Not that we know of yet.

How much money do you hope to make?

We'd like to end up with one booking for each speaker (eight) this year, which will revenue us about $7,000 Canadian.

General

Are you glad you are on the Web for personal and business reasons?

Yes! It is lots of fun, interesting, and the research, material, and opinions available are wild.

Given what you know now, would you do it again?

Yes!

The future

What is your next venture?

Would like to start a mailing list/Newsgroup for speakers to talk about their lives/speeches with other qualified speakers.

What else would you like to say?

Multimedia is taking over many industries, and the meetings industry is the same. There will be more remote locales sent to all over the world, speakers will give talks from their office to the world, to all the little plants. Many organizations will stop bringing their staff all together, just televise the broadcast. The implications are mind-boggling.

INTERNET—BASED SEMINARS BUSINESS

Overview—In the off-line world, seminars are very expensive, yet potentially lucrative ventures. The main cost is to print and mail thousands of brochures to people in the hopes that 1 percent of the people actually pay to attend. Costs also are incurred for the meeting room, refreshments, and the trainer's fee.

An online venture can cut out almost all these expensive marketing costs. You must, of course, pay the trainer to produce the materials and answer students' questions.

Courses can be held with one person who interacts with the teacher, or with a whole number of students who interact with the teacher and each other. You will need to promote the seminars with online marketing techniques, which, as we've discussed in Chapter 3, involve more time than money.

Material can be accessed in any number of ways:

- *E-mail account*—Send course material directly to the student, who reads the material, completes assignments and sends material to the instructor. Each week, a new section of the course materials is sent. For a real-time discussion, the class can be scheduled to meet in a IRC chat room, or with any number of chat software programs produced by various companies.
- *Mailing list*—Send course material to the students via a mailing list, which is an electronic bulletin board. They can send assignments and questions directly to the instructor. They can also interact with the instructor and other students by sending letters to the list in response to questions posed by the instructor and other class members. Students would be required to post answers by certain dates to maintain the flow of dialog. Your ISP can create the mailing list.

An advantage of an online seminar over a traditional one is that the students can turn pages at their convenience and link to other documents and resources, which the instructor has set up, or which other students share.

Rewards—The beauty of running an online seminar business is that you create the course work once, and sell it many, many times. Unlike books, there aren't any incremental costs for creating or duplicating materials. You can have a class with one student or 100 students and make a profit in either case. Also, unlike the off-line world that demands that everyone attend a meeting in a certain room at a specified time with the same beginning and end dates for everyone, the online seminar can involve people who begin when they want to, read the material and complete the assignments when they have the time. In this manner, the online seminar leader is freed from the bonds of time and space that minimize the rewards of the off-line seminar.

Risks—What if they gave a seminar and no one came? You would be out the costs for marketing the seminar and creating the material. Also, your material could be copied and distributed without your being paid.

Special marketing elements for the Home Page—Creating credibility and interest are the key missions of the Home Page. You also can't give away the store. Therefore a Home Page should contain the course overview, objectives, benefits, and deliverables, as well as a session by session outline of material covered. The instructor's biography also should be available. To increase exposure, link to related sites.

Links to Home Pages

Internet Survival Skills–

http://kawika.hcc.hawaii.edu/iss101/welcome.html (free course offered by University of Hawaii)

INTERVIEW—KEN HENSARLING, SEMINAR INSTRUCTOR

Ken Hensarling

http://kawika.hcc.hawaii.edu/iss101/
iss101. html

Hawaii Community College

ken@hcc.Hawaii.edu

1268 Maleko Street

Kailua, HI 96734

Background

What are you hoping to accomplish by being on the Web?

Originally, I developed my Internet training materials as in-house training for our faculty, students, and staff. I began to get numerous requests from others who were using the tutorials and who wanted permission to use them in classes, seminars, etc. At this time very little was available via books on how to use the Internet. Now the market is flooded and new books appear daily. My tutorials still serve the same purposes that they once did and if others on the Internet find them useful I am all for that.

What advice would you give an entrepreneur to succeed on the Web?

Make your information relevant and as up-to-date as possible. Make (your presentation) dynamic instead of simply static pages. Good graphics must be optimized to allow for access over modem lines. Find a real unmet market need and fill that need. Don't simply put an existing service on the net and expect folks to come flocking to your service.

PUBLIC SEMINARS BUSINESS

Overview—Trainers, consultants, and speakers can promote seminar businesses in the real world by creating Home Pages on the Internet. Please see the discussion on Internet Seminars for parallel advice.

Links to Home Pages—Diana Fairechild promotes her public seminars and sales of her book on her Home Page. See the case study that follows for a business plan from a model citizen of the Internet. Her Home Page and interview radiate with warmth and sound advice.

CASE STUDY–DIANA FAIRECHILD, PUBLIC SEMINAR LEADER

Diana Fairechild
HEALTHY FLYING
With Diana Fairechild
P.O. Box 999
808 247-7700
Hana, Hawaii 96713

http://www.maui.net/~diana

diana@maui.net

Background

Who is your primary audience?

My audience is anyone who travels by air or who knows an air traveler.

My seminars are for everyone who wants to enjoy air travel, arrive feeling refreshed, and get the most out of life. They can travel once or as a frequent flier—all will benefit. My book, JET SMART, is for everyone who wants to feel good and look good when they travel by air. All travelers of any age, type of work, and region benefit by knowing how to travel easier, sleep soundly, and eliminate jet lag. The column HEALTHY FLYING with Diana Fairechild is published on the Internet and is moving toward international syndication in print.

How will they benefit from your product or service?

I provide travel wellness information–for healthy people who want to stay that way, and for the less than healthy who want to travel for business or personal reasons. Airline passengers deserve to arrive at their destinations with vigor, stamina, and vitality.

How does your product or service differ from others?

I personally flew 10 million miles as an international flight attendant for 21 years. I know the hidden secrets of how to stay healthy when you travel. I believe I am the only person worldwide providing the service on how jet travel can be easier and enjoyable.

Is this business an offshoot of your existing business, or does it exist only on the Internet?

Offshoot. I am the author of JET SMART, an informative guide to air travel that has sold over 50,000 copies worldwide.

If it is an offshoot, was it meant to generate income on its own or to steer people to your other outlets?

HEALTHY FLYING with Diana Fairechild is offered on the Internet as a free service to airline passengers, so they can travel more safely, more comfortably, and especially more healthfully. This Internet site provides a sampler of the information in JET SMART. JET SMART is for sale on the Internet, and in bookstores worldwide, or with an 800 number.

Where is your office located?

I have a laptop and sometimes I log on in my office, sometimes at the dining room table, and sometimes I sit outside in the garden.

What is your background and training?

I have a B.A. in French literature and I speak several foreign languages. During my two decades as an international flight attendant, while I was circling the earth—literally more than 100 times—I studied esoteric yoga and other healing techniques with acknowledged teachers in Europe, India, Asia, and the South Pacific. I have been subscribing to daily meditation, hatha yoga, and a vegetarian diet for 25 years.

When did you start your business?

1992.

How did you promote your site?

I started with a Lycos search and sent press releases to people who were involved in travel. I was very quickly annotated by a number of travel agents, an aeronautical university, Yahoo, the rec.travel library, GNN's travel page, and I was also offered the position of "guest editor" on Galaxy.

How much did it cost to promote your site?

Nothing.

How long did it take until you got your first sale?

A week or so.

How much has your company made?

N/A

Getting started

Did you create a business plan before going online?

No.

How much time did it take to get up and running?

I got my account in February 1995. My site was online in March in an adequate, but what I now realize was a preliminary form. Six months later the pages represent a state of clarity and organization where I think I can stop fiddling with them, that is, except for regularly updating information and adding new columns.

Did you create the pages yourself or did you get help?

I started writing the pages myself because I enjoy writing. HTML was easy to learn thanks to the "Source" and "View" buttons in Netscape. I also asked for and received assistance from many people.

What advice would you give someone starting a business?

Think about what you want to give to the Internet community. Think about what you would like to contribute. Offer something of value and people of like mind will find your site. People appreciate the content and sincerity of my column.

What skills would a person need to conduct a Web business?

They need to be passionate about their field of expertise and believe that others will benefit from their service.

Your Day

What does your average day look like?

The first thing I do at about 4:30 A.M. is check my e-mail. 4:30 A.M., my time here in Hawaii, is 7:30 A.M. on the West Coast and 10:30 A.M. on East Coast. I find that many people write me late at night and I am always excited at the prospect of connecting with others of like mind first thing in my day.

What does your job entail?

I write columns in response to the e-mail I get from readers. I see myself as an experienced resource for travelers—like their own flight attendant friend. The people I serve travel on all the airlines, and I offer them something which enhances the coffee, tea, or milk.

How many hours a week do you spend working on your site?

I don't keep track because I love what I do. It is part of my day—even the surfing, where I get ideas for enhancing my site. And I often e-mail other sites which I think would like to link me, and they usually do.

This is where the "inter" part of Internet comes into play. We see how our work links up to commercial prospects, and also to life situations, and to people of like mind.

What was the hardest aspect of the work in the beginning?

Mastering Windows, and all the various needed programs of communications and graphics software. Although I had been word- processing for many years, this required a tremendous amount of studying up on my part to arrive at the point that I am so comfortable with all the software that it enhances my thinking and I can easily takeoff in creative trajectories.

What do you like most about your work?

I love helping people. I do not have children of my own, so it is especially rewarding for me that people worldwide are benefiting from my experiences.

What do you like the least?

There is nothing about this I don't like. When I was a flight attendant I met people from all over the world—this was my lifestyle. When I stopped flying, I found I missed ethnic diversity. But now, my site is visited by people from 40 countries—as diverse as China, Korea, and Iceland. This excites me.

What was your greatest moment?

At the beginning of every month my Webmaster sends me the last month's statistics of "reader requests" (hits). My fourth month online, reader requests had increased incrementally to over 20,000. This thrilled me!

How did the startup phase affect your personal life?

It literally became my focus. Most of the people I feel like interacting with now are involved in Internet.

Are you glad you are on the Web on personal and business reasons?

Absolutely. I am glad that I am on the Web because I can live and work remote from civilization where I am not forced to breathe the industrial wastes of our world and the perfumes and other irritants that affect those who are chemically sensitive. It is my wish that the world will come to its senses soon and allow those who react adversely to such pollutants to be able to intermix normally in the workplace, among others in public, and when traveling in jets. The present profusion of chemicals in society is a sad and severe problem that seems to be alluding the consciousness of humanity. This is the subject of my next book.

Given what you know now, would you do it again?

Yes.

What is your next venture?

MaMa Online, `http://www.maui.net/~mama`, an Internet service. I have a partner in this venture, another woman whom I met on Internet; we offer seminars in Hawaii and e-mail/phone consultations to assist others as they create their home pages, then broadcast them out to the global community.

What else would you like to say?

Thank you for finding me and interviewing me via the Internet. It is a perfect example of the linking available to all of us, which I am very interested in.

MARKET ANALYSIS BUSINESS

Overview—Every industry has experts who conduct research and sell the results. Entrepreneurs can create a new online business analyzing markets, ranging from computer chips to the purchasing habits of coeds in midwest colleges. You must have the qualifications and background to be an analyst, just as you must be trained to be a doctor. It is essential that you have a good background in marketing, finance, and analysis, as well as the dynamics of the industry you study.

Rewards—By having fixed costs for creating materials, your income is limited only by your ability to convince companies to purchase it. If the material is highly valued, companies can pay tens of thousands of dollars. If you have good material, it can be resold to many companies.

Risks—If your material is not valued, or poorly researched, you will not sell many reports, or if you do, they will not come back for more.

Special marketing elements for the Home Page—Credibility is the key to making your sales. You have to prove that you–a virtual unknown in a virtual world–have the insight and experience to forecast the future and make sense of the present. Consider writing short articles, press releases and position papers that give away the highlights of your report. This strategy might sound like heresy to you, after all, why would anyone buy the cow if they get the milk for free? However, analysts have been doing this for years. They write a press release which entices the market, which then turns around and buys the whole report because they are number junkies and detail-oriented perfectionists who need to have your facts to justify their multimillion dollar marketing campaigns or company acquisitions.

To add value to your site, add links to companies in your industry, as well as to newspapers and magazines covering the field.

Links to Home Pages

AP Research– `http://www.apresearch.com`
Frost & Sullivan–`http://www.frost.com`
Dataquest–`http://www.dataquest.com`
Maloff Company–`http://maloff.com`

CASE STUDY–AP RESEARCH

 AP Research

Welcome to the cyberhome of AP Research. The definitive source for market research and competitive analysis on PC cards (PCMCIA Cards) and SCSI interfaces.

 About AP Research

 Free Reports & Position Papers From:

AP Research:
- A Brief Analysis of Pager Cards: 1995
- CardBus Summary Report
- CardBus In Retrospect
- Marketing Issues and Trends in Pager Cards
- NEW PC Card Industry: A 1995 Mid-Year Perspective

Figure 8-3. AP Research tells about its services and provides free information and reports. Copyright 1995, AP Research.

Andrew Prophet

AP Research

19672 Stevens Creek Blvd., Suite 175

Cupertino, CA 95014-2464

http://www.apresearch.com

aprophet@apresearch.com

Background

Who is your primary audience?

AP Research (APR) is a firm dedicated to providing market research and custom consulting services to the PC Card (PCMCIA) and SCSI industries. This is a small subsegment of the portable computing industry. The client base is very broad. APR offers custom advice and reports to: corporate management, venture capitalists, marketing managers, financial analysts, strategic planners, product planners, procurement executives and public relations firms. The company was founded in 1982.

How will they benefit from your service?

I research niche markets, review product plans, evaluate product portfolios, prepare competitive analysis, and offer seminars. AP Research concentrates on PC Cards (PCMCIA cards), SCSI adapters, and the underlining semiconductor technology.

In addition to market research, we publish *Baseline Analysis of PCMCIA Card Markets*, a low-cost executive overview of the PC Card markets and recently, a more focused briefing entitled, *Baseline Analysis of Wireless PC Cards*.

How does your product or service differ from others?

AP Research concentrates on the PC Card industry, thus providing in-depth market analysis at a very low cost.

Is this business an offshoot of your existing business, or does it exist only on the Internet?

Like any other specialized consulting firm, AP Research seeks client engagements using all the traditional means including the Web. The Web page is designed to stimulate interest on our services and market research.

What is your background and training?

I was Associate Director of Semiconductor Consulting at Dataquest, a high technology market research firm. My consulting projects covered a wide range of strategic business issues involving semiconductors and personal computers. I am founder of the ASIC Segment of the Semiconductor Industry Service and gained wide prominence as its principal analyst. My academic training includes: a Masters of Business Administration from Santa Clara University, a B.S. Electrical Engineering from Illinois Institute of Technology, and M.S. Electrical Engineering from San Jose State University.

What advice would you give to a similar startup?

Answering this question is difficult. The diversity of products/service on the Web is very broad. I think it largely depends on the infrastructure of the industry. For consulting services such as mine, I think the prospective client needs to feel comfortable with AP Research and the specific type of market research/consulting services available. Obviously, for other enterprises message may be different.

What skills are necessary to run a business?

I think the skill set depends on the type of business. In my case, a strong background in semiconductor market research and consulting is mandatory. I believe this is more important than knowledge of the Internet or the Web.

What education is needed to run your site?

I believe my background as an engineer and market researcher are critical to the success of my practice.

Are you glad you are on the Web for personal and business reasons?

I believe the Web offers my firm the opportunity to cast a wider net and demonstrate our expertise.

Given what you know now, would you do it again?

Yes.

COLLEGE SERVICES

A great many college students have free accounts on the Internet, courtesy of their universities. They comprise a great potential audience for marketers of products that appeal to young adults. They also are candidates for services that help improve their lives as students. The following case studies and business opportunities show the kinds of businesses that attract students and can serve as brainstorms for you to create additional businesses to serve this large market.

CASE STUDY– COLLEGE NET

Jim Wolfston

Universal Algorithms, Inc.

One SW Columbia, Ste 100

Portland, OR 97258

`http://www.collegenet.com`

`jim@unival.com`

503-227-2790

Background

Who is your primary audience?

High school students bound for college, college students wishing to transfer to other schools, college students looking for graduate schools.

How will they benefit from your service?

CollegeNET provides quick and easy access to information about colleges and universities. The CollegeNET database contains the most accurate, up-to-date, and complete set of links to college and university home pages. College-bound students can easily generate lists of colleges by tuition, enrollment, and geography. In the Fall of 1995, CollegeNET will introduce the ability to apply to college.

How does your service differ from others?

It is easier to use and navigate. It has more links to colleges and universities than any other site. It has more schools and other academic resources backlinked to us. The links are set up to financial aid information and other resources. It uses the new ANSI approved Electronic Data Interchange (EDI) definition for college application transmission to the college, ensuring accuracy. It has compatibility with the college's information systems.

Is this an offshoot of an existing business, or does it only exist on the Internet?

Universal Algorithms developed, maintains, and markets CollegeNET. CollegeNET exists only on the Internet. The system is an "offshoot" only to the extent that it is targeted to the same market (college and university administration) as our core scheduling products.

If it is an offshoot, was it meant to generate income on its own or steer business to the parent business?

We are anticipating CollegeNET to generate income on its own.

What is the founder's background and training?

N/A

Getting started

When did the business start?

Universal Algorithms, Inc. was started in 1977. CollegeNET was announced in April of 1995.

Did you create a business plan before going online?

Ready, fire, aim!

How much time did it take to get up and running?

Site is being continuously developed (started).

Who created the Web pages?

Our software developers.

How much did it cost to get started?

Confidential.

Did you need to go to an outside source for startup capital?

Company proceeds.

How is the Home Page being promoted?

Direct mailings, professional conferences, public relations, etc.

How much does it cost to promote the site?

Confidential.

How long did it take to get the first sale?

Within one week of product announcement.

How much money have you made?

Confidential.

What mistakes did you make that you wish you hadn't made?

Of Kourse not!

What advice can you give to someone starting a business?

It depends upon what kind of page.

What skills are needed to run your business?

Unix, Perl, graphics design, strong writing, logical organization of information, hardware knowledge, competitive spirit, pioneering spirit.

My day

What does your average day look like?

An impossible selection of thousands of good choices. I try to cover the most pressing of the thousands of selections and cajole others to help me with the others.

How many hours a week do you spend working on your site?

10-20 hour per week.

What's the hardest aspect of your job.

Coping with negativism.

What do you like the most about your work?

Watching people get pumped.

What do you like the least?

Countering and coping with negativism.

What was your greatest moment?

Smoking the Graduate Record Exam.

How did the startup of this business affect your personal life?

I had none at the time I started.

Given what you know now, would you do it again?

Of course.

The future

What's the next venture?

Starting a social/philosophical revolution.

What are your long-term goals for this Home Page?

CASH FLOW

What else would you like to say?

Watch Out!!!

COLLEGE FINANCIAL AID SERVICE

Overview—Did you find scholarship money online to fund your education? Then the information can be just as valuable as you find sources of cash for others. Several companies in the off-line world offer this kind of database service. You might want to work with them to run an online version. That way you won't have to search for information from scratch; you'll be able to tap into their resources, which will reduce your start-up costs.

Rewards—Your fee can consist of an hourly charge, or a fixed fee.

Risks—You might have to fill out the forms for the less able, but you can charge for that service. Competition can come quickly.

Special marketing elements for the Home Page—Your Home Page should tell your story without giving away your trade secrets—where the money is buried.

Links to Home Pages

I haven't see any. You could be the first!

ADVICE COLUMNIST BUSINESS

Overview—Dear Abby has not hit the Internet yet, so the field is wide open for enterprising know-it-alls. Do you have a good amount of common sense and a kicky writing style? Then you could be the next advice-meister. Hey, if Psychic Friends can be a hit on an infomercial, can this be a bad job?

This business doesn't have to be limited to the lovelorn. How about creating a similar service that draws on your expertise on such topics as car repair, computer solutions, household repair, interior decorating and parenting? You can also specialize in different groups of people, like teens, gays, and seniors.

Here's how the business works. You create a Home Page and tell everyone about it (See Chapter 3). Show you are an expert in a given field. List types of questions you answer. You might show previously answered questions.

Rewards—You can make money either by charging questioners, readers, or advertisers.

Risks—Normal business risks.

Special marketing elements for Home Pages—If you decide to charge readers, you'll need to set up a password or registration system (See Chapter 4). You should consider creating a persona or alter ego for the character you portray online. No one will ask questions of an ordinary Joe, so create a vivid character that people will want to confide in and read replies from.

Links to Home Pages

I haven't see any. You could be the first!

ASTROLOGY CHART BUSINESS

Overview—If astrology can predict the future from stars in space, chart readers should be able to sell prognostications from virtual space on the Internet.

Rewards—You can make money by selling charts on a customized, pay for service basis.

Risks—Check with your lawyer regarding risks and liabilities.

Special marketing elements for Home Pages—Your Home Ppage could look real cool with artwork. Be prepared to include files that explain what astrology is and is not. Educate your new public.

Links to Home Pages

Internet Psychic–

http://www.infohaus.com/access/by-selleres/internet-psychics/ or send e-mail to internet-psychics@sellers.infohaus.com.

INTERVIEW—ASTROLOGRAM

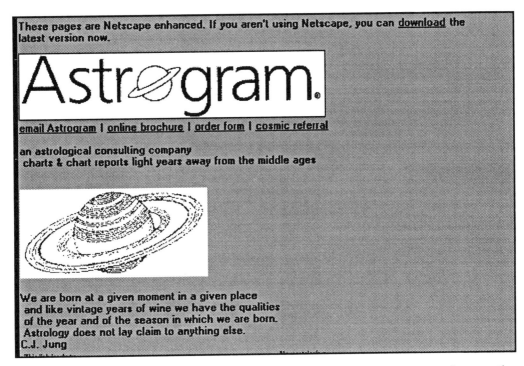

Figure 8-4. Be sure to test your Home Page with different browsers to make sure the page looks good on all of them. Copyright 1995, Astrogram.

Astrogram

P.O. Box 148076
Chicago, IL 60613
312-409-2314

`http://www.dol.com/astrogram`
also
`http://www.dol.com/kiddygram`
`astrogram@astrogram.com`

Background

What is your goal for being on the Internet?

Birthdays are our business. We provide astrological chart reports based on a customer's precise birth data (date, year, exact time and place of birth). Since 1986 we've provided an unusual service that lends itself to being featured on the World Wide Web. Our goal is to be marketing in cyberspace as we move into our second decade. However, our first reason to be on the Web is to position our reports as an upscale, elegant and affordable introduction to the ancient art of astrology and a great source for beautiful birthday gifts! Our second goal was to print less of our glossy brochures and save a few trees. Our ultimate goal will be to provide our reports online when we can design them in a graceful and intriguing fashion.

How has being on the Web helped your business?

Our presence has been acknowledged and two of our reports have been written up (one featured) in Jaclyn Easton's book Shopping on the Internet.

What advice do you have for people starting businesses on the Internet?

To be prepared to invest time and energy in a world that has not yet come into being! Check other web pages and find a talented and dedicated cadre of young designers.

Be prepared to know nothing. Be prepared to jump and then say "Oh! I wonder where I've landed!"

Be prepared to say like Miranda, "Oh brave new world that hath such people in it."

Be prepared to say like Prospero, "Gentle breath your sails must fill or else our project fail which was to please."

REVIEW SERVICE

Overview—If you are the type of person who is always giving your opinion on restaurants, movies, books, and the like, then consider starting a review service. In this business you write reviews and sell them to the public on a pay-per-view basis, or show advertisers that you can create an audience they want to reach and sell them ads. Qualifications should include good writing style and ability to write lots of reviews in a timely manner.

Rewards—You could make money from selling advertising space or subscriptions. You just might be able to get free meals, books, and movie passes.

Risks—Normal business risks. Competition may arise quickly on national issues, like books and movies. However, you might have the field to yourself by specializing in local restaurants, clubs, and bands.

Special marketing elements for Home Page—Your home page should show you to be the expert that you are. Consider giving away old copies of your reviews so people can get a sampling of the quality of your work. Remember, online, no one knows if you have a Ph.D. In literature from Yale or if you are a 16-year-old who can sling a great phrase.

Links to Home Pages

I haven't see any. You could be the first!

BACKGROUND CHECKS AND CREDIT RATING AGENCY

Overview—You can never really be sure who is honest and who is a con man. That might be even more so on the Internet, because you don't see the person face-to-face. Since frauds can prey on people on the Internet, you could create a business that checks people's credit ratings. This could be useful to any Internet business that must enter into relationships involving significant amounts of money, such as roommate referrals, apartment rentals, equipment purchases, singles dating services and the like. Qualifications for this job include the ability to know how to use online services to tap into legal database of credit information (such as TRW), bankruptcy court records, databases of criminal, and the like. It is amazing how much information can be gathered legally from public records or inexpensive credit-rating services.

Rewards—This service can be performed on a project or hourly basis at whatever rates your client can feel comfortable with.

Risks—Normal business risks.

Special marketing considerations for Home Page—Home Pages should stress confidentiality, professionalism, and prompt completion of assignments.

Links to Home Pages

I haven't see any. You could be the first!

BUSINESS PLAN WRITER

Overview—The Web is full of small, start-up companies that are operated by people with varying levels of experience in business. Of the 40 or so case studies in this book, a mere handful created business plans before going online. Perhaps that shows why some entrepreneurs are not doing as well they had hoped. If you have good writing and research skills, there could be an opportunity to start a service to write business plans for online entrepreneurs, as well as to use the Internet to promote these services to businesses that operate off-line.

Rewards—Fees for writing business plans range all over the ball field. You could get thousands from a large company and hundreds from home-based businesses.

Risks—Deadbeats. All consultants and writers should get a significant part of their fees in advance and upon completion of a first draft. Nothing devalues faster than a service after it has been performed.

Special marketing considerations for Home Pages—Build credibility with your bio, testimonials and partial samples of your work. Attract people to your site by writing and posting articles of interest to new businesses. Link to and from sites relating to your potential customers. Alert people in newsgroups in your field of the articles and information available for free. Don't hype your business by announcing its opening in a newsgroup.

Links to Home Pages

I haven't see any. You could be the first!

GRANT WRITER

Overview—Grant writing is a field that will never go out of business. Colleges, researchers, and laboratories live on their ability to get funding by the grants offered by the government, foundations, and businesses. Writing a grant is an art that must be mastered as intricately as playing the flute. Grant writing has its own language and ways of phrasing words and requests to make a point and get the attention of the grantors.

Rewards—Because of the specialty of this work, you won't be swamped with competitors. Prices for services vary by the type of agency you deal with and the complexity of the application.

Risks—Normal business risks.

Special marketing considerations for Home Pages—Prove your credibility by posting your bio, testimonials, and writing samples.

Links to Home Pages

Dr. Pat Rife–http://www.maui.net/~envision/envision.html.

9 WRITING SERVICES

It is truly amazing how many people want to be writers. *Writer's Digest* has 225,00 subscribers who would love to find someone to publish their novels, screenplays and poems. Unfortunately for them, book publishers do not have the budget to print all those new works and bookstores don't offer these writers shelf space. What's a would-be writer to do?

Welcome to the World Wide Web, everyman's printing press. For a small price (see startup costs in Section 1), you can post your poetry, novel, or short story on your Home Page and let the world read it and discover the talent you have.

What's that? You want to get paid? Okay, let's look at how writers can make money on the Internet.

This chapter will explore ways to make money if you are an entrepreneurial writer, book publisher, freelance writer, advertising copy writer, technical writer, news hound, or book store.

BOOK PUBLISHER (SELF–PUBLISHED, REAL WORLD)

Overview—Can't get a publisher for your masterpiece? Publish it online! Here are two strategies: Upload the first two or three chapters onto your Home Page. Take orders for the full copies, which you can send through e-mail or snail mail. Hint: e-mail is cheaper! If you have a full line of books or a garage full of printed copies, the Web is a great place to advertise books. I've gotten orders from Canada, Germany, Israel, and Australia, as well as throughout the United States

Rewards—You can sell books to people all over the world and take home all the money. You don't have to split the income with a publisher, bookstore, or book distributor.

Risks—You'd be amazed at how inexpensive a book can cost to print—as low as $2 a unit for a 200 page book. But you have to order 3,000 copies to get a good price. You are also investing your time and effort to writing the book, as well paying a proofreader and artist to design the cover and interior pages.

Special marketing elements for the Home Page—Consider offering the first few chapters for free online. People can read the work online or print it out. If they want to read the rest of the book, they can send you a check!

Publishers should also print an overview of the book, a table of contents, reviews and testimonials, a sample chapter, the author's bio, as well as how to order the book online and off-line.

Links to Home Pages

Janal Communications–`http://www.janal-communications.com` lists three books and a software program for sale.

BOOK PUBLISHER (SELF–PUBLISHED, ONLINE)

Overview—You don't have to publish a book on paper to be an author. You can create a virtual book that you sell and deliver online. You can print a few chapters on your Home Page that people can read for free and then charge them to see the rest. Or you could sell your book to a larger Home Page that needs content. For example, the Global Network Navigator printed Investment Strategies for the 21st Century by Frank Armstrong. He posts a new chapter every two weeks that readers can view for free. GNN benefits from the increased traffic to their site.

Rewards—Income without the expense of printing, promoting and distributing.

Risks—Normal business risks.

Special marketing considerations for Home Page—See discussion in previous profile.

Links to Home Pages

Global Network Navigator—`http://gnn.com`.

RESEARCH REPORTS, MONOGRAPHS, BOOKLETS

Overview—Books take a long time to write and edit. They are costly to produce. Writers can instead produce research reports, monographs, booklets, and special reports of 8-20 pages.

Rewards—People are willing to spend $5-10 on this type of work. Your per unit profit might even be higher for these reports than for a book. If you send the work out via e-mail, or let people see it if they have a password, then your material costs are next to nothing. As you create more and more booklets, you could have the basis for a book. You will be making money as you are writing.

Risks—Normal business risks.

Special marketing elements for the Home Page—Consider giving a report away for free as a method of attracting visitors and for proving your credibility.

Practical examples and links to Home Pages— See the case study for Herman Holtz, one of the best-selling business writers of all-time.

INTERVIEW—HERMAN HOLTZ, WRITER

Herman Holtz

`71640.563@compuserve.com`

`holtz@paltech.com.`

How effective is the Internet for selling your reports?

I have offered a free report on freelance writing, and am getting quite an enthusiastic response–i.e., requests for the report, which I e-mail to the respondent. The report includes a catalog of my reports and an order form.

It is too soon to judge the total results, but the early results are encouraging. The reports are how-to monographs of five to eight pages each (a few are longer), selling for an average of about $3 each. I also have collections of the most popular reports and one book on disk, each at approximately $10.

The most popular of these reportsóthere are approximately 30 of them–are those dealing with freelance writing. Most of those are not about how to write as much as they are about how and where to market. The reports that are not about writing are on a wide variety of topics: government grant programs, how to use OPM (other people's money), marketing, how to start and run a singles club, and bartering, to name a few.

I have been advertising these on the Usenet, and I am still planning a Web presence. I have been publishing these reports for nearly 20 years, mostly by mail until now. I am still probing ways to market online.

My own claims to fame are a reputation as a guru on consulting, largely the result of my highly successful book, How to Succeed as an

Independent Consultant (Wiley), now in its third edition since 1983, with nearly 200,000 copies sold, plus a continuing series of books for the independent consultant.

DIGIZINE, ONLINE MAGAZINES

Overview—A digizine is a digital magazine. Get it? You can use the digizine to report on areas of interest to you and your audience that they can't get anywhere else. One of the Internet's great strengths is the ability to let you publish your own work and seek representation for your views or interests. Although there are thousands of special interest print magazines and tens of thousands of special interest newsletters and professional publications, none can be produced as inexpensively as one published on the Internet. Whereas the economics of publishing a hard copy newsletter might be prohibitively expensive, a digizine can be a money make.

Rewards—To make money on a digizine, sell subscriptions, advertisements, or links to related pages. Other benefits of publishing a digizine include increasing your credibility and stature in your industry, which could lead to paid speaking engagements and new clients.

Risks—Normal business risks.

Special marketing elements for the Home Page—If you want to make money on advertisements, then make the page free to subscribers, who provide a minimal amount of demographic information in return for the privilege of free issues. You need the demographic information to sell advertisements to companies who want to be sure they are reaching their desired target audience.

Practical examples and links to Home Pages—See the case study on Maui Windsurfing Report.

CASE STUDY–THE MAUI WINDSURFING REPORT

Figure 9–1. Digizines have a fun style all their own.

Tim Orden

http://maui.net/~mauiwind/MWR/
mwr.html

Maui Windsurfing Report direct   mauiwind@maui.net
from the Mecca of windsurfing,
Maui, Hawaii
P.O. Box 1202
Kula, HI 96790

Background

Who is your primary audience?

Windsurfers and wannabe windsurfers.

How will they benefit from your product?

Exposure to the windsurfing community worldwide.

How does your product differ from others?

We are the first, the foremost.

Does this business exist online and off-line?

Only on the net.

Where is your office located?

House and six other houses (the staff).

What is your background and training?

I shed daily, and have for a long time....

When did you start your business?

March 1995.

How much did it cost to promote your site?

A lot of time.

How long did it take until you got your first sale?

We were getting sponsors before we started.

How much has your company made?

N/A

How much money do you expect to make?

No expectations.

Getting started

Did you create a business plan before going online?

NO.

How much did time did it take to get up and running?

Two weeks.

Did you create the pages yourself or did you get help?

We have a staff of seven.

How much did it cost to get started?

Mostly time.

Did you need to go to an outside source for startup capital?

N/A

How did you obtain it?

We're surf bums. Our greatest asset is time and talent.

What mistakes did you make that you wish you hadn't made?

Filling out questionnaires.

What advice would you give someone starting a business?

Use a lot of sex.

What skills would a person have to conduct business?

Time management skills.

My day

What does your average day look like?

Eat, sail, sleep, sail, etc.

What does your job entail?

Eat, sail, sleep, sail, etc.

How many hours a week do you spend working on your site?

15-20 hours.

What was the hardest aspect of the work in the beginning?

Organizing an idea.

What do you like most about your work?

I can eat, sail, sleep, sail, etc...

What do you like the least?

Answering questionnaires.

What was your greatest moment?

Being the Spider's Pic of the day.

How did the startup phase affect your personal life?

My wife hates this.

Given what you know now, would you do it again?

NO.

Where can people find advice about running a site like yours?

In their head.

The future

What is your next venture?

Eat, sleep, sail, sleep, etc.

What else would you like to say?

If it isn't fun, people won't give a shit about it.

FREELANCE WRITING BUSINESS

Overview—Freelance journalists and writers can prospect for new clients on the Internet.

Rewards—Writers can show and sell their works to potential clients all over the world. Having a Home Page is like having a portfolio that people can see whenever they want to view it.

Risks—Normal business risks.

Special marketing elements for the Home Page—Post old articles online so prospects can see your writing style and command of the material. Resumes, bios, testimonials also help.

ADVERTISING WRITING SERVICE

Overview—Are you a freelance writer, copy writer, advertising writer, or the like? Let the world see your samples on your Home Page.

Rewards—You could find new clients who will buy your writing services.

Risks—Investment of time.

Special marketing elements for the Home Page—Include your rates and topics you like to write about. You can also list testimonials from satisfied clients

Links to Home Pages

Online Business Resource Center–http://www.copywriter.com/ab/

CASE STUDY–ONLINE BUSINESS RESOURCE CENTER

Al Bredenberg
Copy and Creative Services
Home Page

Services and Resources for Business, Industry, and the Online World

What you can do at this page:

- ◊ Find out about Al Bredenberg's copywriting services.
- ◊ Go to the Online Business Resource Center. New at the Center: Online Resources for the Construction Industry
- ◊ Fill out a form to tell Al about your project and request his help.
- ◊ Questions? Comments? Send Al an e-mail message.

Figure 9-1. Writers have virtual portfolios of unlimited size to show their works. Copyright 1995, Alfred R. Bredenberg.

Al Bredenberg

The Online Business Resource

Center

18 Kugeman Village

Cornwall, CT 06753-0151

`http://www.copywriter.com/ab/`

`ab@copywriter.com (203) 672-0382`

Background

Who is your primary audience?

Companies that sell their services and products by direct marketing. Businesses that want to use the Internet as a marketing vehicle.

How will they benefit from your service?

I deliver no-nonsense direct marketing copy that sells. I offer a strong business background and first-hand selling experience. I publish material that helps businesses market more effectively.

How does your service differ from others?

I cut my teeth as a business person and manager rather than at an ad agency. I have in-depth understanding of business, industry, and many technical subjects. Rather than creating image advertising, I am committed to direct marketing.

Is this business an off-shoot of your existing business, or does it exist only on the Internet?

This is my regular business. However, since I started working on the Internet, I have begun offering my services doing creative for companies' WorldWide Web sites and online marketing materials. Also, I have written an electronic book, The Small Business Guide to Internet Marketing, which I am selling over the Internet.

Was the site meant to generate income on its own or to steer people to your existing business?

In the beginning, I meant to use my Internet presence to generate leads that I would follow up in the conventional way. Now it is starting to generate some revenue on its own.

Where is your office located?

I operate out of a home office in my apartment.

What is your background and training?

I have been a published writer since 1972. I have been in business and management for over 20 years. I have a masters degree in management from Antioch University. I've been working as a commercial copywriter since 1989.

Getting started

When did you start your business?

I started working as a copywriter in 1989 and have been at it fulltime since 1991.

Did you create a business plan before going online?

Yes.

How much time did it take to get up and running?

Really, I was able to start almost as soon as I had an Internet access account. There's much that a business person can do online using e-mail and participating in electronic forums. I've been on the Internet since 1993, using an account provided by a university I was writing for. In December 1994 I got my own commercial account. I set up my own Web site in May 1995.

Did you create the pages yourself or did you get help?

I did most of the HTML myself, but I had help from my provider, who knows the codes much better.

How much did it cost to get started?

Costs for Internet access and phone charges: $50-100/month. Software: about $200. I worked out a partnership with a provider who lets my Web site live on his server rent-free.

Did you need to go to an outside source for startup capital?

No.

How did you promote your site?

So far the site is what I would call "unannounced." I still have more material to put up before I have it listed in databases and search engines. The site has been mentioned in a magazine article and on some electronic forums. I include the URL with my discussion list postings and e-mail messages. I refer people to my site if I think it might be of interest. I now include the URL on my office stationery.

How much did it cost to promote your site?

So far this hasn't really cost anything. I may have NetPost register the site for me. He charges about $200.

How long did it take until you got your first sale?

About six months. This was from one of the contacts that I made in my first month online. This is par for the course in my business. There's often a long "cultivation" period when I'm developing a new client.

How much has your company made?

I've had $1,018 in revenues as a result of online efforts since receiving my first assignment from this source in May 1995. I'm now working on other assignments which aren't complete yet and negotiating with a number of potential clients.

How much money do you expect to make?

I've set a goal of $50,000 in revenues from 7/1/95 to 6/30/96.

What mistakes did you make that you wish you hadn't made?

All of them! <g> Relying in the beginning on an older and slower PC. It was fine for word processing. But when it crashed I was out of touch with Internet correspondents for a number of days. Now I have a reliable 486 and it's quite a relief.

To be truthful, I'm not *aware* of having made many mistakes. I've checked things out carefully and worked according to a plan.

Ask me again in five years!

What advice would you give someone trying to start a similar business, or any business on the Net?

- Get Internet access and do some exploring and participating. I find many business people are eager to start marketing over the Net before they've even gotten access.
- Take time to work out a plan. Don't jump into it without a clear idea of the options.
- Don't buy into get-rich-quick schemes.
- Do lots of reading about the Internet. I recommend my Small Business Guide to Internet Marketing. Really! I think it's good.
- Remember: Marketing is marketing. You still have to have something worthwhile to sell.
- Don't neglect conventional off-line business and marketing strategies.
- Maybe your product or service isn't suited to the Internet!

What skills would a person need to conduct business?

- Ability to write hard-sell, direct marketing copy.
- Creative problem-solving skills.
- Ability to listen and communicate clearly.
- Basic business and office skills. Organization and time management.

What special qualities are needed to run your site?

- Willingness to learn new skills.
- Recognition that being in business means providing good service for the customer.

Your Day

What does your average day look like?

I spend four to eight hours per day working on writing projects. One to two hours on marketing my own business. I check e-mail at least twice a day and respond as quickly as possible to inquiries. I often spend time in the evening following electronic discussion groups or working on special projects.

What does your job entail?

Much reading and research.

Intensive creative work coming up with concepts, ideas, words, turns of phrase, sentences, the best way to say things.

Writing, rewriting, checking, rechecking.

Delivering the best copy I can and delivering it on time.

How many hours a week do you spend working on your site?

Eight to 10 hours. Reading and answering mail: 25% Reading and participating in discussion groups: 25% Special projects, creating Web and marketing copy, other tasks: 50%.

What was the hardest aspect of the work in the beginning?

Acting and sounding like a newbie and maybe a complete idiot for a number of weeks before I started to feel like I half-way knew what I was doing.

What do you like most about your work?

Every day I get up and I can't wait to get to work!

What do you like the least?

Filling out any kind of form for any purpose.

What was your greatest moment?

Having several Internet experts tell me how much they liked my new Internet marketing book.

How did the startup phase affect your personal life?

A lot of late nights hunched over the keyboard!

Are you glad you are on the Web on personal and business reasons?

Yes. More for business reasons. As far as my personal life, I would much rather spend time with my family, go for walks outdoors, and develop spiritually than surf the Web.

Given what you know now, would you do it again?

Yes.

The future

What is your next venture?

Fully roll out the marketing plan for *The Small Business Guide to Internet Marketing*. Evaluate the plan's effectiveness and consider other publishing ventures if things look good.

What else would you like to say?

Enough already! Thanks!

TECHNICAL WRITING BUSINESS

Overview—If you're a geek, proud of it, and can write, then you can start a technical writing business. Your Home Page can show examples of your work and testimonials from clients, as well as your rates and preferred subjects. You can operate a solo firm in this manner, or grow a business.

Rewards—Increased income.

Risks—None, beyond normal business operations.

Special marketing elements for the Home Page—Show examples of your work and testimonials from clients. A resume would also help build credibility and a list of your interests would help clients learn your strong suits.

Links to Home Pages

See the case study for Manual 3, Inc.

CASE STUDY– MANUAL 3, INC.

 About Manual 3

Read About Our Corporate Philosophy

Learn About Our Services

Access Our Customer Profiles

Find Out About the Technologies We Document

Meet Our Staff

Take an Office Tour

Figure 9-2. Manual presents a clean, easy-to-use menu to find information. Copyright 1995, Manual 3, Inc.

Vincent Crivello
Manual 3 Online
408-293-9654

http://www.manual3.com
vincent_crivello@manual3.com

Background

Manual 3 is a technical writing firm in San Jose, CA. Our full-time, salaried staff primarily consists of senior and junior level technical writers. However, we do have some support positions as well. We provide all services related to information development (e.g. technical writing, online help development, online documentation, technical marketing, writing, technical illustration, etc.).

Who is your primary audience?

Potential customers and customers. Manual 3 produces documentation for several technology companies including, Sun, Apple, Canon, SyQuest, Conner, and Gupta.

How will they benefit from your service?

Reduced costs and shortened development times

How does your service differ from others?

Very few information development firms offer a high-qualified full-time staff with an office equipped with Macs, PC and Sun workstations. This allows us to take projects in-house freeing up customer resources and allowing them to focus on their core business. Our business model also offers an unparalleled amount of flexibility whether working on documentation projects over the long-term or managing publications efforts.

Is this business an off-shoot of your existing business, or does it exist only on the Internet?

Our online presence is simply an extension of our marketing communications and public relations efforts. We also use the Internet as a recruitment vehicle.

Where does your business operate?

We have an office in downtown San Jose equipped with the latest technologies. However, our WWW site is hosted off-site for security reasons.

What is your background and training?

I have a B.A. in political science from San Diego State University. I have worked in various sales and marketing positions over the past five years. I have been using computers since 1982 and have been active in various online services since 1987.

When did you start your business?

The business was founded by Linda Gold in 1981.

How much money has your company made online?

We have only received one direct sales lead from our WWW site. However, we have not been able to accurately measure the exposure we have generated from our online presence. Our WWW site has registered over 2,000 hits since February 1995 (until July).

Did you create a business plan before going online?

I put together a four-page business plan/proposal before going online. I also track the progress of the site as well as competitors efforts.

How much time did it take to get up and running?

From conception to execution: four months. It could have been done in under one month.

Did you create the pages yourself?

We originally outsourced the HTML development because we didn't have time internally. However, all current WWW development is done in house and we provide WWW development services.

How much did it cost to get started?

Startup costs were roughly $3,000 and then $65/month for site mainte-nance. Content development is obviously the biggest time commitment.

How did you obtain your startup capital?

WWW development was funded out of our "Marketing Budget."

What mistakes did you make that you wish you hadn't made?

Choosing our Web developer. We interviewed four different contractors and companies. It made us realize that there are few reliable and estab-lished firms out there providing Web development services.

What advice would you give to a similar startup?

Spend some time on the Net first. Read and research. When it's time to choose a WWW developer, evaluate the company and their proposal very carefully. Always ask for references!!

What skills are necessary to run a business?

Marketing savvy and experience using computers.

What kind of education is needed to run your site?

None–it's outsourced. I do have an extensive background in maintaining various OS's though (Unix, MacOS, Windows).

What kind of special qualities are needed to run your site?

I would recommend outsourcing the effort or it will never get done.

How did you promote your Home Page?

Traditional means: business cards, networking, stationary, postcard announcements, print ads, etc.

How much did it cost to promote your site?

Under $500.

How long did it take until you made your first sale?

Hard to calculate. I would estimate three to four months.

How did the startup phase affect your personal life?

It was a huge time commitment assembling the content for development and then making sure the site was produced properly. With the right WWW developer, the time commitment should be less.

My day

What does your average day look like?

Phone calls, e-mail, Newsgroup browsing, WWW browsing.

What does your job entail?

Sales, Marketing, and now to a lesser degree—MIS.

How many hours a week do you spend working on your site?

Content: two hours. HTML: one hour, Reviews: one hour.

What was the hardest part of the job in the beginning?

The tendency to surf and not get anything done.

How long did it take to get established?

One month of work.

What do you like most about your work?

The "cutting edge" aspect of the business.

What do you like least?

Few people understand what it's all about.

What was your greatest moment?

Seeing the first "hit" report.

Are there any hazards to running your site?

No.

How much money do you hope to make?

I expect that revenues should increase 10 percent for FY96 because of our WWW site.

General

Are you glad you are on the Web for personal and business reasons?

YES!

Given what you know now, would you do it again?

YES!

The future

What is your next venture?

Expanding our site to include project information for customers (budgets, status reports, etc.).

NEWS SERVICES

Overview—Do you have insatiable curiosity about a certain topic that other people care about? If you said "yes," then you can start your own news service on the Internet. You must be able to find information (which is a snap on the Internet and commercial online services), find sources (use Yahoo or another search engine), get comments from newsmakers, and write it up in a factual manner. You can send your digizine (for digital magazine) to people who subscribe to your home-grown mailing list. Remember, e-mail is free. You can also have them read daily updates at your Home Page.

Rewards—Increased income from sales of subscriptions, advertisements or links to related pages.

Risks—Normal business risks.

Special marketing elements for the Home Page—Your home page should extol the benefits of your service. The actual newsletter probably will be sent via e-mail.

Links to Home Pages

For an inside view of how one online newsletter got up and running, read the case history of MESH-Inside Cyberspace published by veteran journalist Don Rittner.

CASE STUDY–MESH–INSIDE CYBERSPACE, NEWS SERVICE

Figure 9-3. Newsletter editors can think of the Home Page as a table of contents. Copyright 1995, Don Rittner.

Don Rittner   http://www.albany.globalone.net/   theMESH/
The MESH-Inside drittner@aol.com 518 374 1088
 Cyberspace
P.O. Box 463
Schenectady, NY 12308

Background

Who is your primary audience?

The MESH-INSIDE CYBERSPACE, a monthly newspaper about the Online/Cyberspace world. Beginner net surfers, old timers, and general audience. Anyone interested in obtaining information or wanting to know where and how to get it on the Net.

How will they benefit from your service?

I have more than 20 years experience in netting and have been on the Net since it was born. We act as a clearinghouse for people wanting to know where specific kinds of information reside on the Net, what issues are affecting the Net, and learning how to use it without spending a great deal of money or time.

How does your service differ from others?

The MESH - Inside Cyberspace exists in multiple formats. The printed version comes out every month. The Web Version is updated daily, there is an Adobe Acrobat version which gets posted on the NET, and a discussion/support area on NEWSLINK, a 24 hour BBS in the Capital District. It reaches many people in a variety of ways, unlike a printed-only publication.

Is this an offshoot of your existing business, or does it exist only on the Internet?

MUG News started out as a user group news service that sent out a monthly news disk to editors of user groups beginning in 1988. The MESH is an outgrowth of MNS, that is, rather than just providing editors of user groups with the latest information about computers and technology, we now provide information to anyone interested in the Net. We still do the disk mailings, and the printed magazine, but spend most of our business activity online.

Was it meant to generate income on its own or to steer people to your other outlets?

Both really. We allow sponsors of the printed magazine to sponsor areas on the Web Site, or just sponsor Web areas and not the printed mag.

Where is your office?

I took the upstairs back porch and converted it into an office. I also have another converted bedroom, the basement as storage, and the attic is full. My wife feels like she is living in the office :)

What is your background and training?

I am a longtime columnist and author specializing in the use of personal computers in science and technology. I have had eight books published and have written hundreds of articles. I am the founder and president of Computer Users for Social Responsibility, Inc., a national nonprofit organization dedicated to the promotion of the wise use of personal computers for the common good. I created and released the first electronic directory of Missing Children in cooperation with Child Find of America, Inc.

Getting started

When did you start your business?

MUG NEWS was started in 1988. The MESH in 1995.

Did you create a business plan before going online?

No.

How much time did it take to get up and running?

After deciding to do the MESH, it was about three months later that the first issue rolled off the press.

Did you create the pages yourself?

The Web version was a trade. A Web designer traded doing the pages for me for an ad in the magazine. I update the site myself.

How much did it cost to get started?

No cash transaction at all–trade. I traded Web space with an information provider so they get an ad in the paper each month for web space. The paper printed version of the paper costs a few thousand each month and is paid for by ads.

How did you obtain your startup capital?

I solicited ads for the first few issues of the printed paper and hired an ad director on commission. The Web site didn't take any cash transaction, so the entire start-up of the paper was minimal. I did have to spend some of my own money for the first few issues to help get it off the ground.

How did you promote your Home Page?

By writing about it in the printed paper and then promoting it using several marketing mail lists and other net promotions (Usenet, mail lists, and chat discussions).

How much did it cost to promote your site?

Nothing!

How long did it take until you made your first sale?

Getting an ad, or sponsor for the Web site, two months.

How much money has your company made online?

We are only in the sixth month of publication (July 1995) but the paper is paying for itself almost 100 percent.

How much money do you hope to make?

Hmm, a tough one. We are doing the paper not so much as a money maker but would like to be able to pay staff, so we would like to make $100,000 a year if possible.

What mistakes did you make that you wish you hadn't made?

Learning HTML myself. It took a little longer to get the web site up since the Web designer had other paying business, so it took about a month longer to get the site ready and public.

What advice would you give to a similar startup?

Get a good designer. The look of a site is 90percent of what keeps someone at your site and coming back. Keep it updated continually.

What skills are necessary to run a business?

Be a good writer, communicator, and a good policeman. Publishing a newspaper is like being a traffic cop. Get a lot of good talented people and keep the traffic (talent) flowing.

What special qualities are needed to run your site?

In my case some knowledge of HTML to update the site. A good knowledge of the industry, computer and online industry, to know where information is and how to get it.

My day

What does your average day look like?

Hectic. I get up around noon, turn on my Mac, log on to my BBS for mail, then AOL, and the other Nets for e-mail. I then go on the Web, surfing, looking for new sites to write about. I also am writing articles for the paper, obtaining permission from authors, sending articles to the editor, calling and discussing layout and design with my designer, updating the

Web page with new stuff, go out looking for ads locally, am working on a couple of books, so am looking for research on that, writing, and editing.

Since I work at home, I take frequent breaks to go down and play with my two boys, age 3 and 1 1/2, and see the wife occasionally :) I am also putting together a weekly Internet radio show that will be broadcast on a local station and the Internet, so work with that. Also, I am getting ready to teach Internet surfing at a local CompUSA. I stopped teaching college a few years ago. I am on the phone during the day as well, talking to third party companies about sponsoring MUG News Service news disks for user groups. I run three online forums, two on AOL (Environmental forum and the Society for Environmental Journalists) and one on eWorld (EcoLinking), so I have to update those as well, answer e-mail, update conferences and libraries, routine stuff. I usually write or surf the NET at night till about 7 A.M. when I go to sleep, only to get up at 11 A.M. or noon to start all over. Each day is different though. Whew, I'm tired just reading this.

What does your job entail?

I am the conductor of my Internet orchestra. As I said earlier, I am like a traffic cop, trying to make sure there are no traffic accidents, and that everything (everyone) is working smoothly.

How many hours a week do you spend working on your site?

I spend close to 15 to 18 hours a day doing this.

What percentages of time are spent on each task?

I would say that 50 percent of my time is writing, the other 50 percent is dealing with people and gathering resources

What was the hardest part of the job in the beginning?

Leaving a paying job with no start up money to go my own way.

What do you like most about your work?

Independence. I love being able to be creative when I WANT to, not when someone tells me to. I love challenges and making things happen. I like to take a concept and make it become reality. I could never work for anyone other than myself again.

What do you like least?

The insecurity of periods when you have no income, thinking maybe there will be no more income.

What was your greatest moment?

Hasn't happened yet.

How did the startup phase affect your personal life?

It was pretty rough but I got lucky. The same month I quit my paying job I got a book contract with a nice advance. I also got married the same year :)

Are you glad you are on the Web for personal and business reasons?

Where else can you meet people from around the world without leaving your chair! I started doing this in the late 70s first starting my own BBS, then getting on CompuServe when it first opened, and then the early Internet and Usenet. I can't imagine NOT being online (but I do have an off-line life as well–I practice martial arts, am a musician).

Given what you know now, would you do it again?

Does the sun rise every morning :) Sure would.

The future

What is your next venture?

I am going to create a multimedia publishing company.

What else would you like to say?

I never give advice to anyone since I don't take advice but one observation I pass on to anyone. As the Nike commercial says, Just "do it." It is better to try something and fail than never try it at all. For every good idea you have there will be 50 people trying to prevent you from acting on it. There is no such thing as failure. The experience is positive since it shows you that something didn't work as planned, but it also means there is another path that will work. One of the greatest things about the NET is you can try almost anything without a great deal of startup cost if you have some imagination and perseverance.

BOOKS FOR SALE

Overview—So you have a couple hundred or thousand books from college and you want to sell them on the Net? And you figure if you sell those, then why not sell more? You're in the right place. Book sellers have reported brisk sales. Book publishers have their own sites (including my publisher, Van Nostrand Reinhold, http://www.vnr.com), where people can place orders via the net or phone or fax.

Remember, you don't have to own a bookstore. You can join a new breed of bookseller that doesn't have a storefront; but exists only online. These companies might or might not have inventory. They mainly function as a front end for a drop shipping business. In other words, they place information about the book, such as title, topic, overview, and price and then wait for the orders. When someone calls, they process the order information and then call their supplier, who ships it directly to the consumer.

In either case, your bookstore can offer collections of books that appeal to specialized audiences, such as business books, comic books, romance novels, art books, oriental literature, or Judaica.

Rewards—You'll benefit from sales. You minimize your risks by not carrying inventory. The only costs you incur are for running the Home Page.

Risks—Normal business risks.

Special marketing elements for the Home Page—The strength of a bookseller's Home Page lies in the power of the database engine that can find books quickly and display the information attractively to the viewer. You'll want to allow the consumer to choose books by category (romance, sports, adventure, etc.), as well as by title or author. Building the database is a task that can be performed by talented database programmers (of which there are a few). The hardest part will be to edit the data for the database, the book title, info, and price. Of course, you'll have to negotiate purchases from the publishers or from local bookstores that agree to work with you. Publishers generally will give discounts beginning at 40 percent for single copy sales. A local bookstore might take the order and ship it for you for a lower discount to cover their costs.

Links to Home Pages
See the interview with Tall Tales - Fine Speculative Fiction–
        http://www.halcyon.com/msk/talltales.htm
See the case study of C.W. Hay Bookseller–
        http://www.maple.net/cwhay/index.html
Dial-A-Book–http://www.dab.psinet/dialabook/
Science Fiction Shop–http://www.tagsys.com/Ads /SciFiShop

INTERVIEW—TALL TALES–FINE SPECULATIVE FICTION

TALL Tales

• Fine Speculative Fiction First Editions

• Michael and Debra Kerstetter, Proprietors

Welcome to the TALL Tales homepage!

Last changed 16 August 1995.

What's New. Catalog #17 is now ready for your perusal. I hope that you find a many things to please and delight you! Things around here are going as well as can be expected when preparing for a new baby. I've got a list of things to get done a mile long and no time in which to accomplish them. Imagine that. And these baby classes... they're taking up all my Saturdays! What happened to the good old days when the father just sat in the waiting room reading a good book? Ah the good life. Actually, the classes wouldn't be so bad except we're the only people in the class with grey hair. It's disgusting! And I'm sorry, but a couple of those fathers don't look old enough to SHAVE much less start a family!! I'm so old. Now that I'm thoroughly depressed, I'll stop so you can get to the catalog. Remember, buy lot's of books: Baby needs a college fund!

Figure 9–5. Homes Pages should display the company's mission statement prominently.

Michael S. Kerstetter

Tall Tales - Fine Speculative Fiction

6219 SE 137th Place

206-228-2760

Renton, WA

http://www.halcyon.com/msk/tlltales.htm

e-mail: msk@halcyon.com

Background

What are you hoping to accomplish by being on the Web?

I'm not a small businessman, I'm a tiny businessman, and a part-timer at that. I deal in a particular subset of a highly specialized genre of literature (quality collectable science fiction/fantasy/horror). I can't establish a growing business concern on just my local customer base, and advertising outlets are also pretty restricted. My main hope for the Web was to broaden my customer base and at least make enough sales to cover my Internet costs.

How has being on the Web been beneficial?

The Web (and mailing lists and USENET) has certainly fulfilled my stated hope. My catalogs go all over the world, even to China and Croatia. I've sold books to customers in many countries who would otherwise never have heard of me. And I've easily sold enough to more than cover my Internet expenses. An unanticipated benefit has been in *acquiring* merchandise from dealers and from individuals through contacts made because of the Web.

What advice would you offer a Web entrepreneur?

Keep your expectations realistic! Only a small percentage of business people are going to succeed in establishing a self-sustaining business based solely on electronic commerce. Even fewer are going to get rich at it. It should be viewed as one tool in your business toolbox, not the whole toolbox itself. But I don't want to minimize the opportunities and benefits, either. The customers I've gained from Internet, while not usually big spenders, are often moderate spenders and very often repeat customers! Also, learn about the resources on the Web. Spend time surfing, checking out bulletin boards and mailing lists, and establishing links and references to your business on other sites. It will take time and effort, but the idea is to get as much visibility as possible. Remember that getting a site on the Web doesn't mean that the world knows you're there or how to get to you.

CASE STUDY–C.W. HAY BOOKSELLER

Welcome to C.W. Hay Bookseller

- About Our Bookstore
- This Month's Featured Selection
- What's up for Next Month's Books
- Order Forms
- Out of Print Requests
- The Reader (Latest Reviews)
- Top 10 National & Our's Local
- BIP the Research Disc
- Book Search

Figure 9-4. This Home Page's menu makes sense of a mountain of books. Courtesy of C.W. Hay Bookseller.

Bill Hay   http://www.maple.net/cwhay/index.html

C.W, Hay Bookseller   bhay@maple.net

Canada

905-728-8011

Background

Who is your primary audience?

Not yet known, but looks like special orders and hard to gets that require research to find, then order and deliver.

How will they benefit from your service?

Not many can be found with the research tools and experience in finding and obtaining this type of book from around the world! We do it every-day in our mail order business and so it falls naturally into our system.

Was it meant to generate income on its own or to steer people to your store?

Really meant to be an addition to our existing sales.

Where is your business located?

Storefront.

What is your background and training?

Twenty years of selling books!!

Getting started

When did you start your business?

Incorporated 1980.

Did you create a business plan before going online?

Yes and no! Pretty much browsed around until I found out about HTML and WWW sites, then decided to float a Home Page out there and see if anyone even looked at it.

How much time did it take to get up and running?

About six weeks part time while I ran my regular business.

Did you create the pages yourself?

Learned from scratch.

How much did it cost to get started?

Other than the cost of books, I just invested my own time.

How did you obtain your startup capital?

N/A

How did you promote your Home Page?

Various listings on the net, Yahoo, yellow pages and any classified space I could find.

How much did it cost to promote your site?

Nothing, if you look around and avoid all the sharks out there who make you think you need them.

How long did it take until you made your first sale?

About a day after the Web site went on line.

How much money has your company made online?

We have begun to see a little response now, $50 per week. I believe we have been on line for five weeks now. I firmly believe this is a word of mouth deal. Provide service and it will amount to something gradually. There are no major quick bucks in this environment as far as I am concerned. Be prepared for the long haul and steady improvement as you go!

How much money do you hope to make?

As above.

What mistakes did you make that you wish you hadn't made?

So far not many.

What advice would you give to a similar startup?

Look at it first, maybe a month. Pick what you like when you see it and make notes of those good and bad things. Formulate where you think you can fit in and then do it!

What skills are necessary to run a business?

Our experience and set up plus some new computer skills.

What special qualities are needed to run your site?

Nothing special.

My day

What does your average day look like?

Small business people never rest!

What does your job entail?

Don't Ask!!

How many hours a week do you spend working on your site?

I don't have time to surf, so line time involves answering mail and taking orders. About 1/2 hour per day at present.

What percentages of time are spent on each task?

N/A

What was the hardest part of the job in the beginning?

N/A

What do you like most about your work?

Novel experience of talking with people around the world.

What do you like least?

Nothing.

What was your greatest moment?

Shipping a book to Osaka, Japan.

How did the startup phase affect your personal life?

Not at all.

Are you glad you are on the Web for personal and business reasons?

Sure! The more business we do the better!

Given what you know now, would you do it again?

Sure.

The future

What is your next venture?

Make the site current, relevant, and attractive for people to want to come to.

POET

Overview—If you're a poet and know it, you can post your poems on your Home Page. We don't know if you'll make any money at it, since people don't seem to want to pay for poetry in book stores either, but you'll be able to get your mission and creative vision out to the world. What could be better than that?

Rewards—Sales from subscriptions, books, advertisements, and links to related pages.

Risks—Normal business risks.

Special marketing elements for the Home Page—Print selected poems, reviews, and testimonials to get people interested in subscribing. If you do readings at colleges, bookstores, or coffee houses, list those dates. See other advice in this chapter as well as ideas from the Business Model-Magazine Publishers in Chapter 4.

PRESS RELEASE SERVICE

Newstips Inc. is a Public Relations company that specializes in companies in and around the computer industry. In addition to performing traditional publicity services, Newstips Inc. produces media receptions at trade shows through its Newstips Events Division. Newstips Inc. also traffics more than 500 review requests in a typical month, through Product Sweep electronic editorial review solicitations. The flagship of Newstips Inc. is its weekly Newstips Electronic Editorial Bulletin, which reaches over 2,000 computer industry journalists every week.

What is the Newstips Electronic Editorial Bulletin?

- What computer industry luminaries are _saying_ about Newstips
- Past _issues_ of Newstips Electronic Editorial Bulletin.
- The Newstips badge card
- Related browsing on the Internet.
- NEW The NetWorld + InterOp Newstips Bulletin NEW
- NEW Web Reply Cards NEW

Figure 9-5. Newstips provides companies with a method to target their news to editors in the computer and software industry.

Overview—PR Newswire and Business Wire both send company press releases about companies to reporters. However, these services are general in nature. They target only a few vertical markets, such as computers and automobiles. Entrepreneurs can create their own news service for their own industry. They will make money by charging companies to print and distribute the news release over the Internet, or any other e-mail service, fax, or mail service the company selects.

Rewards—There is no upward limit on how much money you could make, as you can print and distribute an unlimited number of press releases. PR Newswire charges about $400 to send a press release to its entire nationwide network of reporters. Additional fees can be attained by writing press releases or doing additional publicity services for companies.

Risks—Normal business risks.

Special marketing considerations for Home Pages—The features and benefits of this service must be spelled out clearly, along with the costs. These types of services generally offer many different layers of service and service options, so pricing can become confusing. Be explicit.

Links to Home Pages

Marty Winston's Newstips is an institution in the computer industry. Despite competition from PR Newswire and BusinessWire, Newstips has an active following among companies and reporters who eagerly await each issue. To learn all about this fascinating source of information, go to http://www.newstips.com/newstips. Marty says the Home Page "more than paid for itself" in just a few weeks of going online.

10 DRAMATIC ARTS

As time goes by, actors will give performances on the Internet on a pay-per-view basis, or for free to get exposure for their services. Today, the Internet can be used as a talent agency, a way for actors to promote their services directly to corporations (yes, corporations. Many actors make their living by doing presentations at trade shows and conventions, or starring in corporate videos!) and the entertainment industry. Screen writers, too can promote their services online. You can also start a talk radio business.

TALENT AGENCY

Overview—Entrepreneurs can also start a talent agency for local actors, mimes, street musicians, entertainers, children's party entertainers, models, and others.

Rewards—You could make money by:

• Creating a Home Page and selling ad space to actors,
• Creating Home Pages for actors and charging for your services.
• Selling links from your page to theirs.
• Acting as an agent, you could charge a commission for actual bookings.

Risks—Normal business risks apply.

Special marketing considerations for Home Pages—This is a starting page (See Chapter 4, Business Models, Starting Pages) for people in the entertainment industry. As such, it should be fun and lively. Use your creativity to make it a cool place that would attract people and keep them coming back.

You'll want to have pictures of the actors, since their faces make the first impression. Follow up with more information about their measurements, experience, and desired work.

Practical examples and links to Home Pages

Please see the case study for Red Herring Productions in this chapter.

Red Herring Productions—`http://www.bayne.com/wolfBayne/mystery/`

ACTORS AND ENTERTAINERS

Overview—Actors and entertainers can post their own Home Pages in the hopes of landing jobs.

Rewards—By listing your talents and promoting them to the world, you might be able to get jobs.

Risks—Time and setup costs.

Special marketing elements for the Home Page—Your online marketing materials should include the basic package you have probably already created for getting jobs right now. That includes a professionally taken photo, your acting experience, desired roles, fees, travel restrictions (if any), and the like.

To make your page come alive, draw on your creative resources. You can also include short audio and video files of your best scenes, which viewers can retrieve and play on their computers.

Practical examples and links to Home Pages

Please see the case study for Red Herring Productions—

```
http://www.bayne.com/wolfBayne/mystery/
```

CASE STUDY—RED HERRING PRODUCTIONS, MELODRAMAS

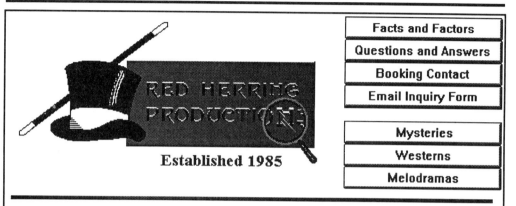

	Facts and Factors
	Questions and Answers
	Booking Contact
	Email Inquiry Form
	Mysteries
	Westerns
	Melodramas

Established 1985

You are visitor number 606 to Red Herring since July 29, 1995.

*Let **Murder** and **Mayhem** Turn Into **Fun***
At Your Next Corporate, Community or Personal Function.

Browse through our catalog to choose from mysteries, westerns and melodramas. Review some fa
answer some questions then find out who to contact to plan your next fun-filled meeting.

Facts and Factors
Questions and Answers
Booking Contact
Email Inquiry Form

Figure 10-1. This classy logo and push-button design create an attractive page. Courtesy of WolfBayne Communications.

Kim M. Bayne

Red Herring Productions
P.O. Box 50287
Colorado Springs, CO
80949-0287
719-593-8032

Red Herring Productions—
http://www.bayne.com/wolfBayne/mystery/
rhp@bayne.com
wolfBayne Communications
http://www.bayne.com/wolfBayne/
kimmik@bayne.com

Background

RHP is an acting troupe that specializes in staging original audience interactive murder mysteries, westerns, and melodramas. Kim Bayne, who completed the interview form, is an actor, the online ad agency and online booking agent for Red Herring Productions, an entirely separate business that she does not own.

Who is your primary audience?

Red Herring Productions targets corporate meeting planners, event managers, trade show producers, or anyone else needing entertainment for a business or special event.

How will they benefit from your service?

- RHP shows are increasingly used to:
- Communicate a message, such as introducing products in a fun and different way.
- Relax conference attendees, especially after a full day of lectures or dry business functions. A melodrama is a great way to relax and unwind.
- Build team spirit, such as in a murder mystery where audience members are called upon to form teams and determine who solved the murder. This is a particularly useful team-building experience for national sales meetings where participants only see each other once or twice a year in person. The audience members get a chance to problem solve together, which builds camaraderie.

How does your service differ from others?

It is entertainment, pure and simple. You can't take it home with you, unless, of course, you count the good feelings, laughter, and feedback you'll get from an event that incorporates humor and fun.

Is this business an offshoot of your existing business, or does it exist only on the Internet?

The owners of Red Herring Productions were expanding their marketing efforts, so I suggested that a Web page would be a unique and inexpensive way to publicize their "products." RHP has been marketed through chambers of commerce, visitor and convention bureaus, meeting planning associations, and event management companies. They've been using "word-of-mouth" marketing tactics, referral bookings, and some direct mail to publicize their programs.

If it is an offshoot, was it meant to generate income on its own or to steer people to your other outlets?

This is hardly comparable to what I regularly earn in my agency. I earn a 10% commission on RHP bookings that are from the Internet or World Wide Web. This is a unique arrangement for me as an agency, because if I was not an actor in the troupe, I would have never agreed to a commission arrangement. I also hope to increase RHP's bookings in exchange for more acting gigs.

I use the Red Herring Web page as one example of my HTML work. Sometimes the RHP page pulls people to my site, but more often than not, people access the wolfBayne or HTMARCOM pages first and then jump to the RHP page out of curiosity. People who visit the RHP page independently usually get connected through random entertainment or meeting planner links, or through one of the online search engines.

Where is your office located?

I currently have a home office for wolfBayne Communications. None of the RHP owners have a separate office specifically for RHP business. They all have other jobs/careers and run RHP in their spare time from their homes.

What is your background and training?

On the professional side, I have been involved in marketing communications since 1981. I've worked on both the agency and the company side of computer and electronics marketing. My masters degree is in Computer Resources Management. On the hobby side, I have been on stage, either singing or acting for fun since I was six. My love for performing arts combined with my work as an Internet marketing consultant brought about RHP's Web page.

When did you start your business?

I have been involved in high tech marketing since 1981. Red Herring Productions has been around since 1985. I booked them at a high tech symposium I helped organize in June 1988. I have been acting in their productions since August 1988. I started wolfBayne Communications in 1993. I put the RHP catalog on the Web in early January 1995.

How much money has your company made?

So far, the response rate has been small, with minimal qualified leads, mainly because I haven't done much more than put up the Web page. RHP owners haven't started using the Web page address in their literature yet. I get mostly inquiries from actors and script writers. One real lead came from a semiconductor company two days after the page went up. The client was planning a sales meeting in Colorado Springs and needed some entertainment. The booking resulted from a combination of things. I had done a few public relations projects for the client several months earlier and my internal company contact mentioned that I was also involved with this troupe. The fact that the client could get the catalog on the Internet didn't hurt either.

Getting started

How much did time did it take to get up and running?

Originally, one of the owners of the troupe e-mailed the text of the catalog from his account at his day job. The RHP page was fairly easy to set up initially, taking only a morning, although I've spent time since its launch tweaking a few things here and there, such as adding an e-mail inquiry form.

Did you create the pages yourself or did you get help?

I just took Mike's e-mail message and did a cut and paste. The HTML was pretty straightforward and easy. Nothing exciting or cutting edge here.

How much did it cost to get started?

My time probably has run into far more hours than I care to admit. I think a similar Web page would run around $500. That doesn't include any online promotional efforts though, which will take more time than setting up the site.

Did you need to go to an outside source for startup capital?

I already was in place on the Internet, and I'm not charging the troupe for storage space because it hardly makes a dent in my monthly bill. The entire RHP Web presence consists of only four files, the catalog, the e-mail inquiry form, the image-mapped graphic and the image map file. There's been some discussion about expanding that, with the addition of pictures, but it's not a top priority for now.

What mistakes did you make that you wish you hadn't made?

I spent far too much time on the RHP pages than I had originally planned.

What advice would you give someone starting a business?

Budget your hours and stick to it! It's too easy to keep going and going and going (picture the Energizer Bunny right here) whenever you think of another "neat" thing you can do to a Web page.

Sing this to yourself whenever you sit down to do HTML (sung to the tune of Shari Lewis' *This Is the Song That Never Ends* from the PBS Show Lambchop's Play-Along):

> * *This is the site that never ends*
> *It just goes on and on my friends.*
> *Somebody started coding it not knowing what it was*
> *And they'll continue coding it forever, just because...*

(Repeat verse from here * until you get carpal tunnel syndrome and your eyes can't focus anymore)

Parody of lyrics written by Kim M. Bayne (satire IS protected under copyright law...look it up!).

What skills would a person need to conduct business?

Acting and/or directing skills and experience. A knowledge of mystery, western and melodrama literature and script writing skills are a must to produce original plays. A good stable of dependable actors willing to work for less than equity wages, a good meal at a fancy resort, and the fun of being in a production.

Don't forget that you also need receptive audiences.

What education is necessary to run your site?

A knowledge of HTML and/or graphic design, good contacts with those that have this knowledge, OR a willingness to learn.

What special qualities are needed to run your site?

To run a murder mystery troupe, you need many people, most of which are contractors, wardrobe, producer/director, business manager, actors of many shapes and sizes, the tolerance of significant others, who don't mind your being gone multiple nights in a row for performances, a good sense of humor.

How did you promote your site?

See above. I currently don't have any plans to do much online promotion, unless, of course it is part of another project I'm working on. The owners of the troupe might send out a news release to the local business press.

How much did it cost to promote your site?

N/A

How long did it take until you got your first sale?

Two days.

How did the startup phase affect your personal life?

It was such a small project that it had no impact.

General

Are you glad you are on the Web on personal and business reasons?

Yes, I couldn't have made it as an independent marketing consultant without the Internet. Red Herring Productions, on the other hand, is continuing to operate as they did before, so it has had minimal impact on their business (mainly because of the promotion factor).

Given what you know now, would you do it again?

Sure. One of RHP's event management contacts was "impressed" that RHP had a Web presence. Another firm found the page on the Web while surfing. They are actually here in town, but had never heard of RHP, so that was a twist for an international medium!

The future

What is your next venture?

I'm currently working on a site for the Business Marketing Association, which will launch by the time this book is out.

SCREENWRITER

Overview—It seems like everyone is writing a screenplay. Why not promote your ideas on the Internet?

Rewards—You might reach the person who can bring your characters to life.

Risks—Someone could steal your idea. You wouldn't have any way to prove it was stolen, either.

Special marketing elements for the Home Page—Your Home Page should tell the world who you are, previously published, or produced works. You might want to limit the amount of creative ideas you give away to protect your scripts. However, you do need to show readers that you have compelling ideas.

PERFORM ON THE INTERNET

Overview—Why not start your own Internet Web Radio show? You can do drama, comedy, or even singing. There are several technological hurdles at this point, such as the problem in delivering real-time audio, which is made easier by VocalTel, which allows people to use their computers and the Internet to talk to one another by dialing a local Internet number. Downloading audio files in real-time is also a problem that will be overcome shortly. You also need to establish an admittance fee and a way of keeping out gate crashers.

Rewards—Charge people on a pay per view basis. If they want to attend, they must type in a password that is good for that night's show. No one does this now, so you would be the first and get a lot of publicity. You can also sell sponsorships, ads, and links from your Home Page or show.

Risks—Technology can be flaky, so productions might be similar to the quality of a 1950's TV show. People might forgive this quality to be part of a new venture, or they might say it isn't MTV and tune you out.

TALK RADIO ON THE INTERNET

- **How to Attend**
- **Enter Internet Roundtable**
- **Upcoming Guests**
- **Biographies and Transcripts**

The Internet Roundtable is much more than just an hour of exciting discussion - it's your point of departure to a journey of the mind. Always enlightening and inquisitive, the Roundtable is a window into the insights of the policy makers, innovators, authors, and artists who shape today's political and cultural world. Open this window and follow any number of fascinating paths ready for your exploration.

Roundtables cover the gamut from best-selling authors to national policy makers. Topics range from the Arts to Zaire, and everything in between. Our goal is to provide an arena for worldwide discussions about the interesting people and issues of today.

Figure 10-2. Internet Round Table is a cross between National Public Radio and Larry King Live! Copyright 1995, Internet Roundtable Society.

Overview—Talk radio is alive on the Internet, although someone really should invent a new term, because it isn't really radio. They are chat sessions in which host and guest type their answers. WebChat software from Internet Roundtable Society allows you to create multimedia chat sessions, complete with images, video, audioclips, and links. You'll also have a transcript of the cyber conversation when you are done, `http//www.irsociety.com/webchat.html`.

Real time audio is coming along quickly. Check out the software from VocalTel, `http://www.vocaltel.com`, which gives you the ability to talk to other people on the Internet by dialing a number that is local to you.

You must be able to interview guests, be entertaining, and moderate the calls from listeners.

Rewards—You can make money selling advertisements on the show and on the Home Page. You can make tapes of the interviews and sell them via the Internet, or get distribution in the retail channel, or via direct mail. If you interview authors, you can sell their books directly from your Home Page.

Risks—Normal business risks.

Special marketing considerations for Home Pages—Talk shows should list the roster of upcoming guests and their backgrounds or links to their Home Pages. Instructions for participating are very important. This means listing what kind of hardware and software are required, as well as how to ask questions and participate in the discussion. Without proper moderating, the conferences can turn into a mishmash of a cocktail party with everyone's messages coming helter skeleter and not making any sense.

Links to Home Pages

Internet Roundtable, a weekly interview show produced by Internet Roundtable Society— `http://www.irsociety.com`

Internet Talk Radio, the first talk radio show on the Internet, specializes in technical topics. You can receive audito transcipts and clips from old shows at `http://www.nsca.uiuc.edu/radio/radio.html`

11 VISUAL ARTS

Since the first stop for many Internet newbies (new Internet subscribers) is the Louvre, Paris' majestic art museum, you would think art galleries would do a thriving businesses on the Internet. Visual artists have an appreciative audience awaiting them on the Internet. This is not surprising because the Internet is a visual medium People like graphics, art, pictures, and the ability to ponder their significance.

This chapter will show how entrepreneurial artists can sell paintings and clip art, operate an art gallery, market photographic services and art photographs as well as merchandise cartoons on the Internet.

Entrepreneurs can also create Home Pages to promote traffic in their retail operations or create online versions of these stores. To get your mind flowing with ideas, here are a few suggested businesses as well as references to similar business overviews and case studies in this book.

SELL CLIP ART

Overview—Clip art and stock photography are used to illustrate slides that accompany speeches, brighten company newsletters, or act as the focal point in advertisements and brochures. The market for these products is unending, as tremendous numbers of people give speeches every day and seek to illustrate their ideas. Although many software programs come with clip art, speakers want their presentations to look unique. Those people are your potential customers.

You can sell clip art on the Internet, such as line drawings in black and white or color, or photographs based on timeless themes, such as cars, nature. However, virtually every topic should be considered for your portfolio.

You can set your own prices for clip art, with higher prices going for more talented work and unique topics. Commercial clip art, sold in software stores, can be quite cheap, about $2 per dozen images. Remember that you can make money by selling in volume.

To succeed in this business, you will need artistic skills, a wide repertoire of samples and marketing ability.

Rewards—Creating newsletters and brochures is one the major uses of computers. Therefore, you will find a large potential audience. You can make incremental income by creating the artwork once and selling it many times. Your cost of goods and time remains the same whether you sell the work one time or 100 times.

Risks—As with any business, people can steal your work and not pay your fee. Further, you might not have any way of knowing they ever used your work unless it came to your attention by accident. Therefore you need to take precautions to protect your work. Consider these two options:

Create a portfolio of clip art that is limited in number, but shows your talent and personality (such as humor). If people like your style, they will order your portfolio.

Disable the art in some way, such as putting your signature in a key portion of the viewing field. Alert your prospects that these are samples and the versions they by will have a clear viewing area.

Special marketing considerations for Home Pages—To protect their work, artists home pages should always contain prominent notices about copyright laws and the penalties for violation.

Artists' home pages will be held to a higher standard than those of other vendors. If your home page isn't visually attractive, then what can a consumer expect from the rest of your work?

Artists can create their own persona online by listing their exhibitions and dates, reviews and testimonials from critics, and clients.

Content for the home page should include portfolios of your work so people can get a feel for your style. The work should be displayed in small, postage stamp sizes so they can transmit quickly to the viewer's screen. To prevent widespread copying and theft, don't include larger versions which would fit neatly into newsletters. Save those for the paying customers.

ART GALLERY

Overview—You don't have to be an artist to sell art on the Internet. Entrepreneurs can start a Home Page gallery of works they arrange to show on consignment. That way, there is no out-of-pocket expenditure for inventory. You could also charge the artist for the space you provide and the promotion you create that attract connoisseurs to your site. You could charge artists for creating Home Pages. Finally, you could charge local galleries for advertisements on your page, or for links to their pages (or you might do this in exchange for a link from their site to yours). The site can also sell art books.

Rewards—Increased sales and exposure.

Risks—You can put art on the walls of the Internet for people to admire, but will people buy art on the net? Fortunately for artists, paintings aren't cheap. I think if the old joke of a blind man selling pencils on the street corner. He holds a signs saying "Pencils, $1 million dollars." A passerby says, "Mister, you aren't going to sell many pencils at a million dollars apiece." "Mister, the blind man replied, "I only need to sell one." Lots of entrepreneurs are trying. Competition should not be a problem given the variety of styles and schools of art, and the prices, and tastes of consumers.

Special marketing elements for the Home Page—For all artwork on the Internet, copyright notices should be posted prominently. Strict warning should be placed regarding the prohibition of copying artwork on the Internet and off-line. Some people actually think they are doing you a favor by posting your art on their sites—even if they give full credit because they think they are publicizing the work. Tell them the cannot do this!

Artwork by its nature will be a large file. This can be a problem as large files take long times to appear on people's screens. You might consider offering a postage-stamp sized view of the painting that people see at first, and a larger view that they can see only if they really want to invest the time.

To attract people to your site month after month, consider posting news of interest to the local art community, like gallery openings, exhibits and classes, and bios of artists that include their exhibitions.

Links to Home Pages

ArtSpeak—`http://www.teleport.com/artspeak`

Art on the Net—`http://www.art.net`

ARTIST

Overview—You don't need a gallery to sell art on the Net. An entrepreneurial artist working in any meda—watercolors, sculpture, clay, mixed media, photography, or the like—can create a home page and sell works directly to the public.

Rewards—By selling art directly, you cut out the middleman, the gallery. You'll keep more money. However, galleries that market correctly will be able to draw more people to see your work.

Risks—Normal business risks.

Special marketing considerations for Home Pages—See discussion in Art Gallery in this chapter.

Links to Home Pages
Anne Burkholder—

http://www.inetnebr.com/lincoln/a_and_e/gallery/Anne_Burkholder

Chris Rigatuso—http://www.art.net/rigatuso

CASE STUDY—BILL SCHWAB, PHOTOGRAPHS

Welcome to the electronic base of
Bill Schwab Photography
You are among the 2012 people to have visited since June 1st. 1995!

We invite you to sit back, relax and spend some time browsing the photographic work of Detroit, Michigan based commercial/fine art photographer Bill Schwab

FINE ART
COMMERCIAL
ABOUT THE PHOTOGRAPHER

Please take the time to sign our
GUESTBOOK
It's great to know who and where
you are! Visitors

LINKS TO GO

Figure 11-1. Photographers can promote their services and pictures on the Internet. Copyright 1995, Bill Schwab Photography.

Bill Schwab   http://www.webcom.com/~snap1/

Bill Schwab Photography   snap1@webcom.com

15134 Colson   Phone: 313-584-0029

Dearborn, MI. 48126   Fax: 313-584-6003

Background

Who is your primary audience?

Designers, Art Directors, Surfers of the Net with photo interest.

How will they benefit from your product or service?

My intent for my site is to offer instant samplings of my work to potentially interested parties as well as to build name recognition in the photographic industry. Normally I have to advertise through direct mail which is wasteful and costly. This way my work is there all the time for potential clients to access when they find a need for services I can fulfill.

How does your product or service differ from others?

A growing number of photographers have a presence on the Web, but most are still making cold calls and direct mail campaigns and are not literate in the world of digital photography. I can transmit reproduction quality images while clients wait potentially eliminating the need for overnight express mail services. This gives an obvious edge in time and ease.

Is this business an off-shoot of your existing business, or does it exist only on the Internet?

If it is an offshoot, was it meant to generate income on its own or to steer people to your other outlets?

Definitely an offshoot at this time although there is room to grow. Basically it is a means to advertise my services to potentially millions of people for a relatively low cost.

Where is your office located?

My business has been home based for over five years although in a separate area build for this purpose as to separate life from business. I also have an off site studio space for when that need arises. However most of my work is done on location.

What is your background and training?

I have a Bachelor of Fine Arts in photography and commercial design plus years of on the job experience in the photographic field. All of my computer training is self taught due to it's mostly being on the cutting edge. Not many textbooks on digital imaging when I started!

When did you start your business?

Mid-1980's for the photo business, January 1995 on the Web.

How did you promote your site?

Business cards, mailings, newsgroup postings, search engines on the Web.

How much did it cost to promote your site?

VERY little. Mostly time and effort. Hard to put a dollar figure on this one.

How long did it take until you got your first sale?

One month.

How much has your company made?

N/A

How much money do you expect to make?

The sky is the limit. Not much at this time though. Most money on the Net seems to be made at this time by the servers we all have to use. I feel this will change as more people become literate in and familiar with this new form of communication.

Getting started

Did you create a business plan before going online?

Business plan grew out of existing business.

How much did time did it take to get up and running?

One week although it is continuously evolving.

Did you create the pages yourself or did you get help?

All pages are self created.

How much did it cost to get started?

Less than $100.

Did you need to go to an outside source for startup capital?

No.

What mistakes did you make that you wish you hadn't made?

None than I can think of.

What advice would you give someone trying to start a similar business, or any business on the Net?

Don't expect immediate return on your investment of time and money. If you do, don't bother! However, if you want an inexpensive way to reach a great number of people world wide. Go for it! The book is still being written on this one and the sky is the limit. I have also found that the knowledge of your presence on the Web will impress even those who know little of it, as everyone knows of the Internet, your presence and knowledge gives a sign that you are with the times.

What skills would a person need to conduct business?

You will need a definite knowledge of computers as well as knowledge of the Internet and how it functions.

My day

What does your average day look like?

Phones, photo shoots, printing, trips to the lab, site maintenance.

What does your job entail?

Much travel, contact with people, scheduling, photographing, collecting receivables, etc.

How many hours a week do you spend working on your site?

Five to ten hours per week

What was the hardest aspect of the work in the beginning?

Most likely the time involved and educating myself in HTML codes.

What do you like most about your work?

All of it!

What do you like the least?

Billing and collections. Hotel rooms.

What was your greatest moment?

There are many, but as far as the WWW, my first serious inquiry over the Net.

How did the startup phase affect your personal life?

There was none! That sums it up pretty well. Starting and maintaining a business that supports you takes loads of time and effort. Don't be fooled. There is always work to be done if you want success.

Are you glad you are on the Web on personal and business reasons?

Most definitely!

Given what you know now, would you do it again?

Yes.

Where can people look for more advice?

Periodicals and magazines. Books (sorry) are obsolete by the time they are marketed. Things are moving way to quickly and magazines keep up better than textbooks.

The future

What is your next venture?

We are at work on a publishing business.

CASE STUDY—THE BORDERLINE NETAZINE

HUMOR NETAZINE

by Gabe Martin_____August '95____FREE!

$ Add a Link to The Borderline and **WIN** $1000

The Borderline is now being published in <u>print publications</u>.

Figure 11-2. Borderline Netazine's Home Page promotes its contest. Copyright 1995, The Borderline.

Gabe Martin

Borderline Netazine

7986 Valdosta Ave.

San Diego, CA 92126

http://www.cts.com/~borderln/

borderln@cts.com

619-695-1840

Background

The Borderline Netazine is the Home Page for cartoonist Gabe Martin, who, at sixteen is one of the youngest entrepreneurs on the Internet! He uses the site to show his cartoons, which can be viewed by anyone for free. He hopes to sell cartoons to "anyone who appreciates the Far-Sideish slant of my humor (and who wants) "a small humorous lift in their day. I like to think that my cartoons are funnier than some of the others on the Web. But of course, I'm prejudiced. :-)"

Is this business an off-shoot of your existing business, or does it exist only on the Internet?

I had tried submitting my cartoon to national syndicators, but as of yet, I haven't gotten an offer. However for the last year and a half I have been doing a monthly cartoon for the San Diego Gas & Electric company newsletter. This work can be quite challenging due to the conflicting goals of making a cartoon that is specific to a given article in the newsletter as well as something that can be used for the more diverse audience on the Internet. It is a paid gig however.

I assume that within a year or so there should be a general mechanism on the Web for charging small amounts (1 cent?, 1/10 cent?) for access to information on the Web (including cartoons). At that point I may decide to charge a nominal fee for the monthly updates or maybe access to the cartoon archive. My primary focus at this time however, is to get exposure for my work and to prove to any potential syndicator that I can reliably produce cartoons on a daily basis.

Where do you run your business?

I operate from home using the computer in my bedroom for producing the cartoons. I use the computers in the dining room for e-mail, Web browsing, etc.

What is your background and training?

I have no formal training in cartooning or art. Since I was very young I've been making birthday cards for relatives. Along the way I decided that they were more interesting if there was a humorous twist to them. That's basically how I got started.

The cartooning side obviously required years of practice along with some innate talent inherited from my mother. I probably inherited my particular sense of humor from my dad. Animated cartoons and cartoon strips also had a large influence on me. My dad is currently handling the business side of things. His experience with computers and his business in general has been a real asset.

When did you start your business?

I had been creating cartoons sporadically for a couple of years when my dad decided that we should put the cartoons up on the Internet Web. Starting Dec. 1,1994 I began putting a daily cartoon up on the Web. I had a "cushion" of 30 or so cartoons that I had already produced. This allowed me to ease into the routine of daily production without too much trouble.

How much money has your company made?

I currently make nothing off of my daily cartoon on the Web, although I do have a couple of minor offers for use of specific cartoons. I do make $50/cartoon/month that I make for the San Diego Gas & Electric Co.

How much money do you hope to make?

Eventually in two to three years - enough for a good living.

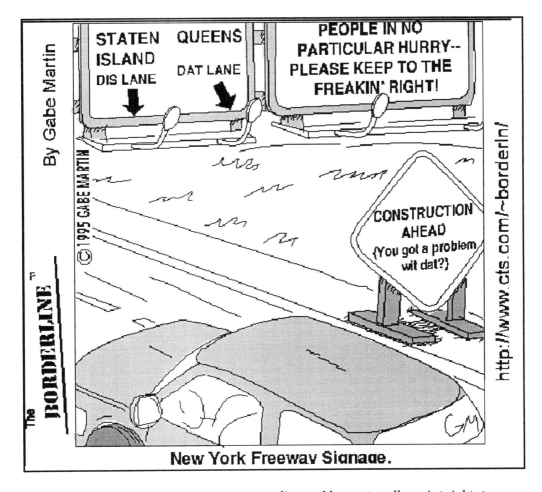

Figure 11-3. Borderline prints its cartoons online and hopes to sell reprint rights to companies. Copyright 1995, The Borderline.

Getting started

Did you create a business plan before going on-line?

No. There were too many unknowns at the time. Going on-line was basically an experiment to see how much exposure I could get for my work.

How much time did it take to get up and running?

It took approximately a month to get everything together. My Internet service provider normally didn't let individuals start their own Home Pages, but since this was just a hobby page, they decided to allow it. However, they made it clear that if I started to make money on the page then I would have to convert to a business (i.e., more expensive) account. Thankfully, after a few months, due to the popularity of my site (judged by the access statistics that they collected), they gave me a FREE upgrade to a business account. Their reason for doing so was that my site brought visitors to their server; visitors that might stick around to see what other services they had to offer.

Being nominated as the "Cool Site of the Day" also helped get their attention.

Did you create the pages yourself?

My dad, who is a PC analyst, took care of most of the technical details. He had to learn HTML and some UNIX, but all of the information was available on the Web (once you knew how to search for it) He also made sure that I knew everything about what he was doing so that I could run the whole process by my self should that become necessary. We still take turns updating the Home Page just to make sure that I can still do it.

How much did it cost to get started?

Since I already had a computer, the only cost for startup was the Internet access account. That cost about $75 for startup fees and the $23/month. for access to the Web, e-mail, FTP, etc. I've recently run up against my limit for file storage so I will have to decide to whether to remove some of the older stuff or continue to pay the additional storage fee (30 cents/Mb/day).

What mistakes did you make that you wish you hadn't made?

I wish I had gotten onto the Web even sooner than I did. There is always more attention given to the first success in any endeavor. Although I was the second (as far as I can determine), daily, Internet cartoon; the guy who does the FIRST, daily, Internet cartoon (Dave Farley—Dr.Fun) continues to get most of the attention/respect/etc. on the Web and recently signed a contract with a major syndicator, United Media. United Media had their Web site up for only a month or so when they picked up Dr.Fun.

What advice would you give someone starting an Internet business?

Move fast! Don't take too long to make decisions. The Web is a moving target; decisions that make sense today may not make sense next month or even tomorrow.

What skills would a person have to conduct business?

Since everything is funneled through a PC, you should have good working knowledge of computers and computer accessories.

How did you promote your Home Page?

I signed up with all of the major lists of sites that I came across. I also spent considerable time searching for sites that already had cartoon-related information on them. The Web Crawler and Lycos search pages were invaluable for this type of searching. Most people that I contacted were very receptive to adding a link to my cartoon page. The plan was to get as many sites as possible to put up a link to my page. This not only got the owner of the page to check out my site, it also would hopefully get some of the visitors to his site to also come.

Although the "cold calls" were productive, they were also time consuming. My dad got the idea of starting a contest on my page. The idea of the contest was that visitors could enter the contest if they put up a link to The Borderline on THEIR Home Page. If the link was on their page when their name was drawn then they would win the prize. The contest was set up with a weekly prize of a Borderline T-shirt and a grand prize of $1,000 (at the end of six months). My dad paid for the T-shirts and shipping (approx. $250) and I put up the $1,000 from my own money (as an investment in my future). So far (half-way through the contest) I've gotten over 500 valid entries for the contest. At the start of the contest I decided that 1,000 entries would make the contest a marketing success. If it is a success, my dad has promised to sponsor another bigger and better promotion.

How much did it cost to promote your site?

Nothing, other than the contest mentioned above.

How did the startup phase affect your personal life?

Long hours. Very little personal life during the startup.

What was the hardest part of the job in the beginning?

Uncertainty as to what might come of all this work.

How long did it take until you made your first sale?

Two weeks. I negotiated my first deal (for money) with someone who publishes a newsletter and wanted to use several of my cartoons that he had seen on the Internet. Hopefully this is just the beginning.

How long did it take to get established?

It took about a month to get a steady flow of daily visitors to the page.

My day

What does your average day look like?

Six to eight hours M-F working on producing the cartoons; usually later in the day. My dad spends another three to four hours a day working the business end of things. He recently received a layoff notice from the company where he has worked for six years and now plans to work with me full-time for at least six months to see if we can work The Borderline into a full-time job for one, or hopefully both of us.

What does your job entail?

Drawing cartoons.

How many hours a week do you spend working on your site?

30 hours/wk. between my dad and myself.

- 10% updating site (daily)
- 60% e-mail (fans, promotions, business contacts, etc.)
- 20% contest management 10% miscellaneous

General

What do you like most about your work?

Making people laugh.

What do you like least?

Investing all the time and effort of putting out a daily cartoon and (as of yet) getting very little in return. Put it down as the impatience of youth.

What was your greatest moment?

Recently I faxed one of my cartoons (Like you) to Art Bell (a national radio talk-show host). He said that even though he didn't normally like cartoons, he really liked this one. He liked it so much that he described it to his listeners (not an easy task for radio). Hopefully that wasn't my 15 (5?) minutes of fame.

Are you glad you are on the Web?

It's a fun place to be and it's the right place to be.

Given what you know now, would you do it again?

Sooner, bigger, better.

The future

What is your next venture?

I plan to expand the monthly features into more a full-fledged humor magazine.

What else would you like to say?

The Web it the perfect place for the entrepreneurs; a huge and growing customer base, little regulation, a level playing field (my page is the same "size" as IBM's!!), and limitless possibilities for the inventive mind.

Where can people look for more advice?

The information is all over the Web. The best places to look are on the Home Pages of the pages of the major Web browser companies. Most of the browser software comes built-in with direct access to the company's Home Page. They have detailed info on how to start Web pages, servers, etc.

12 MUSIC

The success of entertainment sites for rock stars, and the first "virtual concert" featuring the Rolling Stones shows that rock and roll is here to stay on the Internet. A large portion of Internet users are in college, recent grads, or involved with music as a business or hobby.

This chapter will look at how lyrical entrepreneurs can create new businesses on the Internet. Bands can sell records online, music stores can sell new and used equipment online or build store traffic and independent record producers can create an empire. To create an online talent agency for bands, see the materials regarding creating a Speaker's Bureau and the case study for Can*Speak in Chapter 8.

SELL MUSIC ONLINE

Overview—Musicians have embraced online services with a frenzy that is matched by some groups' music. Because many young people are on the Internet, musicians find a natural audience online. Most major music studios promote their top new releases online before the albums are released in stores.

Groups that don't have contracts with major studios can benefit greatly by posting their audio files on the Internet. They can reach a worldwide audience for only a few hundred dollars by creating a Home Page and promoting it by linking to other music Home Pages. They can take orders directly and keep the money that agents, distributors, and music stores would have siphoned off!

The strategy goes like this: post audio files of the songs on your Home Page that people can download and hear on their computers equipped with speakers. Cuts can be for 30 seconds so people get a good feel for your sound. However, you might decide to give away the title cut in the hopes of having people buy the entire album. Experiment to find which works best for your group. You can collect money by mail or credit cards delivered over the Internet, fax, or phone.

Rewards—Unknown local bands can reach a world-wide audience with the Internet. Consumers can hear snippets of songs and read the lyrics before buying the disk. Since the cost of mastering a CD is pretty low and Home Page design is reasonable, this strategy can be a good one that bands can't beat.

Risks—To prevent widespread copying, groups might want to load only a 30 second preview of their best song.

Special marketing elements for the Home Page—Several songwriters place the lyrics to their songs online as well, even for songs that aren't available online so people can get a feel for the tone and texture of the album. Musicians also include biographies or messages to their listeners which show the tone of the performer—a sweet folk singer, or a tear-your-eyes-out heavy metal group. These tactics help to create a persona for the artist and to begin to create a bond of kinship and rapport with the consumer.

MUSIC STORE, RECORD STORE (NEW AND USED)

Overview—Operators of stores selling new and used musical instruments can find a ready market on the Internet. Entrepreneurs can start their own business, without a storefront, by listing ads for used musical instruments. They can find instruments by perusing bulletin boards at record and music shops, pawn shops, garage sales, and flea markets. Entrepreneurs can use one of three business models:

Buy equipment that you like. This step ensures you will have inventory, but it could hurt your cash flow.

Sell equipment on consignment (i.e. you don't pay for anything until you sell it. You receive a share of the sale price—as much as 50 percent—for your efforts).

Sell advertising space on your Home Page to the owners of the instruments. An ad could sell for $25 a month. If you had 100 ads, you'd pocket $2,500.

Obtain a broker. You can get money when the article is bought.

Rewards—Retailers and entrepreneurs benefit from the low cost of advertising their wares to a world wide audience on the Internet. Risks—They must beware of rip-offs from people trying to steal equipment. Profits might also be squeezed by the cost of mailing, insurance, and returns from dissatisfied customers.

Special marketing elements for the Home Page—Because your inventory changes continuously and people's needs change as well, you need to draw people to your Home Page on a regular basis. This can be done by increasing the educational and entertainment value of the Home Page. Include articles on how to be a better drummer, how to form a band, or the like. Post sheet music from local artists who give you permission. Also, consider posting photos of the instruments so people can see that the products are not damaged. Consider giving a warranty or guarantee of satisfaction for a stated period of time.

Links to Home Pages

Apple Music—http://www.telport.com/~apple

RECORD PRODUCER

Overview—Future recording moguls and independent record producers can get their start through the Internet. By rounding up promising talent and placing them online, entrepreneurs can hope to create a musical empire. You must be able to find top talent and arrange for all technical recording operations, as well as promotion.

Rewards—Build an empire and entertain people.

Risks—Instead of finding the next Cher, you discover the next Sonny Bono. Also, because most start-up bands have little money, you might have to front all the cash for creating the CD and promoting it online and off-line.

Special marketing elements for the Home Page—Pictures, biographies, and fan club materials for the groups would be a good way to create personalities for the rockers and relationships with their soon-to-be fans. See other overviews in this section for ideas on selling records online.

FAN CLUB

Overview—Operating a fan club can be a fun, rewarding business that can be started and operated part-time while doing your real job, or going to school. This business can be run online and off-line. You can use the online service to send messages to members and offer products. The best bet is to sell memberships and give people access codes to see more information on the Home Page than non-members would see.

Rewards—Income.

Risks—Check with a lawyer to learn about copyright infringements. What can you do without getting a nasty note from the group's lawyer claiming you are stealing their famous mark?

Special marketing elements for the Home Page—Give something away for free to encourage people to join the fan club. Allow non-members to see a certain amount of information, but cut them off from the really good stuff. Only members who have registration numbers or passwords will get in to the neat stuff.

Links to Home Pages

Industry.net isn't really a Fan Club, but it does show you how to offer different levels of service and information to registered members and newcomers, `http://www.industry.net`.

RECORDING STUDIO

Overview—Recording studios make music for corporations, associations, and the like.

Rewards—Find new clients on the Internet.

Risks—Normal business risks.

Special marketing considerations for Home Pages—Recording studios can attract clients by offering 8-bit sound clips, which consumers can play on their computers. However, they can sell the more interesting 16-bit sound clips.

Links to Home Pages

SF Audio Net Pyramid Sound—`http://www.swaudionet.com`

INTERVIEW—SF AUDIO NET PYRAMID SOUND

Marc Paley—Production Manager

Sf Audio Net Pyramid Sound

39 Gilbert Street

San Francisco, CA 94103

`http://ww w.sfaudionet.com/`

`webmaster@sfaudionet.com`

`sfaudionet@aol.com` or `info@sfaudio net.com`

Background

What was your purpose in putting a Home Page on the Web?

The SF Audio Net is a full service audio production house, specializing in audio content for multimedia applications and advertising. The SFAN caters to multimedia producers and developers as well as advertising agencies, television and film producers. With its diverse team of experienced composers and sound designers the SF Audio Net is committed to musical excellence, innovation, and creative integrity. The SF Audio Net's inhouse facilities are conveniently located at Pyramind Sound recording studios in the city's SOMA district. These state of the art studios insure that all of the SF Audio Net projects are produced and engineered with the highest degree of technical savvy.

The SF Audio Net hopes to increase its exposure to the evolving global markets by having a strong presence on the Internet WWW. Having our own Web site allows us to broaden our target markets to include all those having Internet savvy and WWW access. It also provides content exposure for our inhouse record label, Native Recordings with the hopes of eventually selling our products via the Internet.

How has the Home Page helped your business?

Having our own Web site allows us to download and upload large amounts of digital audio/media to our clients without using overnight mail or shipping. It also allows us to have a real "presence" instead of just using AOL or CompuServe.

What advice would you give to a business starting on the Web?

Our advice to others is to take your time and do it right.

13 FOOD AND DINING

For many Americans, their first exposure to the Internet came from a news report that Pizza Hut was letting people order pizza on their Web Site. The story ran on the front page of many newspapers, including USA Today, as well as on the national news broadcasts.

Today, not only can you order food online, like lobsters, peanuts and hot sauces, you can also learn of new restaurants and bars in your area, or places you hope to visit.

This chapter will look at selling recipes and cookbooks, home-made products, dining establishments, mail order food businesses, Internet cafes, and cooking schools.

For additional online resources, read Food and Wine Online, Gary Holleman, Van Nostrand Reinhold.

SELLING RECIPES AND COOK BOOKS

Overview—When you look in the back of fine periodicals like the *Star* and *National Enquirer,* you always see offers for Granny's special home-made sauces. Send $2 and you'll get the secret recipe. That was then. This is now. Welcome to the Internet, where this same tactic can conceivably work for Epicurean entrepreneurs.

You'll need a host of recipes, a Home Page and marketing savvy to draw people in and make them salivate. If you've ever wanted to write your own cook book, this is your chance. Please see the information on self-publishing on the Internet and getting paid in Chapter 9.

Rewards—You might be able to sell a few books or recipes and make a few dollars from material you've already created. Several Web stores offer recipes as a value-add for viewers, such as Ragu, the spaghetti sauce company. You might be able to sell your recipes to other Home Pages that want to add high touch to high tech.

Risks—Out of pocket expenses.

Special marketing elements for the Home Page—Since people can't taste or smell your recipes on the Web, you need to describe these wonders with the flair of a restaurant menu writer. French fries become "succulent and golden." You can also make people's mouths water with small pictures of the completed meal. If you are a noted chef at a famed restaurant, tell people and post your bio!

Links to Home Pages

Creole & Cajun Recipe Page—

`http://www.webcom.com/~gumbo/recipe-page.html`

Veggies Unite!— http://www.-sc.ucssc.indiana.edu/cgi-bin/recipes

Lacto-vegetarian recipes—

`http://english-server.hss.cmu.edu/Recipes.html`

These examples are free sites. You might want to follow their lead to lure people to your restaurant. If you want to sell books, you might offer a few recipes online and entice people to order the book to get even more recipes.

SELL YOUR HOMEMADE CHEESCAKES

Overview—Do all your relatives love the cheesecake you bake for their birthday so much they lie and tell you they have two birthdays a year? If so, you might have a dessert that is so good you can sell it on the Internet.

Rewards—This could be a perfect source of extra income for a person who loves to bake. Health and safety codes must be observed.

Risks—Normal business risks. Ordering can be sporadic—nothing for days and then a rush. You need to be prepared for both.

Special marketing considerations for Home Pages—Your home page should contain ordering information, testimonials, recipe (or highlights), and a picture of the cheesecake in an attractive setting.

Idea joggers for related businesses—This idea also works for your other home-made products, like jams, jellies, canned fruits, and vegetables, beer, and wine.

GOURMET FOODS AND WINES

Overview—Since the Internet audience is largely affluent and worldly, gourmet foods and hard-to-find items can be good groups of products to sell. Merchants are selling everything: lobsters, chocolates, hot sauces, peanuts, and even garlic.

Rewards and Risks—Established food merchants—especially local and regional producers—can open a new line of distribution through the

Internet. Companies that can't get widespread distribution in grocery stores or national outlets can find willing customers on the Internet.

On the downside, merchants need to careful about returned products that don't match the expectations of consumers. Consider using an overnight delivery service (with packed ice, if necessary) to ensure that foods arrive unspoiled.

Special marketing ekements for the Home Page—Vendors will benefit from showing accurate pictures of their products. They can increase sales by selling gift baskets of related products to raise the price of the average order. You can increase the relationship and interaction by asking for customers' recipes and cooking tips, and printing them in a newsletter that is distributed either online or snail mail.

Links to Home Pages

Please see the case study for Lobster Direct.—

`http://novaweb.com/lobster`

Virtual Vineyards—`http://www.virtualvin.com`

Captain Morgan rum—

`http://www.sports-world.line.com/captain morgan`

Gatorade—`www.gatorade.com`

INTERVIEW—RED HOOK BREWERY

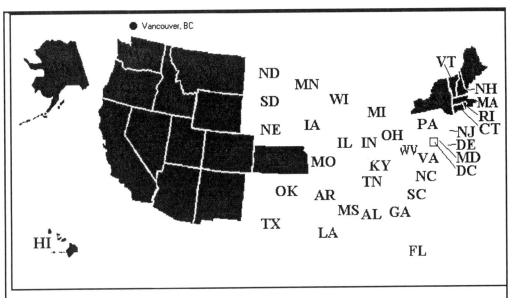

Select the state for a list of local distributors

Figure 13-1. This map shows where you can buy Red Hook Ale. Copyright 1995, Redhook Ale Brewery.

Rick Hauptman

Red Hook Ale

Seattle, WA

http://www.halcyon.com/rh/rh.htm

e-mail redhook@redhook.com

Background

What are you hoping to accomplish by being on the Web?

We seek to be an info site for the company and the beers we make, as well as helping people find them.

How successful have you been?

Quite, for minimal expense we have had over 19,000 hits since December 15, 1995 (through August 15, 1995).

Would you do it again?

YES.

Do you have any advice for entrepreneurs?

Don't try and get rich quick.

Cheers!

CASE STUDY—LOBSTER DIRECT

Welcome to Lobster Direct!
1-800-NS-CLAWS

WORLD FAMOUS NOVA SCOTIA FRESH LOBSTER AND LOX,
SHIPPED FEDEX OVERNIGHT...AT SUPERMARKET PRICES!

Figure 13-2. Lobster Direct puts its toll-free order line high on the Home Page. Copyright 1995, Lobster Direct.

Jeff Morris
Lobster Direct
Suite 3, 109 Ilsley Avenue
Dartmouth, N.S. Canada, B3B 1S8
Canada

http://novaweb.com/lobster
lobster@fox.nstn.ca
1-800-NS CLAWS (1-800-672-5297)

Background

Who is your primary audience?

Seafood lovers, people with cooking/recipe interests.

How will they benefit from your product?

Fresh product delivered overnight, quality information about lobster and salmon, including recipes, cooking tips etc.

How does your product differ from others?

Lots of content on our Internet site, including pictures and text on "How to crack and eat a Nova Scotia Lobster."

Is this business an offshoot of your existing business, or does it exist only on the Internet?

It is an offshoot of our wholesale business, but our first venture into retail and delivery direct to the consumer.

If it is an offshoot, was it meant to generate income on its own or to steer people to your other outlets?

Generate income on its own. We have no actual retail outlets.

Where does your business operate?

Office.

What is your background and training?

Attorney/entrepreneur.

When did you start your business?

January 1995.

How much money has your company made online?

Confidential, but we are shipping lots of orders every week to across North America.

Getting started

Did you create a business plan before going online?

No.

How much time did it take to get up and running?

One month.

Did you create the pages yourself?

We decided to make a computer/friend who can do HTML code and graphics our partner in the business.

How much did it cost to get started?

Cost was under $2,000.

How did you obtain your startup capital?

No comment.

What mistakes did you make that you wish you hadn't made?

No major mistakes so far....we hope this continues!

What advice would you give to a similar startup?

Do not expect instant profits or revenues. Shopping on the Net is still in its early days and you should look at a five year window if you are not selling Internet related products. Develop a marketing strategy to attract attention and traffic to your site and to try to establish a following.

What skills are needed to run this business?

Obviously computer skills and running a retail store.

What education is needed to run your site?

Read and write.

What special qualities are needed to run your site?

Imagination and creativity.

How did you promote your Home Page?

We established in a number of Internet malls, indexed on What's New, Yahoo.

How much did it cost to promote your site?

About $200/month.

How long did it take until you made your first sale?

About three weeks! We thought we would never sell a lobster. Then we got our first order and our sales keep building.

How did the startup phase affect your personal life?

No comment.

My day

What does your average day look like?

Two hours answering mail and processing orders and shipping.

What does your job entail?

As above, writing our newsletter that goes out to about 400 Internet users each month.

What was the hardest aspect of the work in the beginning?

Developing a streamline system to obtain the order and to ship it on time.

How long did it take to get established?

Two months.

What do you like most about your work?

Creativity in our newsletter.

What do you like the least?

Sending out our newsletter...we have to set up a mail server soon!

What was your greatest moment?

Being in Internet World, June 95 issue, in an article on Doing Business on the Net. Never thought we would be mentioned in an international magazine.

How much time do you spend conducting business, marketing, selling, and upgrading your site?

15 hours a week.

Are there any hazards to running your site?

None.

How much money do you expect to make?

We would like to net $75,000 a year.

General

Are customers concerned about security for their credit cards?

Yes.

How do you process orders via credit cards?

We write out slips by hand.

Was it easy or hard to get a machine?

Mail order credit cards take time to obtain and require personal contacts with banks.

Are you glad your store is on the Web?

Yes. It has opened up a new world of communications.

Given what you know now, would you do it again?

Yes.

Where can people find advice about running a site like yours?

Call us.

Lobster Direct
1-800-NS-CLAWS
(1-800-672-5297)

HOW TO REALLY CRACK AND EAT A FRESH NOVA SCOTIA
HARDSHELL LOBSTER!

1. Twist off the claws.

Figure 13-3. Lobster Direct adds value to the customer's experience by answering the age-old question of how to eat a lobster. Copyright 1995, Lobster Direct.

The future

What is your next venture?

We just opened Skyscrapers International Network, a sophisticated Web site for professionals only, `http://novaweb.com/sky`. It is a virtual reality office skyscraper designed by an architect, like a cybermall.

Can you share your cooking tips with us?

Why not try grilling lobster during barbecue season? What's better than surf n' turf! Precooked lobster only needs to be heated on the grill and lightly browned. Perhaps one or two minutes at most. Try using an olive oil, garlic, or lime juice baste while heating.

RESTAURANTS

Overview—Restaurants are a natural business for the Internet. Those that appeal to young, hip, Internet savvy audiences are popping up all over the Internet, especially in college towns and the West Coast, including San Francisco, Seattle, and Portland. Restaurants should market on the Web because travelers and vacationers always ask for recommendations. This is only logical since numerous people use the Internet to make travel plans and reservations.

Rewards—Restaurants can increase sales in several ways by using the Internet.

They can sell meals for take out or pick up.

They can mail-order prepared audiences.

Risks—It can be hard to measure the effectiveness of the advertisements without careful controls or surveys.

Special marketing elements for the Home Page—Restaurant Home Pages should show their sites are cool places to visit, as well as offer good food. Home Pages should include a map, menu, hours, and bio of the chef (they have their "foodie" fans who follow them around). For added value, include favorite recipes and coupons. To create a coupon, simply design one for a page, ask people to print it out. Put an expiration date on the coupon so you don't give away discounts forever. Test various coupon offers with different expiration dates so you can judge their effectiveness.

Links to Home Pages

Burk's Cafe—http://www.halcyon.com/burk

Virginia Diner—http://www.infi.net/vadiner. Please see case study.

My Brother's Pizza,

http://www.halcyon.com:80/mbp/welcome.html

INTERVIEW—ROSEBUD ESPRESSO & BISTRO

The Espresso Bar

Espresso drinks, teas, Italian sodas, desserts, soft drinks, beer, wine. Try our Vice Krispie Treats!

- Mon.-Thurs. 7:30 a.m.-1:00 a.m.
- Friday 7:30 a.m.-3:00 a.m.
- Saturday 9:00 a.m.-3:00 a.m.
- Sunday 10:00 a.m.-11:00 p.m.

Figure 13-4. Rosebud lists its products and hours. Copyright 1995, The Mercury Corp.

John Busey

Rosebud Espresso & Bistro

719 East Pike Street

Seattle, Washington 98122

http://www.halcyon.com/sage/

sage@halcyon.com

206-323-6636

Background

What are you hoping to accomplish by being on the Web?

We hope to gain a relatively inexpensive means of exposure for the restaurant. Our Web page allows us to communicate with our customers and allows them to give direct feedback. It allows those searching for a coffee house or restaurant to have the opportunity to consider ours.

How has being on the Web helped your company?

Our presence on the Web is rather new. For us, it is impossible to attach a revenue figure to this.

What advice would give an entrepreneur to succeed on the Web?

Get listed in as many search engines as possible. Have stylish and efficient presentations.

CASE STUDY—THE VIRGINIA DINER, MAIL—ORDER FOOD

History of The Virginia Diner

A Legend in a Nutshell Since 1929

The Virginia Diner has been a refuge for folks who like down-home cooking ever since Mrs. D'Earcy Davis served hot biscuits an vegetable soup to hungry customers way back in 1929. In those days the little diner was a refurbished Sussex, Surry, and Southampton Railroad car. As business grew so did the restaurant with dining room after dining room added on to accommodate a growing list of satisfied customers.

Figure 13-5. Home Pages can evoke warm, nostalgic images in the minds of consumers. Courtesy of The Virginia Diner Inc.

Bill Galloway

The Virginia Diner, Inc.

P.O. Box 310

Wakefield, VA. 23888

`http://www.infi.net/vadiner`

`vadiner@infi.net`

Background

Founded in 1929, The Virginia Diner sells gifts and peanuts around the world.

Who is your primary audience?

Our audience consists of anyone interested in gourmet gifts and other peanut products.

How will they benefit from your product?

The benefits of ordering our products or visiting our restaurant.

Did you create your home page, or did you get help?

The folks at infi.net were a tremendous help in getting us started. As the Web is a relatively new media, it takes time to develop and as time goes on so does our growth. Since we're new on the net, we've done rather well but it will still take time to develop. So far there aren't any real mistakes to speak of.

What advice do you have for other entrepreneurs?

My advice to someone starting up is that the net is a good place to do business, but don't expect an immediate ROI, as it, like any new business or media, will take time to develop.

What qualities are needed for success?

With any business, education is a must, and of course the qualities needed are those that would relate to your business such as dealing with the public, marketing your products, etc.

My day

My day starts by getting catalogue inquiries and orders and of course answering these inquiries and mail. My job entails the marketing of our products both on and off the net. Dealing with business on the net takes a couple of hours a day. The hardest part of doing business in the beginning was probably becoming computer literate.

As always in the restaurant and now on the net, I still love dealing and meeting new people from all over the world and dealing with them in business. We like the Web and its a good place to do business at this time. Given what I know now,of course I'd do it again, but of course, I'd do it better.

For now, we are looking for a wonderful ROI and hope that the response from the net will always continue to grow.

Figure 13-5. Virginia Diner shows special of the day with artwork. Courtesy of The Virginia Diner Inc.

The future

I wish the best of luck to everyone in business, and if you need some great gift ideas, check us out at http://www.infi.net/vadiner, or if you're in the Wakefield, VA area, stop in—our chicken and ham dinner will definitely make it worth your while.

INTERNET CAFES

Overview—For all those people who think Interneters like to hang out by themselves, think again. Dozens of restaurants and bars from New York to San Francisco to Seattle have begun offering Internet access as well burgers and beers. People pay for their food and their online time as well, about $10 an hour. These elite eateries get a lot of publicity for their owners. As an added draw, Internet cafes feature guest speakers (I spoke at the @Cafe in New York in June as a Japanese TV film crew was in another part of the bar interviewing patrons).

Rewards—As there is a lot of competition in the restaurant business, the Internet gives a cafe a chance to be different and stand out. Also, the longer people stay, the more money you make from their online access time. Normally, restaurants don't like people gabbing at the tables after a dinner when the table could be used for a new set of paying customers. At an Internet cafe, the meter is always running.

Risks—Internet cafes are prone to the same pressures as other restaurants. Good content on the Internet must be matched by good food and atmosphere, otherwise, people will stay home.

Special marketing considerations for Home Pages—See information for restaurants in the preceding case studies. Internet cafes can hold online

seminars as their special real world speakers conduct on-line conferences. Copies of the tapes can be stored as files that can be downloaded
by interested viewers.

Links to Home Pages

@cafe—`http://www.fly.net`

Internet Cafe—`http://www.bigmagic.com`

Paradise Cafe—`http://www.cyberspace.com`

COOKING SCHOOL

Overview—You have your recipes, you've taught all your roommates,
kids or sisterhood how to cook so now you're ready to go public: start a
cooking school online. Also, if you operate or teach in a cooking school,
you can promote your business, or offer classes online as well. The additional exposure can result in enrollments in your classes, or visits by
tourists to your store, which sell your own branded products and cookbooks.

For additional information, see the factoid on seminars in Chapter 8,
Information Industries, and information in Section 1 on how to sell products and services and receive payment.

Rewards—Increased income, additional exposure for your established
business, books or the like.

You can link to other cooking schools, or create home pages for them for
a fee.

Risks—Time, energy, and marketing costs. In other words, minimal exposure. As with any business, there might be dissatisfied customers who
want their money back.

Special marketing considerations for Home Pages—Consider linking to related home pages of cooking schools in different cities, as well as Internet sites offering restaurants, recipes, travel and tourism, wine, beverages, and the like. Add value to the page by offering recipes and cooking tips for free. Also, list newsgroup and mailing lists devoted to your specialties.

CASE STUDY—ASSOCIATION OF BREWERS

Figure 13-7. The Association of Brewers provides a great deal of information for its members. Copyright 1995, Association of Brewers.

Shawn Steele

Information Systems Administrator

Association of Brewers

P.O. Box 1679

Boulder, CO 80306

http://www.aob.org/aob

shawn@aob.org

303-447-0816 ext. 118

Background

The Association of Brewers (AOB), is a 501(c)(3) nonprofit organization that was established 17 years ago (long before I worked here). The AOB has four divisions, the American Homebrewers Association, the Institute for Brewing Studies, Brewers Publications, and The Great American Beer Festival. I administer the Web sites for the AOB and all four divisions.

Who is your primary audience?

Beer enthusiasts, homebrewers (people who brew beer at home), and some professional brewers.

How will they benefit from your service?

We provide information for our members and the general public on our Web site, this includes information on how to brew beer, beer style guidelines, club listings, how to start a club, a list of breweries from around the world, beer recipes (not quite on-line yet), and more. Of course we also have descriptions of the magazines that we publish (Zymurgy and The New Brewer) and of the books we publish, as well as an on-line order form.

How does your service differ from others?

We publish magazines specifically aimed at the Homebrewing and Microbrewing industries. Zymurgy (our homebrewing magazine) has a paid circulation of around 24,000 with a large number of copies sold at newsstands as well. Zymurgy is a membership benefit of the American Homebrewers Association. For more info, contact aha@aob.org.

The circulation of The New Brewer (our micro and pub brewery trade magazine) is around 3,000 and growing fast. The New Brewer is a membership benefit of the Institute for Brewing Studies. The IBS works very hard to help the growing microbrewing industry, which is growing almost as fast as the Web is right now. For more info, contact ibs@aob.org.

Additionally, Brewers Publications publishes books specifically for the homebrewer on subjects such as recipes (both beer recipes and The Great American Beer Cookbook which has recipes that use beer) and The Classic Beer Style Series, which is a collection of several books, each one of which addresses specific beer styles. BP also has industry related books, such as the Brewers Resource Directory, containing general information of interest to the brewery, and several books on brewery operations, including starting a brewery and more, for several types of breweries, including brewpubs, microbreweries, contract breweries, and more.

Lastly, the Great American Beer Festival is America's largest beer festival, with representatives from over 300 breweries attending, bringing with them over 1,400 different beers. The 1994 GABF had something like 20,000 attendees. Contact gabf@aob.org for more details.

Our products differ from others because not a great deal is published specifically for the homebrewer or small brewery, so we are able to provide some information that people wouldn't otherwise get. As far as the GABF goes, it is the largest beer festival in the U.S. which is sufficient to set it apart from other festivals.

Was it meant to generate income on its own?

It was intended to help fulfill our educational 501(c)(3) mission, and to increase our exposure to the general public, especially internationally, which is an expensive market to reach using traditional methods. We hoped to sell our memberships and books on the Web as well (which is happening).

Where is your business located?

Office.

What is your background and training?

Something like 17 years of computer programming experience, covering a large number of areas. I have a large amount of experience in human interfaces for computers, (i.e.: making them more user friendly).

How much money has your company made online?

We've only been on the Web for five months and only been seriously pursuing orders for the last three months. Last month we did about $1,000 gross from the Web stuff. Of course, the indirect benefit isn't really measurable yet. I wouldn't be surprised if our sales go up considerably in the next few months as we add more and more information and create a better index. In particular we plan to start taking ticket sales for the GABF in August which should generate a large response.

Getting started

Did you create a business plan before going online?

No. We had a vague idea that we wanted to be "online," but didn't have a good plan. We used the promotional materials we already had and "ported" them to the Web. Additionally, we had been running a e-mail information server, info@aob.org, since the middle of December 1994, so we already had some of that information in a computerized form. We wanted to provide the information we were already willing to provide for free in a manner so that people could have instant access to it and we wouldn't have to pay postage.

As happens a great deal in an established business, although individual department heads had their own ideas about the Internet (no one had heard of the Web), the managers did not know how to utilize this new media, not to mention the fact that our marketing department kept the World Wide Web and info@aob.org stuff at the bottom of its list of priorities. The IS department (me) was the only person who really knew what the Web was capable of, so it has been somewhat of an uphill struggle, although we have finally figured out ways to integrate our new-found computer connectivity with our traditional marketing methods. (print ads and order forms now have e-mail and Web addresses as SOP. A although I was just handed our new flyer for the 1995 GABF (and I mean just now, as I wrote this response) and there is absolutely nothing about our Web site or e-mail sources of information although the director of the GABF has been speaking with me regularly about getting on the Web and has been very excited about the idea. This is just another example of a learning curve we are going through about this new media.

How much time did it take to get up and running?

I'd guess that it is around 50% of my time since January, although some of that is incidental. I am a full time paid Information Systems Administrator.

Did you create the pages yourself?

They were created in-house. The technical (beer and brewing) experience was important to create an accurate Web site. My experience with computer interfaces helped to create one of the better sites on the Web for beer and brewing (of course most of the others are for-fun sites and we can afford a full time staff to maintain our Web site).

How much did it cost to get started?

As I mentioned, we already had merchandise and this is "merely" a new marketing media for us. Total cost so far has been around $14,500 if you include my salary and the access provider's feed.

How did you obtain your startup capital?

N/A. It was a media project for us.

What mistakes did you make that you wish you hadn't made?

We tried an on-line mall (Branch Mall) to see what it would do for us. So far the fees have been unreasonable and the response fairly underwhelming. We get a much better response from our in-house Web stuff, and it doesn't cost us nearly as much per page.

What advice would you give?

Find someone who knows how to make a Web site interesting to the user. The actual connectivity issue is minor compared to the necessity of creating and maintaining a Web site that people will want to visit. An access provider who is willing to provide space on their Web server will save you a lot of money over having to maintain a dedicated Web server yourself. Avoid groups that are trying to make an instant million off of providing Web access. Some organizations charge $1,000 per page or more, which is extraordinarily unreasonable. Of course those are the companies with tons to spend trying to get you to use their services, so they are also the ones you will hear about first.

An organization with a computer literate staff member should probably consider doing it themselves, but some idea of marketing principles is a must. If the organization is small and has a fun purpose, they may be able to find a college student willing to help them with Internet access for free. If not, they may still want to consider a hot-shot college kid who would be willing to work for pennies, although the organization should make a point to learn what is going on enough that they can temporarily maintain the Web site if they have to look for another employee.

What skills would a person have to conduct business?

As I mentioned earlier, marketing skills, computer skills, and a general knowledge of what people respond to is necessary. I rely heavily on our graphics design and marketing departments when needed, although I can manage without their help if necessary.

What education is needed to run your site?

Our site relies heavily on the ability to update the Web site data from our databases (such as the brewery and club listings) and also the ability for us to take and process orders and automatically check individual memberships. These things all require a thorough knowledge of the computer system(s) you are working with, although they are not necessary to a smaller, simpler Web site. I think I covered the other skills needed above.

What special qualities are needed?

I mentioned graphic artist type skills and marketing knowledge. I believe that there is a fundamental "user interface" type of computer programming skill which is used to create user friendly computer environments. Some Web sites have lots of interesting information, but they are not aesthetically pleasing and can sometimes be difficult to navigate. Special attention must be paid to the different types of browsers and computers out there. Some people may use a text browser, others a graphical interface and many may use Netscape with all the toys. Other computers may provide the user with a small or a large window to view your page. All of these things need to be considered to design a Web site that works well for all of your users.

How did you promote your Home Page?

We mention it in our magazines, brochures, and other advertising. We also have started to "take it with us" on a local server (no real Internet connection) to conferences and festivals. Being aware of it to include it in our regular media is new for us, and taking time to become used to. Additionally we are listed in some of the Web indexes (the free ones).

How much did it cost to promote your site?

A few thousand $$$.

How long did it take until you made your first sale?

A couple months until we really pursued ordering on-line, but then only a couple days until people really started using the feature.

How did the startup phase affect your personal life?

Our organization is a growing one that used to hire computer consultants if something broke. More recently, we have kept a salaried Information

Systems Administrator on the staff to maintain our growing complicated systems. Prior to our Web stuff, I had always been told, "Our eventual goal is that you can get our computer system behaving well enough that we don't need an IS guy anymore." (Not a very reassuring thought to say the least.) Now the opinion of the upper management is more along the lines of, "When you get the Web site producing enough income, we'll hire someone to do the mundane computer stuff and you can devote all of your time to a new World Wide Web department." Much more reassuring to say the least.

My Day

What does your average day look like?

1.   Check e-mail. This comes from lots of sources, not just the Web. Sometimes (like today) it takes hours. I usually get 30-50 messages per day. email checking continues throughout the day.
2.   Help other people with computer problems, report generation, etc. (What I get paid for, I am an IS guy after all).
3.   Phone calls (member problems, sales, etc.), mail (snail mail), and trade magazines get read and dealt with.
4.   Make new Web stuff as time allows.

What does your job entail?

1.   Maintaining and improving the in-house computer system.
2.   Maintaining and improving the Web site.
3.   "Firefighting" of all types, including in-house problems, creating new reports, membership problems, customer service (e-mail usually), etc.

How many hours a week do you spend working on your site?

Twentyish. Orders are filled by customer service 30% making more Web stuff 15% responding to e-mail and specific requests 5% troubleshooting 50% other IS stuff.

What was the hardest part of the job in the beginning?

Connectivity. Our Internet access provider is overworked and makes it difficult to find out what's happening if something is going wrong, and what to do to get started.

How long did it take to get established?

A couple of months before people really paid attention to our site.

What do you like most about your work?

It's fun to be able to provide the information people want to get on the Web and to be in charge of something that is successful

What do you like least?

It's not fun when someone lets me know a link isn't working, that I forgot to check due to some silly typo. Sometimes the detail work gets to be a strain (we have hundreds of individual files), linking and organization of the page can be difficult.

What was your greatest moment?

I liked my boss saying that our site was doing so well that our plan was to make me a full-time Webmaster! Quite a compliment I think and more than I would have expected.

Are there any hazards to running your site?

Since we publish stuff, we have to make sure that our Web site does not give away our copyrighted material. Additionally, we sometimes find our copyrighted or trademarked material floating around the Net and usually work out a friendly, "By the way, that's copyrighted," and they usually respond, "Oh, I didn't know. I'll fix that right away. Mind if I link to your Web page?" We haven't encountered much in the way of other hazards, although on-line ordering has been getting a lot of press and is an obvious concern.

How much money do you hope to make?

I'm hoping that the Web site will pay for itself within the year. As I probably made clear, we also consider the Web site a member service and feel that the incidental exposure will help our organization in general. Additionally, our Web site helps us maintain the 501(c)(3) educational status that we have.

General

Are customers concerned about security for credit cards?

Some are concerned and we don't press the issue. Instead we just ask for a check. If they never send a check, we never send their stuff :-) I think a lot of people don't really give it much thought and most others feel that it won't be their problem if someone takes their card number. I get asked this question a lot and I'd like to point out that it's about as secure as credit card orders by phone. People can read Internet traffic, but that would assume that you actually tried to do so with some sort of criminal intent and had the necessary access to some router somewhere or were willing to break into someone else's system or account to get that access. Similarly, anyone could walk up to the phone lines into our building and tap them. Both are illegal and just about as difficult to do, only the technology is different.

How do you process orders via credit cards?

We already had a system in place for taking phone orders and we do the Web orders very similarly.

Are you glad you are on the Web?

Yes, I'm glad that we're on the Web, and I think it will help the business even more in the future .

Given what you know now, would you do it again?

Yes, but I might try for more preplanning.

The future

What is your next venture?

I can't say right now :-) ask me in August! I can say I definitely have something in mind that will be worth waiting for.

14 PROFESSIONAL SERVICES

While lawyers, accountants, and health care providers can't practice their professions online, they can advertise and promote their services to an audience that can contract with them for work that will be performed off-line.

This chapter looks at how the Internet can help these professionals and service vendors promote their businesses: lawyers, accountants, doctors and health care professionals, insurance agents, financial planners, financial newsletters, masseuses, dating services, and private investigators.

LAWYERS

Overview—Lawyers have learned to use computers and online services in law school as they researched Lexis and other online legal and governmental databases. Many legal resources exist on the Internet and many lawyers are posting Home Pages. It is only natural for this group to move to the Internet.

Rewards—By placing material on the Internet lawyers can attract new clients, referrals from lawyers who have clients who need to consult with an expert, or retain to handle matters outside their normal scope of business. For example, a lawyer might represent a client for a business transaction and then need to find a criminal defense lawyer to provide further assistance.

Risks—Lawyers should check with their state bar association concerning their policy on advertising. Although Internet marketing has not clearly been defined as advertising in the traditional sense, there is enough reason to believe that it will fall under the same ethical considerations as advertising in other media.

Special marketing elements for the Home Page—Home Pages for lawyers should contain information about their specialty or primary area of practice, the cases they handle as well as their educational and professional vita. Extra value will be given to lawyers who post information files, such as articles they've written for legal publications, or papers presented at legal conferences.

Links to legal resources and experts who have home pages will also be appreciated.

Links to Home Pages

http://www.seamless.com—a starting point for information about lawyers and legal resources. It contains many links to lawyers in many specialties in most states.

http://www.seamless.com/alawyer—a marvelous Home Page for lawyer Jerome Mullins of San Jose, whose local number is 408-a-lawyer, a very savvy marketing guy!

INTERVIEW—JEROME MULLINS, ATTORNEY

Expert Criminal Defense for Major Felony Offenses

Dial the letters "A L-A-W-Y-E-R" in area code 408 [252-9937] 24 Hours a day

Figure 14-1. Jerome Mullins beat out every attorney in his area for the best phone number! Courtesy of Jerome P. Mullins, Attorney at Law.

Jerome Mullins
408-alawyer

`alawyer@eworld.com`
`http://www.seamless.com/alawyer`

What are you hoping to accomplish by being on the Web?

I intend to make money on the Web by marketing my law practice and expanding my practice to include multijurisdictional problems in criminal law. For example, one woman in Florida found my Web site by using America Online. Her boyfriend is in jail in Indianapolis with a felony case pending there. He has another case pending in New Orleans, and another pending in Los Angeles. He needs a lawyer for his California case, but more importantly, he needs one lawyer to coordinate the disposition of all three cases. I am interested in this kind of work. I am awaiting his decision to hire me.

The Law Offices of Jerome P. Mullins
at Silicon Valley, U.S.A.

Please sign our <u>guest book</u>.

If you or someone you know is charged with a <u>serious criminal offense</u>, I will discuss the matter at no charge. Please call me any time of the day or night. I will respond promptly to provide you with the defense services you need. It would be helpful if you could provide the following information (if known) about the person accused or arrested: full name, date of birth, day and evening telephone numbers, jail booking number, court case number, next court date, amount of bail and whether bail has been posted.

Figure 14-2. Why is a lawyer on the Net? Here's why: referrals.

How many clients or referrals have you received?

I have received three very solid "leads," one of which has resulted in my being retained locally. One gentlemen saw my Web site and then traveled from southern California to see me in Palo Alto about his federal criminal case in North Carolina. He did not hire me because we differed over tactical approaches to the case. All three "leads" involved rather serious felony matters. Numerous other contacts have resulted in a spectrum of inquiries and comments about the criminal law. I will probably follow up these contacts with brochures, etc.

How has being on the Web been beneficial?

Being on the Web has made me a small amount of money so far, but I expect to make much more. There is a great deal of work for lawyers to do using the Web. I like using it so much that I am considering other lines of business on the Web. I will be on the Web for the rest of my life. I get a kick out of it.

Any words of wisdom?

When more people discover the value of the Web, the word "competition" will take on new meaning in the world of commerce and industry—all to the benefit of the consumer. To compete on the Web it will be necessary for those selling goods and services to attract the public with gobs of good, valuable free information. Every ad must be a "resource center" for the consumer public. I foresee more "subject matter" Web sites, like the spinal care Web site, the dental care Web site, the skin disease Web site, and so forth.

ACCOUNTING

Overview—Professionals involved in accounting related fields can use the Internet to find new clients and to consult or subcontract from others. The Internet could help these professionals: accountants, bookkeepers, tax preparers, CPAs, accounting firms, auditors, and related professions.

Rewards—Accounting professionals can increase their income, gain recognition and sell their services on the Internet.

Risks—The only risks are the out of pocket expenses to create and maintain the Home Page.

Special marketing elements for the Home Page—Accountants can post their areas of expertise, resumes, and articles of interest to their target markets. Professionals who seek to do tax returns for small businesses, for example, could write an article on "10 Ways to Cut Your Taxes" and post it on their Home Page.

CASE STUDY—JOHN SOMMERER & COMPANY, P.A.

John Sommerer, C.P.A.,

John Sommerer & Company

1881 University Drive

Coral Springs, Florida 33071

http://www.accountant.com\~jsomco

cpa@accountant.com

305-752-2885

Background

Who is your primary audience?

Entrepreneurs needing accounting and auditing services, people needing tax advice.

How will they benefit from your service?

Financing, which requires certified audits of financial statements, such as public offerings, and minimizing cash flow required to service tax liabilities.

How does your service differ from others?

We are a small certified public accounting firm, yet we are a full-service member of the S.E.C. and Private Companies section of the American Institute of Certified Public Accountants. As such, we are able to provide accounting and auditing services to smaller firms which would like to "go public" at a fraction of the cost associated with the high-overhead "Big 6" firms. We are big enough to get the job done, and small enough to offer personal service at reasonable rates.

Is this business an offshoot of your existing business, or does it exist only on the Internet?

Our challenge is to let potential clients know we exist and can perform these services. Our Internet efforts are an example of the lengths we go to accomplish this.

Where is your workplace?

We have offices in Coral Springs and Fort Lauderdale, Florida.

What is your background and training?

B.S., M.B.A., Ph.D. candidate ('72-74) in business finance at Columbia University, C.P.A. in New York, New Jersey, and Florida. Public accounting since 1974 with national, "Big 6," and own firms.

When did you start your business?

1982.

How much money has your company made online?

Our Internet activities have not yet generated new clients.

Getting started

Did you create a business plan before going online?

No.

How much time did it take to get up and running?

One week.

Did you create the pages yourself?

Our consulting division did it.

How much did it cost to get started?

Nothing. Used existing hardware.

What mistakes did you make that you wish you hadn't made?

None with respect to this effort.

What advice would you give to a similar startup?

Call for an appointment.

How much money have you made on the Internet?

All of the above, and almost all of the following, is really answered by the fact that our Internet involvement is an outreach effort to make us known to potential clients.

The site is not expected to be its own revenue source.

General

Are you glad you are on the Web for personal and business reasons?

Yes, it illustrates our commitment to innovation and client service.

Given what you know now, would you do it again?

Absolutely!

PHYSICIANS AND HEALTH CARE PROVIDERS

Overview—Health-care professionals can't practice their craft on the

Internet, nor can they give out advice for fear of malpractice suits, because every case is different. However, these entrepreneurial professionals can use the Internet to market their services by telling the world about their skills, backgrounds, and specialties. Home Pages can be used to show the range of services performed, arrange appointments, and create both visibility and credibility. Additionally, there are many sites for preventitive health care and alternative health care.

Rewards—Health-care professionals can gain new clients and referrals from their peers.

Risks—Ethical considerations dictate that each care giver check with state and professional association officials regarding regulations on advertising to see where the Internet falls into their codes.

Special marketing elements for the Home Page—Healers can use Home Pages to establish their credibility by listing degrees, awards, and affiliations with hospitals and clinics.

To encourage office visits, the Home Page should list office hours, a map, and telephone numbers. To encourage people to make appointments, consider using coupons. Dentists, for example, place ads for low-cost cleanings in every print advertising mechanism available, from TV guides to direct mail, so why not advertise a one-time discount on the Internet?

Physicians can also build their credibility by writing articles that help all readers lead healthier lives. Topics can include such useful and non-controversial themes like "10 Ways to Reduce Stress," or "10 Steps to a Healthier Heart."

Links to Home Pages

DentalNet—http://www.dentalnet.com/dentalweb/

Dr. Howard Rosen— http://www.canadamalls.com/provider/rosent.html

Dr. Ted Lewis—

`http://www.bei.net/Oxyfresh/Distributors/ted/home.html`

Dr. Howard Rosen, `74471.226@compuserve.com` uses a Home Page to announce his services. Success has been limited, "nothing so far, but many hits received," he says and "It's fun to get e-mail.

INSURANCE AGENT

Overview—Insurance agents selling all types of products can find an audience online. Look at all the rich, high tech executives who use the Internet, as well as the company employees who need to stash their retirement plans somewhere. There's also the chance of networking with Realtors who need to recommend your services. Lots of work-at-home executives (like me) could use disability coverage (I've already got mine, please don't call. Yes, I bought it, off-line, but that was before I knew about the Internet.).

Rewards—You probably can't sell an insurance contract over the Internet any more than you could sell a policy over the phone. However, the Internet is a great place to make contacts. Please see the rules for marketing on newsgroups (Chapter 3) for additional ideas.

Risks—Please check with your attorney and state agencies regarding the dispensing of advice and the ability to sell policies in states in which you do not live.

Special marketing elements for the Home Page—Lots of information about the practical needs and uses of insurance could draw people to your Home Page. Remember, we aren't talking about the normal gloom and doom brochures that have marked the insurance industry. Be creative in telling people new reasons for buying insurance. Then show them why they should buy from you.

Practical examples and links to Home Pages

Check Yahoo for the latest listings, http://www.yahoo.com.

FINANCIAL PLANNER

Overview—Look at the demographics of the Internet. There are a lot of rich people out there! They could all use your advice. This could be a great service for the right person who can create custom-made portfolios. People could track their investments on a daily basis.

Rewards—New clients.

Risks—Check with your lawyer regarding rules and regulations. If you house portfolios on the site, be sure to protect the data with passwords.

Special marketing elements for the Home Page—Online citizens know there is a sucker born every minute and they don't want to be the next one who get picked. You must create an atmosphere of trust. Show your credentials in your heading, such as Joe Smith, CFP. Present articles on financial planning, along with tips and strategies. By giving away free information, you can attract an audience. With credibility and good advice, you might be able to get a new client.

Practical examples and links to Home Pages

Check Yahoo for the latest listings, http://www.yahoo.com.

STOCKBROKER

Overview—Look at the demographics of the Internet. There are a lot of rich people out there! People have shown a willingness to buy stocks from online brokerage houses on CompuServe, Prodigy, and other online service. Maybe they'll take your advice as well.

Rewards—You can find new clients and prosper from their trades.

Risks—Check with your lawyer regarding rules and regulations concerning sales and dispensing advice.

Special marketing elements for the Home Page—Creating credibility is the key here, as you face a lot of competition.

Practical examples and links to Home Pages
Check Yahoo for the latest listings, `http://www.yahoo.com`.

FINANCIAL NEWSLETTER

Overview—Do you have a good background for analyzing trends, companies and markets? Then you might have the makings of a good editor and publisher of a financial newsletter. While you could go after large markets, the Internet is especially well suited for reaching targeted niche markets, as the case study for NeuroInvestment Newsletter will show.

Rewards—You can make money selling subscriptions to the online or print version. Be wary of selling ads or links, as these moves might be interpreted by your audience as compromising your integrity.

Risks—Normal business risks. Check with your attorney for regulations and liabilities.

Special marketing considerations for Home Page—See Chapter Four, Business Model: Publisher.

CASE STUDY—NEUROINVESTMENT NEWSLETTER

Dr. Harry Tracy

Neuro Investment Newsletter

P.O. Box 458

Rye, NH 03870

http://www.neuroinv.com

neuroinvestment@bluefin.net

Background

What did you hope to accomplish by being on the Internet?

I am hoping that people who use the Internet to acquire information about investments in general will learn about neuroscience stocks in particular. The Internet is about using cutting-edge computing technology to access information about cutting-edge biotechnology information.

We realized that we faced the dilemma familiar to anyone trying to access a very small niche market. At the time that newsletter started, biotech stocks as a whole had been in a slump for two years, and their advances were not getting much attention. To market a newsletter covering just those companies developing treatments for neurological disorders meant defining an even smaller niche in the biotech area, a universe of 20-256 companies, and somehow finding people who wanted to know more about investing in it. Using traditional direct mail or print advertising was a rather expensive process of sifting through large numbers of prospective clients in order to find a select few, and while we have done this some extent, the Internet is a much more cost-effective medium. Instead of our having to find the needle in the haystack, having a presence on the Net has allowed the needle to find us; those people who because of an inherent interest in more scientifically sophisticated companies and/or a willingness to learn about such companies in order to maximize their investment returns, seek out this specialized kind of company research and investment opinion. The truth of this became glaringly apparent before our Home Page was even in operation; we were receiving phone inquiries from people who had heard about the Newsletter in various Internet and commercial online service Newsgroups and were now seeking us out. We turned that realization into an acceleration of our plans to establish a World Wide Web site, and it has really paid off for us.

DATING SERVICE, MATCHMAKER

Overview—If you've been finding love in the all the wrong places, consider starting a matchmaking service. Since the dawn of online services, software has existed to help bring people of all ages and sexes together. Yahoo lists almost 100 dating services. For a list of sites, go to `http://www.yahoo.com`, search through the business category for products and services, and select personals. These services charge about $25 to list your classified ad and could charge additional fees to show your picture. Some businesses try to get viewers to call their 900-pay telephone lines, which can charge several dollars per minute.

Entrepreneurs can start similar services but differentiate themselves by specializing in geographic area, straight or gay, old or young—or have them all!

Rewards—You can make an unlimited amount of money in this type of business—if you target the right audience and charge appropriately, as there are millions of singles eligible for this service. Since many Internet users are college age and have free accounts, there is a large audience out there. However, they might decide they'd rather spend the $25 enrollment fee on beer and videos instead of a chance for a date.

Risk—Check with your lawyer on the legality of privacy and security issues. Remember, we are talking about a legal dating service, not an escort service.

Special marketing elements for the Home Page—This enterprise involves a lot of data entry and financial controls. You will need to create forms and software that collect biographies about people and have it in a format that can be sorted and searched. Next, you need to collect money from the people placing ads. You might decide to charge visitors as well, but that probably would hurt your ability to attract people. If you want to go this route, consider allowing visitors to search the database, but not let them have access to the contact information, such as name, phone, or e-mail, until they pay.

Practical examples and links to Home Pages

For a case study, read about Christian Singles Dating Service, who says there are 972,000 Christian Singles on the Internet.—

http://www.christsingles.com/Two4Christ/

For a list of more than 100 singles centers—

http://www.yahoo.com/Business_and_Economy/Products_and_Services/Personals

CASE STUDY—CHRISTIAN SINGLES DATING SERVICE

Welcome to *Christian Singles On Line*

Figure 14-3. Christian Singles Dating Service reaches out to the lovelorn.

Giselle Aguiar

http://www.christsingles.com/
Two4Christ/

Christian Singles Dating Service Two4Christ@aol.com

P.O. Box 610543

305-940-9663

North Miami, FL 33261

Background

What is your primary audience?

Christian Singles OnLine is a computerized matchmaking service for Christian singles of all ages.

How will they benefit from your service?

It caters strictly to Christians. It's more than personal ad listings, and we provide a newsletter, live chats, and browsing the profiles.

Is this business an off-shoot of your existing business, or does it exist only on the Internet?

It was created based on the Internet but you don't have to have Internet access to join. 70% of the members have access to e-mail at least. Most have Web access.

Where is your office?

Home.

What is your background and training?

My background is in advertising and marketing, but I've been involved with singles for many years.

How much money has your company made online?

$1,910 in 2.5 months.

Getting started

Did you create a business plan before going online?

Yes.

How much time did it take to get up and running?

About three weeks.

Did you create the pages yourself?

I did them myself. In fact, my other business is creating Web Pages.

How much did it cost to get started?

On line set-up $150, $75 per month. About $50 in postage.

How did you obtain your startup capital?

Was able to start without borrowing.

What mistakes did you make that you wish you hadn't made?

Not setting up an accounting program from the beginning. I've had to reenter all transactions since day one.

What advice would you offer someone starting a business?

Do your research. Find out about other similar businesses, check out their pages, find out how they get payment, how easy it is to place an order, etc. Make your site better.

Once the site is up, publicize, publicize, publicize. Register with all the online directories and search engines. Send press releases to all on line publications, send URL announcements to appropriate newsgroups, send releases to off line press, especially related to your business and of course to your local daily newspaper. I got great press in the Miami

Herald and got most of my local members from it.

What skills would a person need to conduct business?

You have to be a people person. Know your way around databases, sorting, etc. Know how to keep members happy. Be very creative.

What education is needed to run your site?

I wouldn't be where I am today without my B.S. in Business Administration and Marketing.

What special qualities are needed to run your site?

Creativity, good organizational skills, diligence, endless energy, patience.

How did you promote your Home Page?

I'm listed in almost every directory. There are new ones popping up all the time, so you have to keep up with them. I will be advertising in online and off line publications.

How much did it cost to promote your site?

So far zero $.

How long did it take until you made your first sale?

A few days.

How did the startup phase affect your personal life?

What personal life? I'm single, no kids, work at home, put in about 15 hours a day on this and the other business.

My day

What does your average day look like?

First thing I do is pick up e-mail and print out any profiles that have come in. Then I go to the post office to pick up checks which I then take to the bank. I send confirmation messages to those whose payment I've gotten. Once a week I enter the matches in the system, update the browser and run matches. This is basically a part-time business. Once a month I write a newsletter and I'm starting once a week chats on AOL.

How many hours a week do you spend working on your site?

About 22 hours a week.

60% on entering and doing matches.

Two hours a day on picking up e-mail, checks and making deposits.

How much time do you spend conducting business?

Another 18 hours spent this way:

86%—marketing
 2% —selling—it sells itself
12%—upgrading the site

What was the hardest part of the job in the beginning?

Finding the time.

How long did it take to get established?

Three weeks.

What do you like most about your work?

I work at home, I may be changing people's lives for the better, it's fun!

What do you like least?

Data entry.

What was your greatest moment?

Hasn't happened yet. The first wedding will be the greatest.

Are there any hazards to running your site?

I try to cover myself with my disclaimer. There may be personal burn-out.

How much money do you hope to make?

$25,000 per year.

General

Are customers concerned about security for their credit cards?

No, we don't take them, yet.

Are you glad you are on the Web?

Yes. It's new, exciting, everyone wants to know more about it. Everyone wants to be on it.

Does age or sex make a difference in running your site?

No. You just need a lot of energy.

MASSAGE THERAPIST

Overview—Sure you can't reach out and touch someone on the Internet, at least until they create a virtual massage machine. However, masseuses can promote their businesses by creating a Home Page.

Rewards—You could expand your clientele.

Risks—For security purposes, home-based masseuses might not want to provide addresses or maps. Also, some people might think the massage service offers X-rated amenities, as the Internet houses many sites of pornography, so your mission statement should be made loud and clear to avoid unwanted patrons. Some people really do want a massage when they call a masseuse!

Special marketing elements for the Home Page—Build credibility by listing customer testimonials, professional, and educational information, such as state licenses and numbers. If you want to add real value to customers, add articles about the value of massage or other topics of interest, such as links to health and nutrition sites.

Links to Home Pages
Golden Sun Body Works—

```
http://www.sfweb.com/\goldsun\index.htm
```

PRIVATE INVESTIGATOR

Overview—Sam Spade has come to the Internet! Round up the usual suspects, sweetheart. Seriously, private investigators and other members of the criminal investigation services can find new clients and network with peers in related fields by using the Internet (i.e. bail bondsmen need private investigators, lawyers need process servers).

Rewards—Benefits include increased exposure and opportunity to build a business.

Risks—Start-up costs.

Special marketing elements for the Home Page—List special interests and abilities, such as speaking foreign languages, gun permits, special training or contacts and background (such as law enforcement positions) and state registered license numbers. Add biographies on staffers to show depth to the service. For entertainment value, consider a game or contest. This field is ripe with possibilities!

Links to Home Pages

See the case study for Agrue and Associates, Investigations.

http:// www.teleport.com/~pagrue

INTERVIEW—AGRUE AND ASSOCIATES INVESTIGATIONS

Agrue & Associates Investigations   http://www.teleport..com/~pagrue/

2061 NW Hoyt Street,.Suite K   503-246-7561

Portland OR 97209

What are you hoping to accomplish by being on the Web?

Exposure and broaden the customer base outside of the local area. Also a way to network with other investigators.

How has being on the Web helped you?

I've been in contact with other investigation firms on the net and have been able to network or at least begin to network with others. I have not made a dime off of the WWW exposure as of yet!

What advice would you give an entrepreneur?

My firm was already very well known prior to the Web. I wrote all my own HTML and pages myself in part for the exposure and in part just because I was having fun doing it. I have dealt with companies on the Web and I would recommend that anyone trying to make a living or just trying to do business on the Web, first research the service or product they intend to sell to make sure that there is a market. Second, make sure that their Home Page is interesting and functional.

15 TRAVEL AND TOURISM

Travel services have always been popular on the commercial online services, and that is true of the Internet. People like the convenience of reading about travel destinations in the comfort of their own home. Many travel agencies have taken advantage of this need by creating Home Pages that offer free information and pictures of exotic destinations. Hotel chains, too, have gone online to post information and pictures about their rooms and rates. Some futurists predict that the travel agent business will be completely reworked as online services and give consumers the power to make reservations with hotels, airlines, and car rental services.

This chapter will explore ways to make money on the Internet as a travel agent, tour provider, travel magazine, and tour operator. In addition, entrepreneurs can create a travel starting page that offers links to travel–related sites and resources on the Internet. They can then charge for advertising to reach the audience this page attracts. For more information, please see the Starting Page Business Model in Chapter 4.

Bon voyage!

TRAVEL AGENT

Overview—The Internet offers travel agents the opportunity to reach a worldwide audience to sell tours, tickets, and adventure. This field will get increasingly crowded. Winners will be able to show their expertise in a special area, like Disneyland, Europe, or wilderness tours.

Entrepreneurs can make money as online travel agents by reselling tours and pointing people to travel related resources. In this manner, they would work out an arrangement with a local travel agent who would make the actual contacts with the travel providers (airlines, hotels, and the like). Travel agents would pass along part of their commission to the Internet entrepreneur. After all, the travel agent is getting additional business without having to spend time and money hunting for clients. The Internet entrepreneur gains as well because he cannot get the discounts or commissions offered by airlines, which have strict controls. However, the entrepreneur could arrange for discounts with hotels, restaurants, and other tour operators who don't mind dealing with an independent.

Rewards—Travel agents can promote their businesses to people around the country who could then book tours and plane tickets with them.

Risks—As with other businesses on the net and off, you must be wary of rip—off artists. Make sure their checks clear and their credit cards are valid before sending tickets, or putting up your own money.

Special marketing elements for the Home Page—People are buying destinations, adventure and romance. Show them pictures of your featured vacations, add music, and recipes for exotic foods. Spark their imaginations by showing calendars with dates of festivals and special events, like Carnivale in Rio de Janeiro, or local celebrations that add color to a city, like Eugene Days in Eugene Oregon, which features the Slug Queen parade and a typewriter throwing contest by secretaries. Consider links to related services, like restaurants, hotels, and city Home Pages. Some companies might be able to charge for these links.

Links to Home Pages

Clawson Travel— `http://www.halcyon/dclawson/advsourc.html`

TravelAssist Magazine— `http://www.travelassist.com/`

Coastliners— `http://www.gvn.com/cu/`

Automated Travel Services— `http://www.ananda.com/plg/travel/`

Travel Online— `http://wwwtol.com/tol/loaded`

CASE STUDY—COASTLINERS

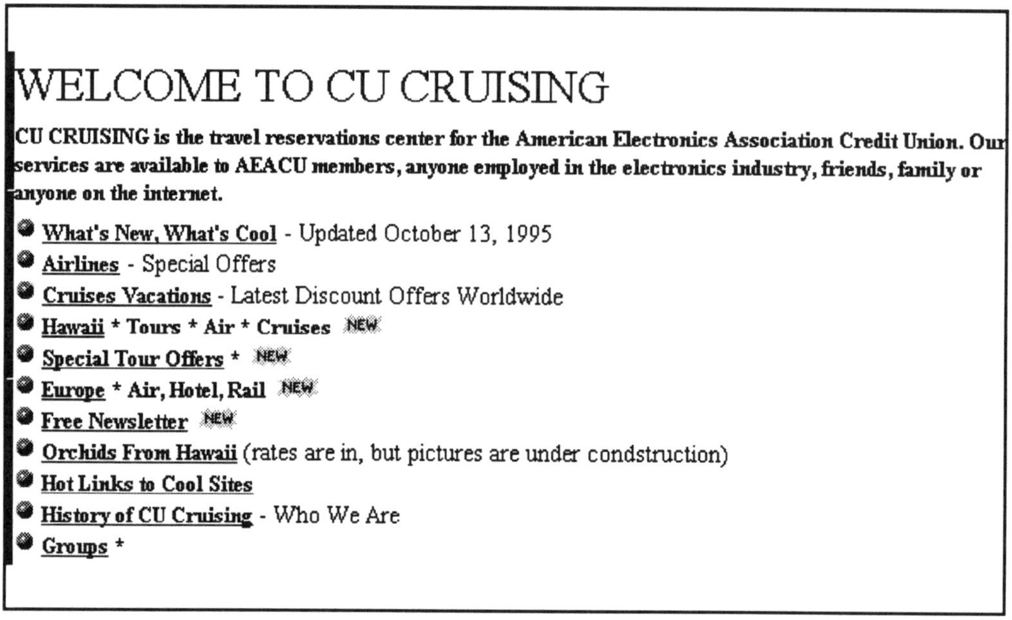

WELCOME TO CU CRUISING

CU CRUISING is the travel reservations center for the American Electronics Association Credit Union. Our services are available to AEACU members, anyone employed in the electronics industry, friends, family or anyone on the internet.

- **What's New, What's Cool** - Updated October 13, 1995
- **Airlines** - Special Offers
- **Cruises Vacations** - Latest Discount Offers Worldwide
- **Hawaii * Tours * Air * Cruises** NEW
- **Special Tour Offers *** NEW
- **Europe * Air, Hotel, Rail** NEW
- **Free Newsletter** NEW
- **Orchids From Hawaii** (rates are in, but pictures are under condstruction)
- **Hot Links to Cool Sites**
- **History of CU Cruising** - Who We Are
- **Groups ***

Figure 15-1. Coastliners Home Page provides information on travel services. Copyright 1995, CU.CRUISING.

Jerry Johnson
800-854-8192

coastlin@realm.net
http://www.gvn.com/cu/

Background

CU CRUISING is a registered dba of Travel Advisors. We also operate another dba COASTLINERS for Coast Federal Bank customers. CU CRUISING was formed as a joint project between ourselves and the American Electronics Association Credit Union (AEACU) to market discounted travel products, i.e., airlines bulk contracts at flat rates and discounted cruises, to the members of AEACU—about 70,000 plus the employees of member firms. At this time there are about 1,500 member firms—Apple Computers, INTEL, and Silicon Graphics to name just a few, with over 850,000 employees worldwide.

Our primary audience will be AEACU members and AEA employees. Our service, however, IS NOT LIMITED to the above but rather anyone that can find our site can take advantage of anything we offer. We have no service charges, no fees other then the cost of the products and we will attempt to create a larger and larger Web site as new products are added. Hot links to tourist boards or other Web sites that we think are interesting...the Atlanta Olympic Games, etc. We also plan to build a single page with a photo and description on every port in the world that a cruise ship might visit so people can learn something about their itinerary. We also will link those pages with URL sites that contain info. about that port. In Hong Kong we will link with a site that contains information about southeast Asia as well as Hong Kong. Kind of cool, don't you think! And of course, anyone that uses our service will benefit—except travel agents.

How does your site differ from others?

How does our site differ from others...what others? In the travel industry, most agencies discovered fax machines in the last two years and Internet, spraynet, fishnet...what are we talking about. When I attend meetings (very booooooring) no one wants to discuss the Infobahn or

Internet. But rather, they are still trying to make tired old marketing programs like cruise nights, work. They don't any more. Those few sites I have found seem to believe that an occasional update is all that is required. That tells me (1) they have little confidence in the potential of a Web site and (2) it's difficult for them to update in that they must supply their server with data which is then loaded and for which the agent must pay for the update. In our case, we do our own loading on a daily basis by one of our staff people that spent the time to learn about Web sites. I don't see other travel agencies as competition at this time...perhaps in the future but then they will be playing catchuppppp.

Does your site exist only online or is an offshoot of an existing business?

Our 3W site is just one more marketing tool of our business although I believe it has the greatest long-term potential. We still use direct mail, advertising, etc., as part of our overall marketing programs. The site resides in one of our offices quite near my desk so I can poke around all the time.

What is your background and training?

Training, none.

How much money have you made?

Not much, in fact less then $1,000.

Something I learned a long time ago about marketing. Unless you have not only the best mouse trap but the only one in the market, MARKETING OF PRODUCTS, goods, and services takes patience, patience, and more patience plus persistence. You also need to present your products in a format or language that is comfortable to your customer. And lastly, when they see your name, product, or in our case our 3W site often enough, new becomes old or familiar and confidence (trust) begins to build. In 1988, we did a mailing (Coast paid for it) to 2.5 million households.

Lots of phone calls but very little business. However, as we continued to mail, the phone calls remained about the same but the booking started to go up. Now we receive bookings without any mailings. We have now reached a life of our own.

Did you write a business plan?

No. We fiddled with the Internet through newsgroups etc. in our shell account from September 1994 to January 1995. Opened our first PPP account through a local provider directly onto the net in January and had our Home Page up in March 1995. We now update nearly daily. We created our pages based on what we saw others doing. Now we are changing our pages as we understand our customer better and what motivates net surfers...minimum click time. We are reducing the number of graphics and will add them later so the download is faster. I find big fancy Home Pages with a giant picture suck. Takes toooooo long to download and my patience is about as long as a 17 year old boy with a hot date.

Our cost to date: $350 including domain registration. Future costs are about $50 a month and we do all the loading ourselves except that our server will scan for us until we have our own scanner.

If someone wants to do what we are doing, first make up your mind to do the following:

1. Read everything you can get your hands on. You can be the dumbest person in the world and still succeed.
2. Learn all you can about what marketing techniques help. Approach the participation in the Internet with an open, blank mind. Old marketing techniques don't necessarily carryover into Cyberspace.
3. Be patient, patient, patient.
4. Update frequently or else your visitors will become booooooooored.
5. GET ON THE FRONT END OF THE LEARNING CURVE. Think of the Internet and Web marketing as a bell curve. Get on and hang on. The curve is expanding and even though you will make progress,

the body of knowledge will probably exceed your ability to keep up....no sweat. Your competitors are probably just sitting around talking about it. You are doing something about it.

6. Remember, the dog that trots about gets the worm. The Internet is like the lottery. It is impossible to win the lottery if you don't play. If you don't experiment with the Internet, fumble and stumble about, you will never be able to use this exciting new tool to your advantage.

7. Think how cool it will be to tell your snobby friends that "You're just getting on the Net, I've been on forever. I guess some of us are just smarter then others."

8. Site promotion. I have searched the net to find any free listing possible, Yahoo, etc. We also now include our site in direct mailings, "CU Cruising is now on the Internet, visit our site..." Then I respond to people like you and hope I will say something that will help you and your book will sell in the millions and you might mention us somewhere and those millions will look in and "BINGO."

We plan an electronic newsletter in about a month just as soon as our list server is ready. Important, make this a FREE service. We capture the e-mail address and then from time to time send out info we think will be interesting. Sales info will be kept subtle and the focus will be on interesting information like the meaning of the word POSH, where it came from, etc. If you want to know, send a new e-mail.

We got our first sale off of an e-mail message in February when AOL posted our site to someplace on their net.

How did the startup phase affect your personal life?

It was fun and my poor brain went bats with ideas...still does.

My day

We have a staff of 18 people. One does all our internal graphics work so she also builds the Home Pages based on my input. I spend about three to four hours a day wandering around the Net looking for places to advertise or link to. I also answer e-mail inquiries. We have two e-mail addresses, and I write copy to be included in our site. For example, AEACU wants to offer a ski trip next year. Sooooo, in about a week we will have three pages, each with a picture showing the three possible sites: Whistler, Copper Mt., and Mt. Bachelor in Oregon. On July 2, a newsletter will be mailed to 70,000 members and the Web site will be listed, as well as a request to visit the ski pages and vote on the one you would like to go on. A reservations mask will also be included for those ready to buy.

The hardest aspect of the work on the website is:

1. Figuring out how to promote the site.
2. Tying to convince other sites to finger us.
3. Writing copy and communicating to a site visitor effectively—holding their attention and creating a place they will want to visit again in the future. I have even thought of having a continuing soap that has nothing to do with our products or services. With characters that would take on goofy social issues or in general get themselves in all sorts of trouble, sort of like a serial story, just to get people to come back to the site to see what new things have developed. I even thought it would be fun to get the audience to participate with possible story lines and if one was used, the person that sent in the idea would become a character in the plot.

How much time do you spend running the site?

About four to five hours a day including updating and looking in for mail. We expect when the Western Pacific reservation site is up, the amount of time spent on our Home Page to increase to eight to 10 hours and more around the holidays (peak travel periods).

What do you like most about being on the Web?

What I like most about my work is the ability to dream and then translate dreams into reality—or at least try. Someone once said our imagination is constrained by the distance between our ears. In our case, we do not suffer from any such constraint. Before Internet, we have always believed our marketing area is wherever our phone will reach. In 1988 we were getting traffic out of Lebanon as well as much of western Europe on projects we were involved in. Internet connection only expands our ability to communicate. We have no fear of doing business outside our geographic area, a problem most of my industry intensely worries about.

In fact, last week I was speaking to the director of a small consortium I belong to. He is planning a Web site for our group (excluding me of course) with the objective of reaching people in our county—that's right—county not country. I reminded him that the net goes all over the world and bla bla bla. Whoops, "I forgot," was his reply. Small thinking and old fashioned marketing at its best.

What do like least?

What I like least is my lack of knowledge and the inability to find answers. I once asked our server (we're not there any more) how to do something simple like reply to a Usenet group. He said, "Buy a book and read it." The server was run by a bunch of teenagers (I guess) that never learned about customer service.

What was your greatest moment?

My greatest moment. Yet to come I'm sure but thus far seeing my Web site up and running and having a friend send me an e-mail to tell me he saw it too. Doesn't take much to make me happy. The day we get 30,000 hits will result in beer for all!!

Are there any hazards to running your site?

I don't think there are any at this time with the exception of credit cards. The financial drain is quite small, and the legal issues are non—issues until someone sues me however, we are careful in what we say and do. Personal hazards — addiction to the project and takes me away from surfing at T Street in San Clemente on Saturday.

General

Are customers concerned with credit card security?

Very much so. Until we have an encryption program that works well we will ask our customers to give us their credit card information via telephone.

Are you glad you put your business on the Web?

I am glad to be on the Web. If nothing else, it is a great experiment and a chance to use my brain a bit...not too much for fear of damage. And given what I know now would I do it again...in a heartbeat. Besides what could be more fun then trying to accumulate little green pieces of paper with pictures of dead people on them?

What else would you like to say?

Just this: The difference between success and failure, particularly as it applies to this subject, is doing something almost right and doing something exactly right. So take your time, learn the system, don't take short cuts, and stay relaxed. Remember, the only place success comes before work is in the dictionary.

TRAVEL RESOURCES MAGAZINE

Overview—Many people are looking for resources to help them enrich their lives. Whether it be travel, cooking, sports, or professional information, a Home Page Magazine, full of links to other sites and chock full of editorial matter can help attract an audience. Once you verify that audience, you can sell advertisements to merchants.

Rewards—If you do this business correctly, you can make money from advertisers. Travel operators also might be able to promote their own packaged tours. Agents also can use this business model to make reservations from Internet travelers.

Risks—Same as with any business.

Special marketing considerations for Home Pages—Create a special marketing hook that makes the magazine speak the same language as your audience. Check out the case study with TravelAssist below and see their Home Page. They have an online "concierge" to help you find information. That word is a lot friendlier and relevant than "online search engine." Also, try to convey a sense of fun, adventure, and relaxation by your choice of words and art.

Links to Home Pages
Search Yahoo or Webcrawler for numerous travel-related sites.

HOTELS, BED AND BREAKFAST, INNS, LODGES

Overview—The hospitality industry is coming onto the Internet as fast as Super Bowl victors go to Disneyland. By advertising its services and taking reservations on the Internet, your stately inn in England can be seen by tourists in Sri Lanka. If you own such an establishment, you are already facing serious competition from the national chains as well as from mom and pops who saw the light years ago.

Rewards—Promoting your services on the Internet can expand your client base. Be sure to have data ports on your phones to please e-mail users!

Risks—The only risk of being online is not being online as your competitors eat your lunch.

Special marketing elements for the Home Page—Major hotel sites are showing pictures of rooms, maps, and toll free reservation numbers. You must compete on this level. Most Home Pages show pictures of the establishment, rooms, and smiling staffs. They list rates and include reservation numbers and e-mail reservation forms. To add value, you could include links to Home Pages of local tourist attractions, cities, shopping, and entertainment centers. Links from these sites can help your business grow (e.g. "Coming to Sante Fe? Stay at the Inn of the Animal Tracks! Click here for a tour!"). To help add more flavor to your site, list menus, recipes, and afternoon snacks.

Links to Home Pages
Guest House Cottage and B&B—
http://www.halcyon.com/dale/breaktfast.html
Marriott International— http://www.marriott.com
San Francisco Hotel Reservations— http://www.hotelres.com/

TOUR GUIDES AND SERVICES

Overview—Travel guides offering tours of Hawaii by helicopter, river canoeing adventures, and the like can be found on the Internet. You can create a tour that takes advantage of your favorite activity, like biking along country roads, wine tours of Napa Valley, or walking tours of delicatessens in New York. Create a Home Page and then market the site.

Rewards—Creating a tour business can be a nice sideline to your current job—and you'll get paid for doing what you like to do. As some kinds of tours can accommodate large numbers of people, you can make a decent day's income. For example, a walking tour of your town's architectural district can accommodate 30—40 people (more if you can project your voice above the urban roar). If they paid $15 a head, you'd make $450 for a morning or afternoon's work on a weekend. Other groups that must be kept small for safety sake, like a bike tour, can charge slightly higher fees. A helicopter tour of Hawaii, on the other hand, might be able to fit only four people, but can command $150 a seat!

Risks—Ask your insurance agent about liability for injuries.

Special marketing elements for the Home Page—Pictures and written descriptions of the highlights of the tours, comments from previous tourists, and menus of restaurants visited would add visual appeal. Prices, times, and itineraries would need to be included. For an added marketing boost, consider creating a game of the places you'd visit, such as a treasure hunt. You could also charge for links to sites you visit, or create Home Pages for them.

Links to Home Pages

Blue Hawaii Helicopter Tours—
http://www.maui.net/blue/bluehaw/blue.html
Rainbow Canoe Expeditions—http://maui.net/~canoe

16 SOFTWARE AND CONSULTANTS

It shouldn't be a surprise that software publishers are a true success story on the Internet. After all, doesn't everyone who uses the Internet have a computer? What a perfectly matched target audience!

This chapter will look at how to sell software online, a one-man software publisher in Australia who is selling software worldwide to critical acclaim, a 10-person software retailer that exists only on the Internet, computer consultants, and software games tips.

SOFTWARE PUBLISHING BUSINESS

Overview—Software sales are among the largest category on the Internet. After all, everyone who uses the Internet uses a computer! What a great match of demographics.

Rewards—Selling software through the retail channel can cost $250,000-$500,000, which is way too much for most midnight engineers (and small software companies). The Internet can give these entrepreneurs the exposure they need to make it in the virtual world or real world. More than a dozen multimillion dollar software companies got their start posting shareware (try software before you buy it) on the commercial online services. Numerous other publishers have used this marketing method to make good livings and to supplement their daytime jobs.

Risks—Software publishers the world over live in fear of having their works pirated (copied without permission). This could happen on the Internet. However, publishers can take precautions such as posting files that will lock after a given period of time, or not working unless the works have been paid for and registered.

Special marketing elements for the Home Page—Software publishers should pay attention to letting people know the benefits of their products, which too often are shrouded in a set of meaningless features.

Home Pages should point out the system requirements for the software. If software demos or time trials are posted for downloading (retrieval), the file size should be posted as well as an estimate on how long the file will take to transmit. This will avoid confusion later on as the consumer waits 30 minutes or longer and wonders if the machine is working or locked up.

Instructions for payment should be posted.

Links to Home Pages

Quarterdeck— http://www.qdeck.com
Sausage Software—http://www.sausage.com. Please see case study
     in this chapter.
Stac Electronics—http://www.stac.com

For More Information

How to Publicize High Tech Products and Services, by Daniel Janal, Janal Communications.

How to Sell Your Software, by Bob Schenot, John Wiley and Sons.

The Shareware Book, by Bob Schenot, Compass New England

The Association of Shareware Professionals, 545 Grover Road, Muskegon, MI 49442, Phone: 616-788-5131, Fax: 616-788-2765, CompuServe: GO SHARE

CASE STUDY—SAUSAGE SOFTWARE, SOFTWARE PUBLISHER

Steve Outtrim

Sausage Software

P.O. Box 36

Briar Hill VIC 3088

AUSTRALIA

http://www.sausage.com

sausage@scully.rucc.net.au

Background

Who is your primary audience?

People who want to create HTML documents for the World Wide Web.

How will they benefit from your product or service?

HotDog provides a graphical interface to the HTML command language. In simple terms, they can click a few buttons instead of typing a slew of obscure commands.

How does your product or service differ from others?

HotDog is a 100% commercial venture. Most other HTML editors have been created as shareware or freeware, written in the author's spare time. Obviously, someone working on their program whenever they get a free minute is going to find it much harder to produce great software than a company that can devote much more time, money, and resources to development.

The feedback we've got from our users is that HotDog is easier to use, more pleasant to look at, and much more useful than its competitors.

Is this business an offshoot of your existing business, or does it exist only on the Internet?

We exist only on the Internet (well, we sell through CompuServe and by fax, but since we're selling Internet software, we'd be dead without it!).

Where does your business operate?

I run the business from an office at home. Sausage Software is structured very much as Charles Handy described the "Shamrock Organization" in his book The Age of Unreason.

I am (at the moment) the sole full-time employee of Sausage Software; any work I can't handle is subcontracted out globally, via the Internet. These subcontractors work for me, but they're not technically employees.

Some are people working from their bedroom in their spare time, some are professional consultants, and some are employed by organizations we contract work to, so they work on HotDog as part of their job.

What is your background and training?

I have a degree in accountancy and management. I've been programming since 1981 (self-taught). I've only had two full-time jobs—systems programmer on a Unisys mainframe for the New Zealand Inland Revenue Department, and office manager for a food-industry business here in Melbourne. Part of my role at the latter job was to develop a financial system for them. I left with the intention of starting my own business to sell this package, but the accountancy market is pretty mature and the barriers to entry are high.

I spent three days thinking about how the world is going to change in the next few years, and almost every idea I could come up with was in some way tied to the Internet. I should qualify this by saying I was by no means an Internet junkie or "guru" —most of my time on the Net was spent talking to my cyber-buddies in alt.drunken.bastards.

But I really believe that the Net is going to change dramatically over the next couple of years, and the opportunities for making money here are phenomenal.

Anyway, I settled on HotDog quite by accident. I was creating some HTML pages for my personal account, just to say who I am, what I like, and all the other stuff that no-one really gives a damn about.

I spent a while looking for a good editor, and eventually found a program. This was functional, but not brilliant. It was written in Visual Basic, which is my programming language of choice. I thought "Hell, I must be able to do better than this," so I spent a few days banging together a little program.

When I was finished, I decided to test the waters on the Net. I posted a single message in comp.infosystems.www.authoring.html, asking if people were interested in helping to test a new HTML editor for Windows. I expected I'd get maybe 10 replies. Within three days, I had 150 testers (by the time HotDog was released, I had over 800). I'm not stupid—I realized very quickly that I was onto something here. There was (and still is) an enormous pent-up demand for decent HTML tools, and it seemed like there were a lot of people very unhappy with the current software.

Getting started

When did you start your business?

March 1995 (but the idea for HotDog came in May 1995).

Did you create a business plan before going online?

Yes and no. The business plan was there, but I didn't specifically create a plan like "OK, this is how I'm going online, this is who we should use, this is how many hits a day we're going to get, etc." This information was in my head. The business plan is more useful to tell the bank, accountants, and other nontechnical people what my business is about. These people don't want to know about projected transfer volumes, hits per week, or indeed anything about the Internet (which, as they see on the news every night, is full of rapists, terrorists, and pornographers!).

This is actually one of the difficulties I've found. Since my business is totally centered around the Internet, it's not easy to explain to someone who doesn't know what the Net is.

How much time did it take to get up and running?

Well, it's hard to define "up and running." Getting a virtual Web server took two to three weeks, but I'm still waiting for some of the things I require here. Development of HotDog, from the day I decided to write an HTML editor, to the day it was officially released, took eight weeks.

Did you create the pages yourself?

I created the initial pages myself, but they're now being done by a professional company.

How much did it cost to get started?

- Virtual domain (three months) U.S. $130.
- Permanent Net connection (28800 PPP): AUD $1,200, including modems and phone lines (this is a luxury that's starting to become a necessity for me).
- Development software: U.S. $1,500 (approximately; I already had most of this).
- PC: AUD $5,500 (I'd had this for two years).
- General start-up expenses: $10,000, but I'm paying these as I go; I didn't have to have $10,000 in cash to start the business.

How did you obtain your startup capital?

I funded everything myself. All of the money has been spent from sales. I didn't have any money at all when I started the business!

How did you promote your Home Page?

By announcing the product in appropriate newsgroups, and registering with Yahoo and the other search sites. Now people who like the product are linking to our site from theirs.

How much did it cost to promote your site?

N/A

How long did it take until you made your first sale?

This is probably different for us than for a lot of people you'll be directing this survey to. We didn't put up the Web Site, then wait for people to buy the program. We pre-sold a number of copies to people testing HotDog, so our first sale came a week or so before the product was "officially" released.

How much money has your company made online?

In the 3 weeks since the product was released, about $19,000. I was expecting about a third of that.

How much money do you hope to make?

My goal for the year is $1 million in turnover (that's Australian dollars). We're not actually selling anything physical, so we don't have a cost of goods sold. Probably 30% of turnover will go towards R & D for future products. I'm hoping for a 50% net profit before tax ratio.

What mistakes did you make that you wish you hadn't made?

Our alpha program was way too open. We got people who joined, but weren't interested in testing the program; they just wanted to evaluate a new editor. This meant we had to field a lot of e-mails along the lines of "How dare you release a program with so many bugs!" The whole point of the alpha program was to fix the bugs, so when people actually evaluate the product, it's relatively bug-free.

It was pretty depressing to get these negative comments instead of constructive criticism, but more importantly there's a lot of people out there who don't understand what alpha and beta testing is, and will never buy our product because of all the bugs they found when they tried an earlier version.

Our alpha program for our new product, HotDog Pro, is closed. The only way to get into it is to purchase the program in advance. This means that the people using it are genuinely interested in helping us fix all the bugs because they've made a financial commitment to the product themselves.

What advice would you give to a similar startup?

DO IT! There's no formula for being successful on the Internet. You need to understand the basic rules of doing business on the Net, like don't send people junk e-mail, don't repeatedly post advertising material to newsgroups, don't make inappropriate posts, and try real hard not to flame anyone no matter how much they piss you off. But if you think you have a great idea, try and bounce it off people in newsgroups or mailing lists (which is effectively free and a very rapid market research). If you get an encouraging response, go for your life!

What skills are needed to run a business?

Well, programming skills obviously, and you need to understand the syntax and the theory of HTML. I'm finding that I also have to be responsible for other companies' bugs. We get a lot of people blaming us for bugs in Netscape, Trumpet Winsock, and Windows.

You can't really say "Talk to Microsoft. I don't want to know." But it's frustrating when you get the "Your product is a load of crap" messages because of something completely out of your control! So I guess a thick skin is a useful skill.

I think a high standard of ethics is very important—a lot of people are wary of doing business over the Net, particularly with someone in another country; in my experience, this is more of a problem for Americans than anyone else, but I guess that's because the rest of us get used to purchasing things from the States. You need to do everything in your power to reassure them. If your customers are impressed with your integrity and service, then they'll tell their friends, or vouch for you in public forums like newsgroups, when people express concern.

I find writing skills to be very useful, too. I think if your English and general grammar skills were below average, you could alienate a lot of people and just generally give an unfavorable impression of your professionalism.

What special qualities are needed to run your site?

I think graphic design skills are important (that's one of the reasons why someone else is doing our site). An understanding of basic principles of business law and copyright is useful.

My day

What does your average day look like?

Get up 9-10 A.M.
Answer e-mail for two hours.
Have lunch for an hour.
Program until about 7:30 P.M. Watch some TV, have dinner.
Either program or answer more e-mail.
I work on the business seven days a week.

What percentages of time are spent on each task?

20-30. Hard to say, I haven't really measured it.

What was the hardest part of the job in the beginning?

Learning to use the Net - mailing lists, UNIX, PGP, things like that.

What do you like most about your work?

I can run the business whenever it suits me, and really from anywhere in the world. I guess you'd call this "freedom."

What do you like least?

Waking up in the morning to find 200 e-mail messages waiting for replies, then finding that most of them say "Your program doesn't work. How could you do this to me?")

What was your greatest moment?

Well, some of the reviews we're getting have been pretty nice. I guess the greatest moment was my first sale. It's an amazing feeling, to know that you can create something out of thin air, and people will pay you for it. It's very, very satisfying.

How much time do you spend conducting business, marketing, selling, upgrading your site?

Not much (but a lot of time on upgrading the product). I'm planning on hiring some full-time programmers very soon; this will free me up to concentrate most of my time on marketing.

How did the startup phase affect your personal life?

The fact that I had no money made me cranky! Other than that, there weren't any major effects.

Are you glad you are on the Web for personal and business reasons?

Absolutely. I've never been happier. Not only am I making money, I'm having a helluva lot of fun! As far as business reasons go, I think I'm in the right place at the right time with the right product.

Given what you know now, would you do it again?

In a second.

The future

What is your next venture?

We're going to continue building the business as providers of authoring and design tools for the information superhighway. I also want to diversify into multimedia programs for the educational market. I think making interactive Dr. Seuss-style books would be an incredible amount of fun.

What else would you like to say?

Hey, I've enjoyed talking about myself! I would like to say that I believe the Net needs some sort of regulatory body to ensure that businesses who get "wired" behave properly. In Australia we have a Fair Trading Act which prevents you from making false statements and generally enforces ethical behavior. There's nothing to stop a competitor from publicly denigrating my product in a newsgroup; neither is there anything to stop a business from taking orders but never delivering the products. Sure, you could prosecute them under their local laws, but who wants to fly to Taiwan to sue a Taiwanese company?

This idea could be implemented like a Chamber of Commerce, an elected body who hear complaints from consumers about businesses. If you're not doing the right thing, you can't be a member of the Chamber of Commerce. That way, consumers who are wary of doing business with a company can check with the Chamber of Commerce. If the business is a member, then you're probably a lot safer dealing with them. I'd happily pay to join an organization like this.

ONLINE RETAILER

Overview—Hardware and software retailers can sell products online. You don't even need to have a storefront, as the case study on software.net will show. Please see the additional case study on software.net in Chapter 4 as a model for starting this type of business.

Rewards—Increased sales via online ordering and increased traffic to your store. Companies that do drop-ship ordering will not need to carry large amounts of products in inventory. Entrepreneurs can target special audiences, like parents, teachers and accountants to offer a one-stop shopping solution and resource center for customers.

Risks—Normal business risks.

Special marketing elements for the Home Page—Since you don't have a salesperson online to answer questions, the Home Page becomes your salesperson. It should contain a mountain of information about each product, its features, benefits, audience, and system requirements. It should also include payment options and information about return privileges, if any.

Links to Home Pages

software.net— `http:www.software.net`

CASE STUDY—SOFTWARE.NET

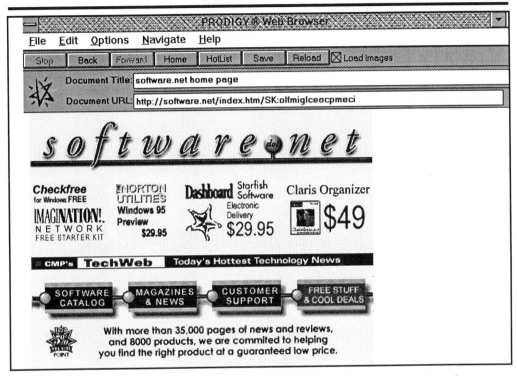

Figure 20-2. Sales items are displayed prominently on software.net's cyber store. Copyright 1994, 1995 CyberSource Corporation.

William S. McKiernan

software.net

CyberSource Corp.

1050 Chestnut Street; Suite 201

Menlo Park, CA 94025

http://software.net/index.html

billm@software.net

415-473-3067

Background

Who is your primary audience?

Corporate, government, university users.

How will they benefit from your product or service?

Electronic distribution of software offer over 8,000 software titles and 35,000 pages of product information.

How does your product or service differ from others?

Electronic distribution.

Is this business an offshoot of your existing business, or does it exist only on the Internet?

Only on the Internet.

Where is your business conducted?

Office. We have 10 people right now with plans to grow to 30 by first quarter 1996.

What is your background and training?

President of public software company, (took them public-McAfee Associates) Harvard M.B.A,, C.P.A.

Getting Started

When did you start your business?

April 1994.

Did you create a business plan before going online?

Yes.

How much time did it take to get up and running?

Six months.

Did you create the pages yourself or did you get help?

Engineering team.

How much did it cost to get started?

Approximately 100k (including merchandise).

Did you need to go to an outside source for startup capital?

Self funded to begin.

How did you promote your site?

Through traditional public relations and reciprocal links.

How much did it cost to promote your site?

$25,000.

How long did it take until you got your first sale?

Few hours.

How much has your company made?

$15,000 per week.

How much money do you expect to make?

Lots—plan is to do $3 million this year.

What mistakes did you make that you wish you hadn't made?

Nothing catastrophic yet.

What advice would you give someone trying to start a business?

Focus on customer needs.

What skills would a person need to conduct business?

No fear.

What special qualities are needed to run your site?.

Yes.

Your Day

What does your average day look like?

Not for the faint of heart.

What does your job entail?

A little of everything.

How many hours a week do you spend working on your site?

60.

What percentages of time are spent on each task?

Hour each on 60 million different things.

What was the hardest aspect of the work in the beginning?

Working without sleep.

What do you like most about your work?

Inventing a new channel, being independent.

What do you like the least?

Lack of support infrastructure.

What was your greatest moment?

Turning the server on and then seeing the site the next day on the floor of Comdex.

How much time do you spend conducting business?

They are all intimately related.

How did the startup phase affect your personal life?

Fortunately I have an understanding wife.

Are you glad you are on the Web on personal and business reasons?

Yes.

Given what you know now, would you do it again?

Definitely.

The future

What is your next venture?

Distributing other digital content via the Net besides software.

What else would you like to say?

This is not a business for committees and task forces. You do. You make mistakes. You learn. You do again. It's like working in a giant laboratory.

COMPUTER CONSULTANT

Overview—What better place to look for a computer consultant than on the Internet? A Home Page could be the ideal marketing tool for the consultant who can write software from scratch, install a network, and provide a myriad of other services for the home, small business, large business, government, or educational marketplaces.

Rewards—You could find new clients.

Risks—Normal business risks.

Special marketing elements for the Home Page—Show people you know what you are doing by posting your bio, testimonials, and qualifications. To cut down on the number of tire kickers, you might want to list your prices and specialties.

Links to Home Pages

Faludi Computing— `http://www.faludi.com`

INTERVIEW—FALUDI COMPUTING

Robert Faludi   `http://www.faludi.com`

Faludi Computing-Macintosh   `info@faludi.com`

Internet Consulting

242 Townsend Street   Phone: 415-512-8212

San Francisco, CA 94107   Fax: 415-512-8215

What were you hoping to achieve by putting your company on the Net?

Faludi Computing provides Macintosh consulting services to San Francisco businesses. We specialize in wide area communications systems and Internet.

We put our company on the net to provide cheap, fast, and easy wide area communications. Our internet connection serves as our link to the world, both for outgoing connections to other businesses services, and incoming connections to our own services and marketing information.

How has being on the net helped you?

We regularly get work from companies that have seen our Web page and contacted us for more information. The best part of an Internet connection, however, is that we have been able to keep on top of developments in technology in a way that would be impossible without the incredible two-way communications with hundreds of other companies both in San Francisco and around the world.

What kind of background is needed to do what you do?

We do business Macintosh consulting. I would recommend three years of Macintosh experience combined with some business management experience. We need to know about computers, but it is even more important to understand the types of problems that businesses are using computer communications to solve.

What kind of income can one expect to make?

$20,000 —$1,00,000 :-) There's plenty of business out there, but not a bit for those who aren't working very hard to keep themselves informed and clients happy.

What is the best part about your job?

Exposure to a technological and cultural revolution. And control of my own hours and working environment.

What is the worst part about your job?

Some people wouldn't like the long hours. The worst part for me is that all the tools we use are constantly under development. It takes a lot a patience to deal with so much half-baked software, although it has greatly heightened my appreciation for well programmed work.

How many hours do you work a week?

Don't ask. Actually, I probably only work 50—60 hours, and I get to choose exactly which ones those are.

SOFTWARE GAMES TIPS

Overview—You might not want your co-workers to know that you are an expert gamesman (who learned the finesse while on the company clock). However, you can tell the Internet world about your prowess and your ability to provide answers to the thorny questions that help people unlock the mysteries of Myst and other games.

Rewards—You can make incremental income from creating a tip and selling it many times. The cost of distributing the answers on e-mail is nothing. This field can be a good one as there are dozens of tips books on the retail shelves. This proves there is a market for advice.

Risks—Normal business risks.

Special marketing elements for the Home Page—You need to create a system for getting paid. Please refer to Chapter 3 for payment plans. You might offer answers online and/or via phone.

Links to Home Pages

This is a new business. You could be the first! Stake out your game territory now!

17 INTERNET CAREERS

INTERNET INDUSTRIES

A whole new field of jobs has been created by the Internet to provide services to people who want to do business on the Internet. These businesses include:

- Internet Service Provider
- Digital Mall landlord
- Web Farm
- Internet Advertising Agency-Internet Presence Provider
- Webmaster
- HTML programmer
- Illustrator
- Demographics and database marketer
- Internet software tools developer
- Multimedia conference coordinator
- Internet Service Provider

Overview—This company provides the local telephone number connection for consumers to access the Internet. Although many companies are large, there are a phenomenal number of one— and two—person companies. They do best when they operate along the back roads of America where a long distance call to connect to the Internet is a very expensive proposition.

Qualifications—Superb technical skills. Operating this equipment is not easy. Additionally, you should be good at marketing, hiring, and managing people.

Rewards—Recurring income from leasing space on your T-1 line.

Risks—Heavy start-up costs. Lots of competition.

DIGITAL MALL LANDLORD

Overview—Digital Malls are conglomerations of merchants who want to sell products and services on the Internet. By co-locating on a mall, businesses benefit from traffic to other people's stores. Digital Mall landlords must attract businesses, sell space, provide customer support, hire programmers and designers to create mall stores, take orders and process credit card information, as well as market the site to consumers and provide security against online thieves.

Qualifications—Excellent programming skills, people management, financial abilities.

Rewards—Recurring income from leasing space on your T-1 line. Extra income opportunities from sales of programming, marketing, artistic services.

Risks—Heavy start-up costs. Lots of competition.

WEB FARM OPERATORS

Overview—Web Farms are like Digital Malls, but provide fewer support services. At their most basic level, they are a business incubator for companies that need a space to house their stores, but not need the support services offered by a full-service provider, like a Digital Mall.

Qualifications—Excellent technical abilities to make sure the connections to the Internet operate properly. Good management, sales, and people skills.

Rewards—Recurring income from leasing space on your T-1 line.

Risks—Heavy start-up costs. Lots of competition.

CASE STUDY—LAUNCH POINT INTERNET SERVICE CENTER

Alan Crofut

http://www.lpoint.com

http://www.sfweb.com

Launch Point Internet Service Center   cpu@lpoint.com

221 Main Street, Suite 1040   Phone: 415-995-8535

San Francisco, CA 94105   Fax: 415-995-8548

Background

Who is your primary audience?

Anyone with products or services to promote, information to publish online.

How will they benefit?

We provide the technical wizardry behind the high speed internet connection. This saves our clients from having to spend lots of money and time on their own system. We create websites from scratch, the graphic content, the HTML programming, and database and CGI programming, as well as the ongoing administration and changes. We are a one stop shop, if you need us to be. We also work with our client's art departments and marketing departments.

This way, if a company brings us an idea drawn on a napkin, we can create a full Web site from it.

How does your service differ from others?

Our attitude is that soon enough all of this will be simple enough to put into every office. We work with our clients towards that end. We try to educate our clients if they want, that way they get more control and eventually will take over their own site.

Is this an offshoot of an existing business?

No, but I do service calls on an hourly basis to offset the roller coaster ride called equipment budget for Internet Access.

Where is your office located?

Office building South of Market near the downtown Financial District and Multimedia Gulch. A good location for San Francisco. Easy access to clients and consultants.

What is your background and training?

Networking for 10 years. Service calls on other networks, now I have one of my own.

Getting started

When did you start your business?

One year old, started as a school. In February we started putting up Web sites.

Did you create a business plan before going online?

Absolutely. And spent far more than the budget and got far less in return.

How much time to get running?

Organic process over the coarse of a year. I still feel like we are finding our niche. Lately we have been concentrating on moving pictures and sound. Multimedia on the net is coming up, so we are moving organically towards that vertical market. We are always in a state of growth, because the Internet is.

How much did it cost to get started?

Telco T1Dial-in setup	$3,000
Provider setup	$1,000
Computers and peripherals	$22,000
Routers, CSU, modems	$6,000
Cabling	$2,000
Software	$7,000
Monthly Net Access	$1,800
Monthly office overhead	$1,500
Salaries	(Laugh)

Did you need to go to an outside source for startup capital?

It would have been easier, but everyone I've talked to so far wants to be way over compensated for an initial gamble in an unknown industry. So, I have been funding this from service calls and setup fees. I also trade services and do any kind of strategic ties I can. The only outside source I have used for capital has been credit cards.

How much have you made?

Barely begun to show a profit. Lately we have been bringing in over 10k monthly, but that is new. I expect it to grow, but don't count on anything. The Internet trade winds have been good to us, but there could be storms.

What mistakes have you made?

Not marketing enough. Paying too much attention to the Tech end and not selling enough. Few other sites of my size can boast the solid hardware platform and fast bandwidth allocation that we have. We are committed to a fast, secure site. But that alone does not pay the bills.

What advice would you give entrepreneurs starting a business on the net?

Get capital. Hire good talent. Get help. Take regular vacations before you forget how.

What skills would a person need to be a success?

Tech—Hardware and software. Programming helps a lot.

Sales—Sell the services.

PR—Promote yourself and your client sites.

Design—Graphic content and layout.

Teaching—People don't buy what they can't understand.

What education is needed?

Computer hardware and software. Specialized software, like Windows NT Admin or UNIX. Full knowledge of how the Internet works.

What special qualities are needed?

Patience, drive, abstinence, graphic and film education, advertising eye, a high degree of entrepreneurial spirit, and a legal mind. A good renaissance man or woman can do this, it is learning all the time.

How did you promote the business?

Word of mouth. Web registration. Direct mail offering to give demonstrations. Occasional speaking engagements.

How much do you spend on promotion?

$500. I should spend more.

How did the startup effect your life?

I no longer have a life. People who have no e-mail address have not heard from me in a long time. On the other hand, I have not been happier in years. Blind drive can uncover very interesting attributes in a persons character. I consider my life exciting, even though it wouldn't seem so to a young single person on a nice salary. At any moment, the deal I am involved in may bring me PLENTY of money. It is happening, and to people with less than I have going for me.

Your day

What does your average day look like?

In the office about 9 A.M. Phone and mail till 11A.M. Meet with prospects or do service calls till 4 or 6 P.M. Program HTML, Site admin, other tech work in office till midnight. Plan the next day before going home.

During that day, I educate people, answer the same questions quite a few times, do project management for ongoing Websites, coordinate the outsourcing, solve tech support calls, schedule other people, call prospective clients, touch base with clients and never eat lunch.

At night, all tech work is done, including putting up the actual pages. This is the most rewarding part of the biz. And at night, it is very peaceful. Weekends are spent doing more programming and graphic work, or taking care of invoices and planning the coming week. Saturday and Sunday are workdays. I always try to plan for one day during the week when I can sleep late, but rarely get it.

What does your job entail?

Checking all hardware on our internal network daily. Checking all client Web sites daily. Scanning the news and trade pubs for pertinent info. Try new software versions. Setup sales calls, plan marketing strategies, perform specialized demonstrations. Tech support for clients, programming, graphic content, Internet use. Project Management phone calls, faxes, follow—ups, scheduling time Percentage of time spent:

Checking Launch Point	8%
Get clients	6%
Maintain Clients	15%
HTML Programming	15%
Graphics	25%
Tech Support	10%
Project Management	20%
Invoicing, Accounting	2%

Hours per week. Over 80 on the average. 10 to 18 hours per day. 7 days per week, usually.

What was the hardest aspect in the beginning?

Planning important purchases without a budget for it. Reading about overnight successes of people with less hardware and expertise.

What do you like most?

The roller coaster ride—not knowing what is around the corner. Our next deal could be huge.

Planning for the future, plotting the course for Launch Point over the next few years on the Internet, and knowing it is all possible.

Providing communication for clients. Web Site programming is INSTANT GRATIFICATION! Both sides of your brain get exercised, and then people all over the globe can see what you have done. That is exciting.

What do you like least?

Paying the huge bills.

What was your greatest moment?

A few months ago we realized we were cutting edge, having arrived quite by well planned accidents. But the feeling was gone in 15 minutes, and I'm sure we are not as cutting as we were. But we are definitely on the Wave. I couldn't tell you where the beach is, though. Before that, the first Home Page we did for ourselves was a big high. It was all using shareware and a 486 server. When that happened, I felt like we had really accomplished something.

What risks are there?

Unstable biz environment, and no previous boilerplate to go by.

Legal Issues—Not settled and change often. Mercy of big biz, our government, and loose interpretations of old laws.

Financial—Unpredictable hardware costs. Bandwidth is a slippery commodity, in many forms and costs.

Technical—Can leave you behind if you let it.

Personal—Lose all friends who aren't online.

How much money do you expect to make?

A comfortable living. It is a rare service provider that is getting rich. If they are, check them carefully. Unless you have some real sweet clients, the numbers just don't add up to instant success here. What I am trying to do is build equity and client base over the next few years, and any real profit will result from the sale of Launch Point.

Are you glad to be on the Web?

Personally I am glad to be a part of the largest cooperative project on the planet. There are millions of people working in concert online, at a time when it is hard to merge in rush hour traffic. Business wise, I am happy to be involved in something akin to the land rush of the 19th century. This is history, and I'm glad to be a part.

Given what you know now, would you do it again?

Absolutely, and with more money.

Where can people learn how to do what you do?

Seminars, courses, trade shows, on the job training, USENET discussions and technical books all support what I do. Anyone who tries to be a provider should bring along many hats to wear.

The future

What is your next venture?

1. Teleconferencing
2. Motion pictures and sound
3. 3—D animation
4. Combine CD ROM with Web site programming
5. Internal and private Web sites for multiple corporate locations

What else would you like to say?

Keep the Net as free as possible in cost and abilities. Keep your site fast. Don't oversell your bandwidth. Work with cooperation in mind.

WEBMASTER

The Webmaster is the person who runs the day to day administrative and technical operations of the Web site. Depending on the company, their job description could include handling mail from the public, training employees and revising the pages, updating the page with content and advising others. They are part administrator, part artist and designer, part taskmaster, and part magician.

CASE STUDY—WEBMASTER, PHASE TWO STRATGEISS, INC.

Coleman Jolley

Phase Two Strategies

170 Columbus Avenue #300

San Francisco, CA 94133-5148

coleman_jolley@p2pr.com

415-772-8400

Background

Coleman Jolley is Webmaster for Phase Two Strategies, Inc., a public relations and marketing firm based in San Francisco.

What kind of person makes a good Webmaster?

You are essentially the art director and chief programmer of the Web site. You might be assigning these out, but you are in charge of the lay of the land.

What skills are needed to be Webmaster?

I would want to see someone with a background in desktop publishing so they have familiarity with conversion of files, because the Web is a different environment. You have to take into account that graphics are optimized for screen and not print. There should be an appreciation for Quicktime and MPEG and video formats. You are asking for people who know a little bit about everything.

It is something you research on your own. There are books on how to learn HTML and there are a lot of resources on the Web. I'm not aware of any school that teaches these subjects. Some of the art colleges are just adding it on now.

What kind of salaries can Webmasters make?

Right now it is a fairly new and exciting field. You can make $35-50 an hour or up to $100 an hour if you have a hefty portfolio. Webmasters can expect to earn $28-35,000 annually. Heavy commercial sites with UNIX implementation might pay $40-50,000. Wages will drop as these skills become more common.

What skills will Webmasters need to develop?

Commerce servers are the new thing. Webmasters will need to program the CGI (Common Gateway Interface) scripts, which allow you to implement forms and download information into databases and interact with Visa or Mastercard in real time so people can purchase with their credit cards.

What makes a Home Page good from an artistic point of view?

You have to think of interaction and showtime. It is a little bit different than graphic designers are used to. For example, designing tables is different on the Internet.

To me it is kind of the Renaissance of computer use because before the Web, you had artists who didn't know how to use computers and computer users who didn't know how to be graphic designers. You have to have a little of both skills. People have mutated into that—a new evolution of people who are not quite programmers and not quite graphic designers. I think that is what Webmasters are in their heart of hearts.

WEB ADVERTISING AGENCY INTERNET PRESENCE PROVIDER

Overview—In the old days of the Web, (old days can be defined as three months from today, regardless of when "today" is), the companies that created Home Pages and cyberstores for businesses were called Internet Presence Providers. Today, they are called Web Advertising Agencies. Perhaps the pioneers were afraid of the negative connotations the word "advertising" in the hearts of old-time Internet users. However, smart marketers quickly realized that no one knew what the term "presence" meant and that clients wouldn't spend $25,000 for a "presence" but would pay that much and more for a "cyberstore," "Home Page," or "Web Site." These companies can create the marketing plan, design for the Home Page, all HTML conversions, and CGI scripting that creaes catalogs and order forms.

Qualifications—Outstanding marketing acumen, ability to transmit ideas and concepts to HTML programmers and artists, sales skills to land new accounts, financial abilities to run a profitable company and charge what the job is worth in a market that is increasingly price competitive, and management skills.

Rewards—Madison Avenue advertising agencies that are getting into the Web business are charging $25,000 and up for a Home Page.

Risks—Prices are falling, competition is increasing. To succeed, base your sales pitch on quality, not price.

HTML PROGRAMMER

HTML designer—is a person who creates the HTML coding for the Home Page. This process unites the Home Page, sub pages, art and marketing materials, and transforms it into a format the World Wide Web can understand and display to consumers.

Qualifications—Persons who want to do this should understand HTML programming and have a good flair for design.

Rewards—HTML programmers can earn $50-$75 a hour, but prices are falling as more people learn these skills.

Risks—They also face competition from software programs that automatically convert text files into HTML. While these program might not be perfect, they certainly reduce the amount of time needed for human intervention. I predict that most desktop publishers will develop the skills needed for HTML programming within the next 18 months.

INTERVIEW—HTML PROGRAMMER

Dale Beasley   http://www.halcyon.com/dale/stphil.html

22700 28th Ave. So. #210   dbeasley@halcyon.com (Dale Beasley)

Des Moines, WA 98198-4418

206-878-4664

What skills does a Web designer need?

Knowledge of basic HTML extensions, how to use an HTML editor, how to create tables, image maps, and forms, and keeping up with newest extensions.

However, saying all that, it is my understanding that many commercial servers such as AOL, CompuServe, et. al, do not often support the latest extensions. It would probably behoove a real professional to write Web pages that would look good on these servers with an option for those who do support Netscape with the newest extensions.

What advice would you give an entrepreneur to succeed?

Keep pages relatively short—people get bored reading too much. Include pictures to help convince the viewer of the beauty of place.

How long did it take to learn and master?

I learned what I know so far in about a year. I did so because I teach school and have more time during the summer to spend time investigating and developing. I am not a master. I still have a great deal to learn.

What pay ranges can HTML programmers expect to make?

I've been participating on the HTML Writer's Guild and the past few months many HTML developers were arguing this topic. I got so bored reading the arguments that I quit reading them but I think the consensus seemed to be, charge what the market will support. If you're good and in demand, charge as much as you can. If you're just starting or aren't that capable, get what you can.

What are you favorite resources for learning about HTML?

I use newsgroups, looking at other developer's pages that I admire and studying how they're composed. alt.html.writers.guild.list (moderated).

ILLUSTRATORS

Illustrators—Artists who understand the need for creating interesting, interactive artwork that makes few demands on a computer system's overhead. Because pictures need to be a small file size, they must understand the need to limit colors and other intricacies of the new art form.

Qualifications—Excellent artistic ability and how to translate it to a computer screen.

Rewards—Established artists can make $35-$100 an hour on their own.

Risks—Because many artists want to break into this field, it is not unheard of to find artists working for $10 an hour.

DEMOGRAPHICS AND DATABASE MARKETING ANALYSTS

Overview—Demographics and database marketing analysts are high level marketers who have adapted their craft to the Internet. They specialize in creating one-to-one relationships with consumers. They are adept as finding every household, for example, with a Volvo and an ice-cream maker.

Qualifications—Number crunchers on steroids.

Rewards—People who are in this field have backgrounds in direct marketing (junk mail) and live by numbers. They can make $75-150 and hour an up if they have a proven track record.

Risks—Increased competition.

INTERNET SOFTWARE TOOLS DEVELOPER

Overview—The Internet is an immature technology in search of solutions and applications for millions of people around the world. It is the beneficiary and victim of hype that raises expectations of people who think they can do things as easily as in the off-line world. What a tragic surprise awaits those pioneers! The Internet needs software tools to make it easier and more reliable to use.

Rewards—There is a bright future for entrepreneurs to start a business writing software tools for the Internet. Although the Web is a relative newborn, companies like Netscape Communications, which makes browser software for the Web, went public after only 16 months and had a valuation of more than Maytag and Broderbund! Smaller success stories abound, but many companies and individuals are getting rich by running businesses that make the Internet begin to live up to its promise.

A benefit to writing software that helps the Internet is that you have the ability to use the Internet as a printing press and distribution mechanism. These two steps are so costly in the off-line world, that many software publishers with dynamite programs have failed because they couldn't raise enough money to make it in the marketplace.

Your software might be a tool that works immediately to help users, such as Yahoo, InfoSeek, or Webcrawler, the directory search tools. In these cases, let people use the software for free and charge advertisers for the right to post a small ad or link to their site. In this manner, you'll make money by attracting large numbers of readers, instead of making money selling the software.

Another business plan is to let people use the software for free online for a given time and then charge them for subscriptions, which is part of the business plan for InfoSeek.

Risks—There are no new ideas. You will face competition—perhaps intense challenges—from people who are just as smart as you are. The software industry is full of products that won because they were first to market, not the best on the market.

Special marketing elements for the Home Page—Sit down, software developers, you aren't going to like this advice one bit. Give your software away—at least for a limited time. That is the best way for people to try it and recommend it to their companies and friends. Netscape Communications retained a 70-75 percent market share for its browser by giving a limited version away for a limited time period and asking for donations thereafter. In a matter of months, they succeeded in positioning their product as a standard.

The Home Page needs to explain how the software helps people. It should then describe the system requirements, how to download and install the software, and how to pay for it.

Reviews from magazines, as well as testimonials from users will help convince consumers to try the product. Screen shots of the program in action help consumers understand what the product does and looks like.

Links to Home Pages

Walter Shelby Group Ltd.— `http://www.shelby.com/pub/shelby/`

(See the case history that follows)

Internet Roundtable Society—`http://www.irsociety.com/Webchat.html`

CASE STUDY—WALTER SHELBY GROUP: SOFTWARE DEVELOPER

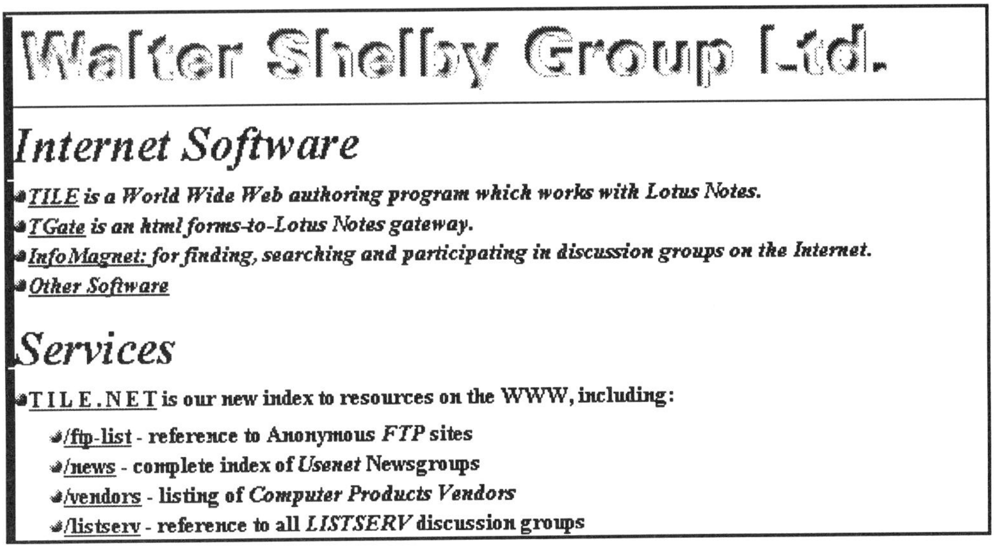

Walter Shelby Group Ltd.

Internet Software

- *TILE is a World Wide Web authoring program which works with Lotus Notes.*
- *TGate is an html forms-to-Lotus Notes gateway.*
- *InfoMagnet: for finding, searching and participating in discussion groups on the Internet.*
- *Other Software*

Services

- T I L E . N E T is our new index to resources on the WWW, including:

  - /ftp-list - reference to Anonymous *FTP* sites
  - /news - complete index of *Usenet* Newsgroups
  - /vendors - listing of *Computer Products Vendors*
  - /listserv - reference to all *LISTSERV* discussion groups

---

Figure 17-1. Walter Shelby Group leads viewers easily to menu selections on its Home Page. Courtesy of Walter Shelby Group Ltd.

John Buckman

Walter Shelby Group Ltd.

4618 Maple Avenue

Bethesda, MD 20814

http://www.shelby.com/pub/shelby/

info@shelby.com

301-718-7840

Background

Who is your primary audience?

People publishing on the Internet who have databases to publish, in Lotus Notes or other formats.

How will they benefit from your product or service?

Most times, when people publish a database on the Web, they reinvent the wheel by writing their own HTML exporting program. TILE allows you to easily create WWW sites from databases, and manages the indices, reports, and forms your site needs to make it easy for your users to find the data they need.

How does your product or service differ from others?

There is no other product out there that creates browseable WWW sites from databases. Everything else takes a "search" approach: fill out a search form and I'll display what I've found. We let users browse the database along any number of categories. For a telephone book, for instance, you could browse by telephone prefix, by last name, by first name, by city, as well as free-text search.

Is this business an offshoot of your existing business, or does it exist only on the Internet?

Net-only.

Where is your office located?

Home converted to office.

What is your background and training?

Masters in philosophy. I've been programming for profit since I was 14, working for Yale University.

When did you start your business?

1987 for the business, 1991 for the Internet business portion.

How did you promote your site?

WWW directories, lists, but mainly by putting up public-service WWW sites that people will want to go to.

How much did it cost to promote your site?

Only time. Others are eager to offer services for free in exchange for publicity.

How long did it take until you got your first sale?

We had sales ready when the software product came out of beta testing.

How much money has your company made?

N/A

Getting started

Did you create a business plan before going online?

No.

How much did time did it take to get up and running?

Four months.

Did you create the pages yourself or did you get help?

Ourselves.

How much did it cost to get started?

Free. Once again, trading services.

Did you need to go to an outside source for startup capital?

I had previously worked as a Lotus Notes and database programming consultant, which is lucrative, and worked 100 weeks to pay my (then) three employees minimal wages.

What mistakes did you make that you wish you hadn't made?

Find a provider I could depend on. This has been a very, very hard mistake to fix.

What advice would you give someone starting a business?

Find people who return your telephone calls, and work with them. Responsibility and professionalism seem to be absent from almost all companies working on the net. This is especially true for the bigger companies.

What skills would a person need to conduct business?

The ability to teach yourself, and, most importantly, thoroughness. 80% of our current business is repeat business or directly obtained by reference from current customers. Every single customer has to be happy, and you have to always have time to talk to them.

My day

What does your average day look like?

I work from 9 A.M. to 11 P.M., with one to two hours of breaks. I do this 6 1/2 days a week.

What does your job entail?

Everything from tech support to sales and programming.

How many hours a week do you spend working on your site?

10 hours a week for e-mail. I have someone else who answers most of it, and she takes about 20 hours a day. About 10 hours a week working on our sites.

How much time do you spend conducting business, marketing, selling, upgrading your site?

About 10-20 hours a week.

What was the hardest aspect of the work in the beginning?

Learning to do everything, too much to learn.

What do you like most about your work?

The potential for success.

What do you like the least?

The risk.

What was your greatest moment?

That's a hard one. Getting anything written about you in the major press (be it USA Today or PC Magazine) is always a great victory.

How did the startup phase affect your personal life?

I had/have none. :)

Are you glad you are on the Web on personal and business reasons?

Yes.

Given what you know now, would you do it again?

Yes.

Where can people find advice about running a site like yours?

At the site itself (`http://tile.net/`) since that's the purpose of the site. People are supposed to be impressed by the site, and want to do it themselves.

The future

What is your next venture?

Concentrating on this for the time being. Have found that doing too many things is what kills the business.

MULTIMEDIA CONFERENCE COORDINATOR

Overview—The teleconferencing business, which allows people in different locations to see live broadcasts and interact with people in different locations, is booming, but it is expensive. The Internet can cut the costs by using such software programs as VocalTel (or WebChat for text and files only).

Rewards—This can become a very lucrative business for a person who understands how to use and install the technology and knows how to market services.

Risks—Normal business risks.

Special marketing elements for the Home Page—Prepare a demo of a conference that can be viewed online, or sent via videotape to potential customers.

Links to Home Pages
This is a new business I created. Run with it.

18 INTERNET SALES

Nothing happens without sales, as the old saying goes. The same is true for the Internet related business. There is a tremendous need for sales people who can transmit the benefits of the Internet to a wide range of potential audiences—from consumers to merchants, but nothing will happen without someone making a sale. The first wave of Internet entrepreneurs is full of people from technical and engineering background who not only don't have sales abilities, they have a disdain for sales in general! This chapter will explore the job opportunities, overviews, qualifications, duties, where the jobs are and, salaries.

JOB OPPORTUNITY—ADVERTISING SALES

Overview—As the Internet becomes more and more commercial, Home Pages will need sales people to sell advertising space. Even as this book is being written, there is a new trend toward charging for links to and from Home Pages (links had been free, and still are at many Web sites). As this industry matures, there will be a need for people to manage sales people, make sales calls both to Web site operators to sign them up as clients, and to potential advertisers who would pay to link to the sites.

Qualifications—Salespeople should have a firm footing in both sales strategies, and netiquette. They must thoroughly understand the mind-set of people who operate businesses on the Internet. One group might be very net savvy and understand the dynamics of links of the economics of advertising in this new media. Others, from traditional businesses, must be educated on the technology and new marketing paradigms of marketing on the Internet (See Chapter 2).

The number of new Home Pages grows at a phenomenal rate every month and the size of the Internet audience grows exponentially as well. Demographers are just beginning to create reliable tools that track the number of visitors. This step is essential as the basic model for advertising is based on the cost per thousand of consumers who see the advertisement, or, in this case, the Home Page, which displays the ad, or the link to the advertiser's site. Different rates will be charged for each level of service.

Duties—Sell advertisements and links to potential advertisers,

Where the jobs are—Traditional advertising agencies, online advertising agencies, traditional mailing list brokers (including Worldata Corporation, a leader based in Pompano Beach, Fla.). This is the kind of business you can start yourself by making arrangements with both advertisers and Web site managers.

Salary—Our survey showed a variety of income opportunities ranging from straight salary to a combination of salary and commission. The potential for income is unlimited because commission work doesn't have a ceiling, earnings can be directly related to the effort, skill and energy of each salesperson.

JOB OPPORTUNITY—CONSUMER AND BUSINESS NETWORK SALES

Overview—As the battle for signing up consumers to online services grows, customer sales representatives will be needed to sell Internet access services to two groups of customers: businesses and consumers. Businesses will be sold on the idea of using ISPs to house and maintain their Web sites. Consumers will be sold subscriptions to local and national ISPs.

Qualifications—Sales skills, presentation skills, speaking skills, understanding of the Internet and numerous services and Home Pages that can benefit different audiences, technical knowledge of the Internet.

Duties—Demonstrate the service to large groups of people, sell products.

Where the jobs are—Internet Access Providers targeting business and consumer use, both on national and local levels, commercial online services (e.g., CompuServe, America Online, Prodigy, Microsoft Network, eWorld, and others).

Salary—Commission or salary base plus commission. Unlimited potential for income.

JOB OPPORTUNITY—ADVERTISING AGENCY SALES

Overview—Online advertising agencies and traditional advertising agencies both need sales people to sign new clients who buy the creating thinking and execution services provided by these full-service centers.

Qualifications—Sales and prospecting skills, ability to understand technical and Internet marketing concepts.

Duties—Find prospects and make appointments, demonstrate agency's expertise and understanding of the Internet and prospect's business, and write proposals.

Where the jobs are—Advertising agencies, digital malls, Web farms, HTML programmers, designers, illustrators.

Salary—Salary or salary base plus commission. Unlimited potential for income.

JOB OPPORUNITY—CONTENT SALES

Overview—Content is king on the Internet. As more Home Pages go online, they will need editorial matter to attract readers and make their pages informative. A need will arise for people to create the content (like a writer or marketing company) or for an agent to find useful articles and pictures that can add value to the Home Page.

Duties—Find out what client's needs are and find the material.

Qualifications—Ability to understand a client's needs, act as acquisition editor to purchase or license material, ability to work with Home Page marketers in understanding their market mission, ingenuity in finding or commissioning material. Talk to a lawyer about copyright issues, fair use and first rights.

Salary—You can be paid by project, by hour or by word (usually for writing)

19 TRADES PEOPLE

This chapter was originally called "Businesses you'd never expect to see on the Net." You would wonder what a tow truck company or plumber would be doing on the Internet. Making friends and influencing people is the answer. This chapter shows how several trades people are using the Internet to promote their businesses.

TRADES PEOPLE, I.E. PLUMBER, ELECTRICIAN, PAINTER

Overview—I wouldn't have suggested that a plumber create a Home Page, but after seeing Hill's Plumbing Home Page, I've changed my mind. Hill's prides itself on being the plumber of choice on Vashon Island. They are staking out a position in a specific market and they are using the Internet to reach out to people who live there and have a computer account. Using this strategy, they will dominate their market.

Rewards—You can reach your techno-literate audience and probably be assured of being the only plumber (or electrician, painter, gardener, handyman) in your neighborhood to be on the Internet. You'll build instant rapport with your clientele because you speak the same language of the Internet.

Risks—On the downside, visitors to your site might not be from your service area and could waste your time with questions. If you are renting space at a digital mall, you could be charged for these people who couldn't possibly be your customers. On the other hand, you could refer them to trades people in their areas, and receive a finders fee.

Special marketing elements for the Home Page—Hill's adds tremendous value to the standard idea of a guest book or register. To capture a person's name and begin building a relationship, the Home Page asks you to submit a question about plumbing. When Hill's answers your question, they have begun a dialog that will be essential in building trust, credibility, and a phone call when the washer leaks!

Practical examples and links to Home Pages

Hills Plumbing—http://www.halcyon.com/hill/hill.html

INTERVIEW—A TOWING COMPANY, INC.

Eugene E. Kashpureff

A Towing Company, Inc. USA

P.O. Box 24106

Seattle, WA 98124-0106

http://www.halcyon.com/ekashp/

http://vbn.com/~towing/

ekashp@halcyon.com

206-935-8697

What are you hoping to accomplish by being on the Web?

Get rich (not too quick), and serve the public while doing it.

How has being on the Web helped you?

Made the front page of the Seattle Times Business Section on July 31.

What advice would give an entrepreneur to succeed on the Web?

Get an unlimited usage access account, look into virtual domains, study your potential market, plan on working hard.

20 HANDLE WITH CARE

While most of the businesses, jobs, and careers discussed in this book can lend themselves easily to the Internet, two business must be given special notice because of the potential for violating Netiquette and disturbing the sense of positive commercialism that is developing on the Internet.

These two businesses are Network Marketing and Mailing Lists. They pose potential danger for their owners if they do not conduct their businesses within the generally accepted bounds of online behavior, which is *don't send unsolicited advertising via email or post it in newsgroups and mailing lists..* (See Chapter 2 for more information on Netiquette)

Already these media are polluted with the tell-tale signs of network marketing businesses, headlines reading "Get Rich Quick," "Fortune to be Made," and "Money in 900 numbers." The proprietors of these businesses are not getting rich from the savvy Internet crowd. Instead, they are wasting the time of the Internet consumers. Don't do it!

This chapter will look at how network marketers and mail list vendors can operate productively on the Internet.

NETWORK MARKETING

NIKKEN

The Sleeping Giant

Millions of people the world over benefit from using Nikken's unique wellness products. Since 1975, Nikken has been developing products to help people gain, and maintain, a higher level of wellness. If you know someone that may benefit from these products please tell them, you'll be glad that you did. Do your shoulders, arms, and/or wrists sometimes ache from typing or moving the mouse?

- **Try the Magboy or Kenko Relax Products.**
Does your backside sometimes hurt from sitting for long periods?

- **The Kenko Seat and ThermaTech Seat were designed to provide comfort.**
Do your feet get sore and tired?

- **Magsteps may help you get the relief your looking for.**
Do you sleep? Would you like to improve your quality of sleep?

The Nikken™ Product Line

- **Nikken Sleep Systems; Designed to help you get the rest you need.**
- **Nikken Accessories; One great product line deserves another.**
- **Relax Products, Thermatechnology, and Electrocare.**
- **N2 Nikken/Nowtrition Products; Wellness from the inside out.**
- **Product Pricing / Order Entry.**

    Gold which buys health is never ill spent.
    - **Specialty Items.**

    Custom order items available from Nikken.

Figure 20-1. Nikken shows how network marketing can be conducted properly on the Internet without violating Netiquette. Courtesy of Total Health Marketing Nikken Independent Distributors.

Jim Clements, Marketing Director

`http:/www.xmission.com/`
`~total/health.html`

Total Health Marketing
Nikken Independent Distributors
1929 East. 9400 South
Sandy, UT 84093

`thm@xmission.com`
801-553-8716

What was your purpose in putting a home page on the Web?

Total Health Marketing, is an organization of Nikken independent distributors. Nikken is the supplier of leading-edge wellness products to one in ten Japanese homes. Network marketing has been selected by Nikken as the means of product promotion and sales in North America. With operations in twelve countries on four continents, annual sales exceeding one billion dollars, Nikken is estimated to be in the top five network marketing companies worldwide.

We use our Web pages primarily to direct people to learn more about the Nikken and its product line. We also use the Web to help keep our down-line informed of changes that may affect them. These products are new to our culture.

How has the Home Page helped your business?

In the past sharing information was primarily done by mailing audio tapes, video tapes, and brochures to people who requested more information. The Internet provides a way that we can direct people to our Home Pages and the information there will answer most questions that they may have about the company, product, and business opportunity. This is a great savings of time and money

What advice would you give to a business starting on the Web?

Do not become disillusioned if the orders do not start pouring in. There has been much hype regarding the Internet/WWW, reporting how businesses are booming on the net. The only business profiting on the net are mall sites and ISPs (Internet Service Providers). This hype is being used by this business to promote their services and charge inflated prices.

Many businesses will probably remove their web pages from these mall sites after their initial contracts expire since the return is not what they had been led to believe.

In my opinion, business will eventually boom on the net for the retailer as well. That day is probably still a year or so in the future. Hopefully Win95 and other programs will make gaining access to the web easy to use by the real buyers, women with credit cards.

Until that day. Put up a Web Site and advertise its existence whenever and wherever possible. When the buyers do come and if they are looking for a widget, they can do a search on the Web and you want your widget to be referenced everywhere they look.

Internet users have been wary of multi-level marketing companies posting unsolicited notices to "get rich quick" in newsgroups. What is your attitude on this matter?

I do subscribe to several newsgroups which may attract people that may benefit from the products that we offer. I listen, learn, and contribute to the conversation when I can. The extent of advertising in these groups is a four-line signature line which identifies me as a Nikken Independent Distributor and provides URL information on our WWW site and FTP site.

It is upsetting to see some of the newsgroups trashed by spam and the kinds of posts that you mention. MLM is nothing more than a means of product distribution. It is not a get-rich-quick business. One of the reasons that MLM has developed a bad reputation is that too many people incorrectly promote it as such. It has the potential to generate a good income, as with any other business, if you work at building the business.

Actually the services provided by the Internet greatly support the MLM business. There is no better way for the parent company to disseminate information to the large number of distributors in the field.

I think that the growth in the Internet will assist in the growth of network marketing companies as well.

MAILING LIST SALES

As time goes on, the Web will become more and more commercial and the business plans of the off-line world will meld with that of the Web. In most cases, these blendings will be smooth, as seen from the numerous examples in this book. That's why we're saving the most irksome for last—mailing list sales.

It won't be long before mailing list companies get into the act as well. These are the companies that rent your name from a magazine subscription or software product registration form, for example, and sell it to an advertiser who wants to reach those profiles of consumers. In the off-line world, we'd call this "junk" mail. If you want to read the mail, you do. If you don't, you toss it out and no harm is done.

That isn't the case in the online world. People don't like getting unsolicited e-mail from advertisers because it takes time to read and delete the messages. On some commercial online systems, people have to pay to receive messages—even those they don't want. You can imagine how upsetting this would be. Sending unsolicited e-mail is a breach of netiquette (see Chapter 2) which is not a good thing to do—unless you like getting hate mail in return.

However, selling names is a profitable business. Companies can get 10-15 cents a name. If you have 100,000 satisfied customers, you can sell that list for $10,000-$15,000 in full to several companies that want to reach your audience. That can be a great deal of money—especially since you don't have to do anything special to cultivate those names beyond what you do for normal business.

So how can mailing list companies perform their job in the online world? Easy. Ask the customer for permission before placing the name on the list. If permission is denied, don't use it. Period.

You can be very straightforward about this. As people read your home page, let them know they can receive information about new products or services from companies that they might find interesting if they submit their names, addresses, or email addresses. If they submit the information, you are on your way to creating the mailing list.

Now comes the entrepreneurial part. You can create a mailing list company that gathers the names from Home Page owners, manages the names (purges out of date names, sets up computer label forms, invoicing, etc.), and finds companies to buy the names. Brokers fees are about 15 percent. On a $10,000 order, you would receive $1,500. Not bad for a few hours work, especially since you can sell the list over and over.

As long as you obey netiquette, this business could work.

GLOSSARY

Baud: The speed at which modems transfer data. The speed is listed in BPS or bits per second.

Download: Retrieve files from a computer.

FAQ (Frequently Asked Questions): A file that contains questions and answers about specific topics.

Flame: Abusive hate mail.

FTP: File Transfer Protocol: Retrieve files from the Internet

HTML: Hypertext Mark-up Language: The standard format for documents on the World Wide Web.

Hypertext: A system where documents scattered across many sites are directly linked.

Hypermedia: A system where documents, pictures, sound, movie, and animation files scattered across many sites are directly linked.

ISDN (Integrated Services Digital Network): Technology that makes it possible to move multiple digital signals through a single, conventional phone wire.

Leased line: A permanently installed telephone line connecting a LAN to an Internet Service Provider.

Lurking: Reading messages in a forum or newgroups without adding comments.

Modem: A device that connects a computer to a phone line and enables users to transmit data between computers.

Mosaic: A software program that allows users to browse the World Wide Web.

Netiquette: The etiquette of Internet.

Newbies: Newcomers to the Internet.

Service Provider: A company that provides connections to the Internet.

Signature or .sig: A personalized address at the bottom of a message often containing contact information and a short commercial description.

SLIP and PPP (Serial Line Internet Protocol and Point-to-Point Protocol): Two common types of connections that allow your computer to communicate with the Internet.

Smileys and emoticons: Typographical versions of faces that display emotions in text messages.

Spam: Posting or mailing unwanted material to many recipients. A flagrant violation of Netiquette.

TCP/IP (Transmission Control Protocol/Internet Protocol): The standardized sets of computer guidelines that allow different machines to talk to each other on the Internet.

Sysop (SYStem Operator): The person who administers a forum. Same as Webmaster.

Upload: Send a file from your computer to another.

URL (Uniform Resource Locator): A type of address that points to a specific document or site on the World Wide Web.

Usenet: A collection of discussion areas (bulletin boards) known as newsgroups on the Internet.

World Wide Web (WWW or W3 or The Web): A hypertext and hypermedia system that enables users to find information about companies.

JANAL COMMUNICATIONS SEMINARS AND CONSULTING

Daniel Janal provides a variety of services for companies that need to succeed with online marketing. This section describes the services available.

To contact Daniel Janal, send e-mail to: update@janalpr.com or 76004.1046@compuserve.com. You can also call 510-831-0900 during normal business hours in California.

Speaking and Training Seminars

Here are the speaking and training programs I conduct. Each program lasts 45 minutes and can be combined to fill any time slot. The final topic, How to Sell Software Online, is a full-day seminar.

Session 1: How to Succeed As an Online Marketer: Understanding New Marketing Paradigms

The new advertising and marketing differs tremendously from the old advertising especially in regard to creating images and interactivity. This session shows four key differences between the two ways of thinking, as well as 10 ways to think like a new marketer and incorporate this new thinking into your online marketing program.

Overview includes business reasons to be online (sales, customer support, and distribution of marketing support materials).

Discussion of Internet demographics, tools, and trends.

You'll learn what works and what doesn't in the emerging field of interactive advertising.

Presentation format: Lecture with overhead slides, screen shots of relevant Home Pages, and examples drawn from Home Pages of your competitors or industry, when possible. Questions and answers.

Handouts: Slide presentation with notes section.

Session 2: How to Add Value and Content to Your Home Page

Successful Home Pages don't just show marketing materials, they add value to the customer's experience at your site. This session will show case studies of successful Home Pages and present proven strategies for creating enhancement experiences for consumers who visit your Home Page.

You'll learn how to build customers for life with these winning strategies.

Presentation format: Lecture with overhead slides, screen shots of relevant Home Pages, and examples drawn from Home Pages of your competitors or industry, when possible. Questions and answers.

Handouts: Slide presentation with notes section.

Session 3: How to Publicize Your Home Page

If you build a better Home Page, will people beat a path to your door? Not unless you promote and publicize it! This session will present eight strategies for promoting your site.

You'll learn how to get people to come to your Home Page and how to find out who they are through registration techniques, contests, and guest books.

Presentation format: Lecture with overhead slides, screen shots of relevant Home Pages, and examples drawn from Home Pages of your competitors or industry, when possible. Questions and answers.

Handouts: Slide presentation with notes section.

Session 4: Creating Direct Relationships with Customers and Analysts

Reporters kill most press releases they receive. Here are ways to get your message to your key publics WITHOUT the media's help.

You'll learn how to create customers for life by creating meaningful information exchange and dialogs.

Presentation format: Lecture with overhead slides, screen shots of relevant Home Pages, and examples drawn from Home Pages of your competitors or industry, when possible. Questions and answers.

Handouts: Slide presentation with notes section.

Session 5: Why Your Company Should Be Online

Selling products is only one reason to be online. This session explores how companies can save time and money by transmitting software and marketing materials online, providing customer support, and building image using the Internet.

You'll learn why your company should be online.

Presentation format: Lecture with overhead slides, screen shots of relevant Home Pages, and examples drawn from Home Pages of your industry or competitors, when possible. Questions and answers.

Handouts: Slide presentation with notes section.

Session 6: The Internet: A Candid Assessment

Demographics, hit rates, and other misinformation create an inaccurate view of the Internet and its potential for marketers. This session tries to dig closer to the truth of who is online and what they are buying.

You'll learn what's hot and what's not; as well as be able to separate the hype from reality of online sales.

Presentation format: Lecture with overhead slides, screen shots of relevant Home Pages, and examples drawn from Home Pages of your competitors or industry, when possible. Questions and answers.

Handouts: Slide presentation with notes section.

Session 7: Designing a Home Page from the Marketer's Perspective

Find out how to incorporate your Home Page strategy into the integrated marketing plan.

You'll learn the fundamental steps in creating an online marketing plan, designing the page, and flowcharting the sub pages, using art to support your message and avoiding costly design mistakes.

Presentation format: Lecture with overhead slides, screen shots of relevant Home Page,s and examples drawn from Home Pages of your competitors or industry, when possible. Questions and answers.

Handouts: Slide presentation with notes section.

Session 8: Designing a Home Page from an Artistic and Creative Perspective (Part One)

A complete introductory course in HTML programming in 45 minutes! Learn all the basic commands for creating the Home Page, attaching art, linking to related elements and other Home Pages, creating downloading capabilities (FTP).

You'll learn how to put up a cool home page in no time at all!

Presentation format: Lecture with overhead slides, screen shots of relevant Home Pages, and examples drawn from Home Pages of your competitors or industry. when possible. Questions and answers.

Handouts: Slide presentation with notes section.

Session 9: Designing a Home Page from an Artistic and Creative Perspective (Part Two)

Add forms, tables, email responders, and other cool tools to your home page.

You'll learn how to add ordering and interactive features to your home page.

Presentation format: Lecture with overhead slides, screen shots of relevant Home Pages, and examples drawn from Home Pages of your industry or competitors, when possible. Questions and answers.

Handouts: Slide presentation with notes section.

Session 10: How to Sell Software Online (Full day seminar)

Selling Software Online shows you how to sell your software on the Internet and commercial online services.

You'll see how other companies have succeeded by selling software through the online services, either direct from the company, using online distributors, or by using the strategies of Shareware, freeware and get-it-out-there-ware. Solutions for security, registration, and piracy will be discussed.

You'll learn how to sell, distribute and promote software online.

Presentation format: Lecture with overhead slides, screen shots of relevant Home Pages. Questions and answers.

Handouts: Slide presentation with notes section.

JANAL COMMUNICATIONS

Fact sheet

Positioning

Founded in 1986, Janal Communications is an online marketing and public relations agency that helps software publishers, hardware manufacturers, and online service providers sell more products and create customers for life by creating and implementing online marketing programs that are cost efficient and editorially effective in traditional media and online.

Structure

The company has three departments:

Public Relations— publicity services

Online Marketing—marketing and Web page creation (content, art and hookups available through affiliated companies) for all companies

Speaking and Training Seminars—in-house and public seminars covering publicity and marketing, both traditional and online

Speaking Engagements (partial listing)

- University of California at Berkeley
- University of California at Santa Cruz
- Software Publishers Association
- Business Mailers Co-Op Conference
- Softex 2000, Brazil
- Web Insight

- Barnes and Noble Bookstores
- Internet World
- @Cafe
- Computer Literacy Bookshops
- Soft-letter Marketing Summit
- Ragan Communications Seminar
- Public Relations Society of America
- Apple Computer

Private Company Seminars (partial listing)

- Software Publishing Corporation
- Intuit

Internet Clients (partial listing)

- Gold Disk
- Software Publisher
- Programmers Paradise
- Software Catalog
- Launch Point
- Internet Presence Provider
- Austin-James
- Software Publisher
- Road Scholar
- Software Publisher

Public Relations Clients (partial listing)

- America Online
- Learning Company
- Association of Shareware Professionals
- Prentice Hall
- AT&T Multimedia Software

- Productivity Software
- Equis International
- Gold Disk
- Road Scholar Software
- Trimble Navigation
- Grolier Electronic Publishing
- Ziff Institute

Services Profile

Janal Communications provides expert, personal, hands-on, cost-efficient online marketing, and public relations services to companies that want to reach on-line audiences.

Janal Communications helps a company create its personal marketing plan and helps the company execute the plan.

Services can be retained on an hourly, daily, or project basis.

Capabilities include:

- Market research.
- Competitive analysis.
- Company and product positioning.
- Web page flow chart design.
- Plan and create editorial and marketing materials.
- Create contests and promotions.
- Publicize and market Web Site.
- Editorial introductions and product placements.
- Press kits, press tour

INDEX

Enter the "Best Internet Business Idea" Contest

Have you ever considered starting your own business on the Internet? If the answer is yes, then this contest is for you!

Van Nostrand Reinhold (VNR) is sponsoring the "Best Internet Business Idea" contest to help you get started. Winners will be selected from five categories and will be awarded prizes from CompuServe, NetGuide, Entrepreneur, and VNR. The GRAND PRIZE will be awarded to the Most Outstanding Online Business entry.

Contest Categories:
- Most Creative Online Business
- Most Educational Online Business
- Most Humorous Online Business
- Most Likely to Succeed Online Business
- Most Useful Online Business

Here's What You'll Win:
- One–year CompuServe connection sponsored account worth $1,200
- One–year subscription to *NetGuide*
- One–year subscription to *Entrepreneur*
- Your choice of five VNR Internet books

The GRAND PRIZE winner will receive all of the above prizes, PLUS a one–time free home page set–up by VNR and a one–hour consultation by online marketing expert, Daniel S. Janal.

All winning entries will be announced at the Spring Internet World 1996 convention. (You need not be present to win.) Winners will be notified by May 6, 1996.

How to Enter:
Send your name, address, telephone number along with the following information to VNR Online Business Contest, 115 Fifth Avenue, New York, N.Y. 10003 or e-mail jjeng@vnr.com
- Category(ies) you wish to enter
- Type of product or service and its price
- Market for your product or service
- Reason for starting your business

Contest Guidelines:
1. All entries must be received by March 1, 1996.
2. Each entry will be judged by a panel of experts from VNR and the Internet community.
3. All entries will be considered for the Most Outstanding Online Business entry.
4. Only one winner per category.
5. All winners will be notified by May 6, 1996. For names of all winners, send a self–addressed stamped envelope to : VNR Online Business Contest, 115 Fifth Avenue, New York, N.Y. 10003 or e-mail jjeng@vnr.com
6. VNR is not responsible for entries that are not received.
7. VNR reserves the right to use your entry in future editions of *101 Businesses You Start on the Internet* and in National publications. Winners will also have the opportunity to link their home page.
8. No purchase is necessary. This contest is subject to all federal, state, and provincial laws and regulations and is void where prohibited. This contest is not open to employees of VNR, ITP, and other VNR distributors, or the families of any of the above.
9. Prizes awarded are not exchangeable. Certain restrictions apply under the jurisdiction of VNR.
10. CompuServe sponsored accounts are under the jurisdiction of CompuServe Corp.; some restrictions apply.

Co-Sponsors

CompuServe   **NetGuide**   **Entrepreneur**

CompuServe brings the world to your PC.